BITES

of

BUSINESS™

Improve Your Success Diet

TIPS AND INSIGHTS FOR ASPIRING, NOVICE, AND EXPERIENCED MANAGERS

DR. BEN A. CARLSEN, MBA

Stanyard Creek Publishing
Miami . Nassau . Los Angeles

BITES of BUSINESS™

Copyright © 2010 by Dr. Ben A. Carlsen, MBA

www.bitesofbusiness.com

ISBN: 978-0-9742949-2-6 (hardcover)
ISBN: 978-0-9742949-0-2 (paperback)
ISBN: 978-0-9742949-3-3 (e-book)

Library of Congress Catalog Number: 2010935843
Carlsen, Ben A.
Bites of Business
1. HF5001-6182 Business, 2. HF5549-5549.5 Personnel Management

Published by: Stanyard Creek Publishing, Miami, FL, Nassau, BA, Los Angeles, CA
www.stanyardcreekpublishing.com

Printed in USA
Cover design by: Rmada Concepts
www.RmadaConcepts.com

ACKNOWLEDGEMENTS

There are many people to thank for their support, contributions, and encouragement. This book would not have been completed if it wasn't for people like:

Felecia Sheffield, PhD., who got me started writing articles, after I had neglected to author professional publications and presentations for a number of years.

Hendrick Ferguson, who provided support and encouragement, has written a book himself, is an accomplished songwriter and publisher, as well as a creative force and motivating influence.

Elsie Delva, a professional colleague and close friend, who consistently provided support, encouragement and inspiration... and she's a great proofreader.

Allen Calvin, PhD., my favorite instructor in my doctoral program; a true intellect and a skilled businessman.

Arthur Agatston, MD, who saved my life, and kept me healthy.

Robert Bugental, PhD., my favorite instructor in my MBA program. He looked like Moses, and helped lead me out of the wilderness.

Sid Levinson, mentor, friend, astute manager, and someone who recognized my potential early in my career.

Brian Ross, EdD, an excellent researcher and educator; my friend, colleague, former boss, and consistent supporter.

Mike Broyard, P.E., a very disciplined professional who provided detailed editorial input which I largely ignored, but greatly appreciate.

Fausto Manzo, one of my students, who made the most of his education, and contributed significantly to mine.

My family, individually and collectively, who indulged my eccentricities, and offered their unconditional love and support; in particular, Ben Carlsen, Sr., my father, who taught me the value of hard work, sacrifice, and persistence.

And...my cousin Fred who asked me to take a ride with him when he went to the University of Washington to apply for admission. (And so did I.)

<u>DEDICATION</u>

This book is dedicated to employees, managers, entrepreneurs, executives, teachers, and students of business. Through their unrelenting efforts the business world generates remarkable products, services, innovation, and an enviable standard of living, for all of us to enjoy.

CONTENTS

FOREWORD

In today's World, there are very few business books rising to the level of successful practical daily application like "The One Minute Manager" (written by Ken Blanchard & Spencer Johnson) and "Who Moved My Cheese" (written by Spencer Johnson). What is the basic key to the success of these two books? They both speak in very plain terms to business (and even non-business) types, allowing them to quickly understand and execute their precepts. Bites of Business falls into this very same category.

As a long time corporate manager who has successfully managed some of the World's most vaulted brands (e.g., IBM, Coca-Cola, General Motors, The Olympics, Mercedes-Benz and Porsche), I understand and appreciate the value of a good basic business book. This is especially true, if it can take readers to another level of fundamental understanding, execution, growth and ultimately success. As a long time personal colleague of the author, I recognize that Dr. Ben Carlsen's book easily accomplishes this and so much more. How many times have you been faced with a challenge as a manager or entrepreneur and said to yourself, if I could just find the right solution to this problem? Bites of Business offers these solutions, and so much more.

Think of dining in a gourmet five star restaurant. You start off with the first course; an appetizer, to scintillate your taste buds. It jump-starts your entire fine dining experience. This book will do the same thing for your expanding business acumen, if properly read, understood and applied. How does he as an author accomplish this, by his many years of experience as a successful manager, educator, administrator, mentor, and student of both business and popular culture

We are living in a time of severe economic hardships, business difficulties and failures, political rivalries, and intense international competitiveness. As a businessperson, if you can arm yourself with more arrows in your personal quiver, wouldn't it increase your chances for success in the marketplace? Just a quick glance at the table of contents, reveals these arrows: Understanding Business & Management; Managing Yourself; Managing Your Employees; Creating Your Own Business; and Managing Ethically, to name just a few. They are all created and written with your success in mind. Specifically how to further empower and embolden you, to be a better business leader.

It is my hope that Bites of Business will, much like the appetizer within a gourmet meal, only whet your appetite for further insights and information on how to become an even better businessperson or entrepreneur. The only thing constant in life itself is change. If you are not attempting to better yourself or your business, then the competition will catch up with and surpass you. This book will help you successfully run in the race of business, and hopefully propel you upward and onward to a long lasting lifetime of success.

Michael A. Russell is the principal and owner of FastLane Marketing Consultants, LLC, a full service agency meeting the needs of large, medium and small businesses and is located in Hallandale, Florida. Russell earned an MBA degree in marketing management, from Clark Atlanta University's Graduate Business School of Business Administration in Atlanta, Georgia. He also has served as a long time marketing guest lecturer, visiting professor and adjunct professor at educational institutions of higher learning, such as, New York University in New York City, Fairleigh Dickenson University in Hackensack, New Jersey and at his Alma Mater Clark Atlanta University. He has resided in South Florida since 2006.

PREFACE

I'm not a "pure" academic. I've been in business and in management or leadership positions almost all of my adult life. As a kid, I was, like many of you, an entrepreneur of sorts, making money with a lawn-mowing service, (I even had business cards printed up ["Save your Pennies - Ask for Benny's"...]), selling greeting cards, hawking "chances" on punch-card lotteries, etc. As a teenager, I was working as a deckhand on fishing boats in Alaska and in Washington State. This was a natural introduction to the larger world of business, as my father was a commercial fisherman, and captained his own boat -- the "Yankee Maid." The summer jobs paid my way through high school and college, and made me feel more responsible, productive, and independent. I also learned the concepts of "risk-reward," (fishing is very unpredictable), productivity, teamwork (with a crew of seven) management, leadership, accountability, profit/loss, etc. Too bad more young people don't have this opportunity.

While in college, at the University of Washington, I also worked part-time jobs at Seattle Children's Home, and at Frederick & Nelson's department store. This was the beginning of a life-long pattern of part-time and/or full-time employment while pursing my education, as is the norm for millions of working students.

Upon graduation from college, at age twenty-one, I left home, in Seattle, and headed south to California. There, with sixty dollars in hand, I knew I would have to find employment-- FAST! Initially I sought junior management positions, but as time was of the essence, I accepted whatever I could immediately get, and that was a job on a loading dock at Barker Bros. furniture store in downtown Los Angeles. Barker Bros. was good to me, and in only a few months I was offered a position as Supervisor in the Carpet Department - my first management position. From there on it was a series of management positions in the private and public sectors, interspersed with further education, part-time teaching, and college instructor positions at various colleges and universities.

My education has been both academic and experiential, covering decades, and embracing the private and public sectors, various professions, numerous leadership levels, and multiple industries.

In the final analysis, I suppose I'm an educator. This is whether I'm in the classroom, the Boardroom, or the office.

I hope you will enjoy and learn from this book-- about yourself, business, management, career, and life.

INTRODUCTION

Ever wonder what it takes for businesses to succeed and for individuals to succeed in business? This book provides insights, advice and tips for the experienced, novice, or aspiring business manager. Whether you, the reader, are a business student, employee, leader, middle-manager, or an executive, you are sure to find practical, relevant, and useful information in the following pages.

The origin of this book is in a series of articles, starting in 2008, written to inform and assist business leaders, managers, and owners. It is based on experience and knowledge gained in over thirty years as a manger and more than twenty years as a consultant and educator.

Poor management abounds. In every profession and industry, in almost all businesses, and certainly in government; mismanagement is the norm. Yet, the effective and profitable conduct of business requires management and leadership.

Businesses begin with human imagination and initiative. They survive and thrive, because of these elements, combined w th good fortune and good management. Every business can improve, and so can every employee and manager.

This is a book about business, although it focuses upon the human factor. After all, businesses do not run themselves, and business is not only about making money, it is also about the underlying relationships that permit profitability. The relationships between the employees and their customers, the relationship between the employees and their bosses, the relationships between the employees and their work, the relationships between and among employees, the relationship between the suppliers and the company, the relationship the company has with its shareholders, regulators, competition, the community...and the list goes on. So, we put a human face on business, management, and leadership.

"Bites of Business" consists of easy to read and digest essays. It truly is "bites" of business. Short, to-the-point discussions, messages, advice and tips. It is specifically designed for busy executives and managers. It's what might be termed an "easy read," This is by design, and intended to facilitate "grazing" rather than reading the book in a linear "cover-to-cover" fashion.

The book is organized in Chapters beginning with "Understanding Business and Management," proceeding with "Managing Your Business," "Managing Your Employees." "Managing Yourself," "Creating Your Own Business," and "Managing Ethically." There's even a chapter about studying business and selecting a college. Each chapter consists of various independent, related, brief, subjects. The purpose of this is to allow the reader to "pick and choose" topics of interest or import, without having to read all that precedes it to understand what's being discussed. The reader may find this "grazing" rather than linear approach, less time consuming, more efficient, and useful. After all, you're not reading a novel, but a business book, and the book should reflect the principles of "effectiveness" and "efficiency." Besides, in business communications, I've always believed you should: "Identify the villain before the end of the story."

Although you can read one portion, or an entire chapter, to get information about a particular topic, it's important to realize that the entire book is an important resource. For example if you're planning to start a business, Chapter Five, Creating Your Own Business might be a good starting point. However, if you already have, or plan to start a new business, you also need to know about Management (Chapters Three, Four and Five), Business Ethics (Chapter Six), etc. Everything is interrelated.

A new management model (paradigm) is introduced in this book. This model builds on the generally accepted compilation of management functions/responsibilities. Most of you have probably heard of POLC - the peculiar acronym for the basic functions of management. The POLC (**P**lanning, **O**rganizing, **L**eading, **C**ontrolling) model is included in practically every introductory business or management textbook, and millions of college students have struggled to remember what each letter stands for when they're taking a "pop" quiz, or a final exam. I always find it's easier to remember letters which are organized to make sense, i.e., form a word. So, POLICE is the word/acronym used to represent management responsibilities. You'll learn more about this later in the book.

Now that I've whetted your appetite for more, let's get into "Bites of Business."

1

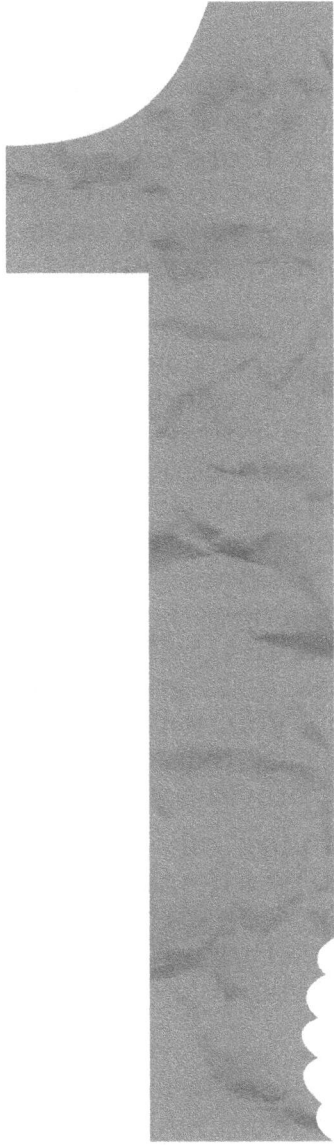

UNDERSTANDING
BUSINESS AND
MANAGEMENT

UNDERSTANDING BUSINESS AND MANAGEMENT

The concept of business is simple. The practice of business is not. The following is a brief primer on Business and Management. Although you are undoubtedly familiar with these terms, a succinct and focused discussion follows. Further, a new view of management, based on established concepts and principle is introduced.

Business

What is Business? It is pervasive in our society and the basis of our economy. It is conducted locally, nationally and worldwide. It can be complex but is fundamentally simple. Business involves producing goods or services, which can be exchanged for money or other consideration. Businesses are created to make money. In fact, the primary objective of business is PROFIT. The other primary objective for business is GROWTH. There may be secondary objectives, but profitability and growth are supreme. So if someone asks you "what is the purpose of business?" hopefully you will respond "Growth and Profitability." And when they follow-up by asking how you do this, you can say by "providing goods and/or services."

Of course, there are many other elements involved in business. There needs to be a demand for the goods, and/or services the business provides. They must be accessible, and competitively priced. But perhaps the singular most important factor in business success is management.

Management

What is Management? There is little disagreement that it involves the process of "getting things done through other people." And most experts would say that certain basic functions are common to the process. The generally agreed upon basic management functions are: Planning, Organizing, Leading, and Controlling (P.O.L.C.)

The POLC paradigm has endured well and has an important place in management texts and treatises. However, perhaps it is time to revisit this model. And, we will be doing that in the next few pages.

2

MANAGING YOUR
BUSINESS

"POLICE" YOUR WAY TO BETTER MANAGEMENT

It's easy to define managemnet as "getting" results through the efforts of others, but it's challenging to practice management effectively.

Management Functions

The generally agreed upon basic management functions are: Planning, Organizing, Leading, and Controlling (P.O.L.C.)

Managers must engage in Planning to set the direction of the organization so that mission, goals, and objectives can be attained. They also must Organize staff and resources into an effective mechanism for the achievement of these directions. To provide effective coordination and inspiration the organization demands a Leader. Finally, to make certain resources are not squandered, and that progress is made efficiently, Control is essential.

P.O.L.I.C.E.

Here come the management POLICE. In addition to being an easy to remember acronym, there are two more important management functions which have been incorporated.

The first is **Informing**.

The Information Age is upon us. In today's era of rapid and pervasive communication, information is essential. The manager must constantly communicate by Informing, and being Informed.

The second addition is **Enhancing**.

The manager's role should be more than just additive to the organization. It should be synergistic, and enhance the ability of the organization to compete, survive, grow and prosper. The manager's presence must make a difference. Merely being present as a functionary, performing the essential tasks of POLC, will not necessarily result in excellence. The manager's efforts must benefit, improve and enhance the prospects and reality of the organization.

POLICE Power

The power of the POLICE is well recognized. They patrol our streets, maintain the order, and apprehend miscreants. The power of P.O.L.I.C.E. in management is in the application of its components. Remember to consciously, conscientiously, and consistently apply POLICE Power in your organization.

Many police departments have a motto like "To Protect and Serve." Perhaps you never thought of yourself as a Policeman, however, you would do well by protecting your business, and conscientiously serving it, and its stakeholders. This way your business will be safe and secure. With this type of **POLICE** protection your employees will enjoy an environment in which they can grow, prosper, contribute, and succeed. Not only will you be performing the essential functions of management, you will recognize an expanded role, obligations, and responsibilities, in a new context.

As a manager you are the **P**lanner, **O**rganizer, **L**eader, **I**nformer, **C**ontroller, and **E**nhancer. You are the **POLICE**!

PROFITABILITY: THE PRIMARY BUSINESS OBJECTIVE

Profitability: Isn't that what you're in business for?

Businesses that don't make profits don't stay in business long.

How can you improve your bottom line?

The Purpose of Business

It doesn't matter what business you're in: Retail, manufacturing, service, resale, wholesale, etc. You must make $$$$.

The purpose of business is two-fold: Growth and Profitability. Every business wants and needs to make a profit and most, if not all, want to grow. If someone were to ask you "what is the purpose of business?" would you say Growth and Profitability? Let's hope so.

The Organizational Mission

Of course the business purpose, common to all business enterprises, is to grow and prosper. But the purpose should not be confused with the Mission. It is important to make some distinctions. Although the Mission is sometimes referred to as a "Statement of Purpose," in reality it is more a description of "how" you're going to make money.

The Mission is a broad statement which generally refers to the type of business, the products and or services produced, and frequently some indication of quality (e.g., the "best" auto parts supplier in the West). And, the Mission may identify the more specific aspects of the particular firm. Its basic intent is to define why the organization exists, what it hopes to achieve, and perhaps values, essential nature, etc. However, the business has an overriding purpose of making money and growing. Of course it is difficult to rally employees around the profit motive. If you were to say "we're here to make money," instead of "to produce the best tires in America," or "provide top quality healthcare to our patients," it would be inconsistent with a favorable image.

Making Money

Money is the lifeblood of the company. It is essential to survival, growth and well-being.

Businesses make money by selling products and/ or services. Production, quality, customer service, marketing, etc., all have elements of cost and potential savings or profit improvement. The formula is simple: sell more products or services and you have more income. That does not necessarily mean that you make more profit. So the equation must be expanded to include the cost(s) of doing business. Income minus expenses = profit. Management must strategize, and position itself to successfully compete in the marketplace.

Some Considerations

Here are some considerations, or "rules of thumb" to ensure, promote and maintain profitability:

--Keep sales high. (marketing, customer service, production -the 5 P's: Product, Price, Placement, Promotion, People)

--Keep costs low. (cost containment, cost reduction, waste reduction, employee involvement).

--Maintain and increase your customer base (customer care, reliability, marketing)

--Protect and enhance your reputation. (dependability, reliability, fair-dealing)

--Be competitive. (competitive pricing, product differentiation, state-of-the-art products)

--Consistently improve your products/services. (quality assurance, quality control, innovation, benchmarking)

--Increase employee productivity. (performance standards, measurement, incentives, efficiency and quality control)

Finally

You may think you already know all of this. And, hopefully you do. But a good refresher is always useful, and it is easy to fall into bad practices. The importance of being cognizant of, and attentive to, your basic business purpose will pay PROFIT dividends (perhaps in more ways than one!).

IN BUSINESS CASH IS KING!

Following the "Panic of 2008," and continuing with the "Credit Crunch" into 2009-10, many Americans have rediscovered the notion that "Cash is King." With credit difficult to obtain and asset values declining, the only sure bet is cash. Businesses are particularly vulnerable to any credit contraction as they require money for expansion and day-to-day operations, and their customers also need credit to purchase the company's goods and/or services. So they're hit with a double "whammy" - no outside funding for the business operations and weakened customer demand for their products.

Credit is Important

It has been said that credit is the "lifeblood" of business. And, there's a strong case that can be made. To expand or even maintain your enterprise money needs to be available. Typically these business needs can be met through financing (credit lines, or short-term borrowing). Businesses carry customer accounts on a credit basis, finance inventory, buy supplies on credit, finance expansions or acquisitions, etc. But a dependence on borrowing, or advancing, funding can make your business vulnerable. Just look at the construction industry. Development funds have almost exclusively been obtained through financing of some sort, and now that these funding sources have become more risk aversive, many construction/developer companies are in trouble. Of course there are many other industries dependent on credit availability, and many individual companies within each sector with substantial financing needs. Part of this need can be attributed to a demand for growth and profitability tied to shareholder expectations. And, while this is all fine in good times, it can turn around to be a significant negative in bad times.

The Importance of Reserves

We are all aware of the advice to accumulate and keep six months income in the bank in case of personal job loss or emergency. However, most individuals have not followed this advice and likewise, most businesses haven't either. The *Pollyana* assumption that things will continue to get better leaves too much to chance. A viable business must be in a strong cash position to survive a moderate to severe downturn, although many cannot even sustain a mild correction.

Part of your business planning should include a strategy to create a satisfactory reserve/ contingency account. This will provide you with the security of knowing that your business will not fail due to short-term cash needs, and enjoy the flexibility of having ready funds when opportunities arise.

Setting Up Your Cash Reserve

Cash flow is essential to establishing a reserve account. Without a sufficient cash surplus (i.e., positive cash flow) you cannot accumulate any savings. Cash resulting from sales, accounts receivables, asset sales, etc., needs to be closely monitored and tightly controlled. The surplus of income over expenses will yield a capability of creating a reserve to be used in time of need. There are many ways to improve cash flow and cash management. The most important consideration is to avoid losses. Bad debts are a primary culprit. A single non-paying customer can easily wipe out the gains from many who pay on time. Therefore, it is essential to have tight payment and credit standards to minimize the amount outstanding at any time.

You can try to improve the accounts receivable/ accounts payable cycle so that cash on hand can be enhanced. Your objective is to get the money in the door as fast as possible and delay the payables as long as possible. This is usually accomplished by tightening credit requirements for your customers, and taking the maximum amount of time to pay your bills. Of course everyone is trying to do the same thing so you need to be astute, strategic, and controlling.

It's important to analyze your reserve requirements from a realistic perspective. Undoubtedly you want to put your "money to work," and excess capital sitting on the sidelines is unnecessary and counter-productive. However, depending on the volatility of your business, the state of the economy, competitive and customer factors, trends and forecasts, you will want to adjust your reserves accordingly. In a stable business , in a stable environment, three or four months operating capital may be sufficient, while in a less predictable situation six months, or even more, may be prudent.

The Bottom Line

By now you have probably arrived at the conclusion that "Cash is King." Credit lines can be restricted or evaporate. Loans can be unavailable or made only with onerous terms. Business conditions can deteriorate. Emergencies happen.

So don't procrastinate, take the tough steps required to build your cash reserves.

BUSINESS STRATEGIES FOR TIGHT MONEY

Small businesses are having tough times. And, the primary reason for failure is undercapitalization. How can small businesses weather the current financial storm?

The Economy

The U.S. economy stinks! And the prospects for the near term aren't much better. Even the worldwide economy is fragile and suffering. Business loans are currently tough to obtain and qualifying can be downright challenging. The banks don't want to loan funds, and the interest rates, if you do qualify, are high. There isn't much you can do about this environment, but there is a lot you can do about your personal situation.

Strategies for Survival

Businesses need to position themselves to survive the economic downturn. This means thinking proactively, thoroughly analyzing your situation, and taking decisive actions. Here are ten strategies designed to help.

First, take a realistic look at your financial condition. Have your accountant review the books, particularly "cash flow," to ascertain how much latitude you have, or if you need to take drastic action to reduce expenditures.

Second, don't cut back on advertising. This is a common curtailment, although it's a short-sighted one. You need to bring customers in your door (whether it is a "virtual" or a physical door) and differentiate yourself from the competition.

Third, keep your established customers. Give them special attention, frequent contacts, superior service and incentives to continue to do business with you. Provide loyalty rewards in a form that is appropriate and meaningful (e.g., discounts, gifts, special status, preferred customer standing, 24 hour service, etc.).

Fourth, maintain a close relationship with your banker. Although lending has all but dried up, as you know, the clients with the best relationship often get the best treatment.

Fifth, conserve your cash. Build and maintain a reserve, for difficult times like these. Don't make unnecessary expenditures. Plug the leaks, cut costs, and reduce inventory to minimal, practical levels.

Sixth, renegotiate with your suppliers. See if you can get lower prices and better terms. They're probably suffering too and will be more inclined to reduce their margin in order to maintain a customer.

Seventh, maintain and increase your networking activities. Now is not the time to drop your *Chamber of Commerce* membership. Networking with other businesses can pay off in numerous ways, including learning how others are coping with tight financial conditions.

Eighth, re-engineer your business. Step back and take a fresh look at the nature of your business and the way in which you conduct it. Perhaps you'll have an epiphany. Ask yourself if you're in the "right" business, and if you have the correct products and services. Do you have the appropriate location? Are you appealing to your "true" customers? Should you redesign your layout? Re-examine your product mix. Rethinking your entire business is something that should be done periodically. Remember the story about the "buggy whip" manufacturers after invention of the automobile. They eventually realized that they were in the wrong business.

Ninth, seek help when necessary. You don't have to go it alone. If you need help get it! Perhaps the expense of an outside consultant is justified, or maybe the *Service Corps of Retired Executives (SCORE)* will do. In any event, if you're struggling, or drowning, get the help you need.

Tenth, realize that you're a survivor. We all know that small business fail at incredibly high rates; the fact that you're still in business means that you've done many things right.

PLANT AN APPLE SEED: GROW AN APPLE TREE

The Bible says: "Whatever ye sow, so shall ye reap." Sometimes we forget this simple advice. Plant the seeds of responsibility, pride, and accomplishment and you should be able to receive a harvest of these attitudes and behaviors. Plant the seeds of negativity and despair or hopelessness and you'll likely get those too.

You Get What You Deserve

Some people have unrealistic expectations. Remember the pop definition of insanity - "To keep doing the same thing and expect different results"? This popular saying contains more than a grain of truth. Your actions will cause results which are in accordance with those actions. So, back to the analogy: plant an apple seed - grow an apple tree. If you want bananas, plant a banana tree.

Organization Culture

The culture of an organization is in large measure a reflection of its leadership.

Managers have a responsibility to provide effective leadership. Your actions as a leader will ultimately affect your organization and the people in it. Part of leadership is to inspire and motivate. If you, as a manager, plant the seeds of motivation and inspiration, you can, with proper care expect to grow a healthy crop of both. There are always weeds, insects, disease, blight, drought, etc., to contend with, so you need to take special care, and preventative actions. And, bad morale can spread like wildfire.

On the other hand, building a positive organization with a "can do" attitude takes patience and support. Because there are so many bad managers, employees typically mistrust their organizational leadership. You will have to "win them over" by consistently nurturing what you want to grow.

Organization Success

The success of your enterprise is a result of many factors. However, the most important one may be your attitude. Just like individual success depends on attitude so does corporate success. The initiatives and projects you endorse and support will more than likely succeed. Those that you ignore will be ignored by your employees. The seeds you plant include: interest, enthusiasm, confidence, success, persistence, achievement, etc. These are your apple seeds. If you inadvertently, or purposefully, plant other seeds, you'll produce entirely different results. Likewise if you focus on one result but expect another you should not be surprised at the outcome.

You can also plant the seeds of contempt, mistrust, and negativity. Expect to get a "bumper crop"!

The seeds of success are often simple and straight-forward. Plant an apple seed and expect an apple tree. Enjoy your "Golden Delicious."

DON'T GOUGE YOUR CUSTOMERS

In challenging economic times, businesses, particularly small businesses, sometimes resort to counter-productive strategies. One of these is price-gouging. In order to make up for decreased sales they charge inflated prices for those customers who remain. This is a bad idea.

The Dilemma

Businesses make money through price and volume. These two factors are inextricably connected. If you want to be profitable you must sell products or services at high enough prices to generate profit. There are two basic ways to do this. Either you sell many items at low markup, or fewer items at higher profitability. In today's economic environment with customers at all levels watching their budgets and reducing their consumption, the temptation is to raise prices to make up for reduced volume. Stories of this practice abound. Whether it's repair on a Mercedes, or a purchase at the discount store, consumers are complaining about being overcharged or even "ripped off." For those not in the retail business, the same phenomenon is being experienced in B2B (business to business) transactions.

The Customer Relationship

The business/customer relationship is a fragile one. Customers decide to do business with a particular firm based on a number of factors. Some of these are: Price, Product, Service, Proximity, Loyalty, Quality, Reputation, Dependability, Personal Rapport, etc. Because of the fragility and complexity of the relationship, perceptions of unfairness are precarious. The relationship dynamics are subject to change, sometimes in an instant. Should the customer feel that the relationship is unfair they will be inclined to visit another source. Very few businesses are in a monopolistic position, and customers almost always can exercise a choice in who they want to do business with. Established relationships are being tested as price considerations increase in importance. The business must understand that price points must, therefore, be closely monitored to gauge their impact.

Price Wars

With price increasing in importance as a consumer decision factor, and with so many businesses closing or downsizing, price "wars" are becoming widespread. The bankruptcy of retailers like *Circuit City*, *Mervyns*, and *KB Toys*, puts pressure on remaining firms. Although there are fewer competitors, the interim impact is on pricing. How do you effectively compete with a business offering "going out of business" sales?

Marketing experts, always looking for a competitive edge, are trying many strategies. Recently, (starting February 4, 2009, and continuing periodically) the *Denny's* restaurant chain offered free *"Grand Slam"* breakfasts. You can't beat zero cost, and despite the one day loss the restaurant giant calculated that the publicity, goodwill, customer loyalty factors, etc., would more than offset the temporary loss. Besides, they wanted to show off their public spirit, capture new customers and gain market share. They believe that if customers understand that they can have breakfast at *Denny's* for a cost approximating a fast food restaurant they will come back. So, there are varied responses to the business decline. Some are experimenting with novel approaches while others, in a desperate attempt to maintain profitability, have used exploitative techniques.

What can be done?

Businesses can learn from the current challenging circumstances. For example they can learn (or relearn) to:

- Treat the customer fairly
- Value long term relationships, and appreciate customer loyalty
- Step up customer service
- Re-examine priorities
- Increase marketing efforts
- Publicize and market the business
- Focus on core business competencies
- Price merchandise and/or services competitively
- Stress uniqueness
- Contain and manage costs and overhead
- Compete effectively (especially with long- term competitors)
- Consider loyalty and repeat business incentives
- Retain the best employees
- Re-examine and reinforce strategic alliances and partnerships
- Think and act creatively with new approaches and strategies
- Not yield to temporary profit squeezes by gouging customers

Marketing textbooks stress the "5 P's" i.e., Pricing, Product, Price, Place, and Promotion. The new realities include a whole lot more of the alphabet.

THE SINS OF OVER, OR UNDER, ANALYSIS

We've all heard the saying: "paralysis by analysis," meaning that you can substitute analysis for action and continue to come up with "unknowns" which prevents movement. This inertia can be counterproductive, costly, and result in missed opportunities.

Analysis is Important

Now, we wouldn't want to disparage analysis, because, after all, it is important to gather and evaluate data and information before taking action. This approach prevents many missteps and provides some assurance of the quality and appropriateness of our decisions. So, obviously, we won't be recommending dispensing with analysis, but rather limiting it by removing redundancies and overkill.

Making good Decisions

It is difficult to make good decisions without analysis. The decision maker must understand the problem and the data which will be utilized to arrive at an accurate conclusion. And, a person would have to be quite lucky to arrive at an optimal decision without first knowing, and assessing the significant variables, influences, and options. Whereas the "*scientific method*" may be fine when timelines are lengthy, a more truncated methodology can be beneficial for shorter deadlines.

Decisions always have more than one value. Two important considerations are: 1) Quality, and 2) Timeliness. The best decision if it is not timely will have lessened, marginal, insignificant, perhaps even negative, value. For example, an investor who decided to invest in residential real estate in Las Vegas would probably have made a more profitable choice had he decided on this course of action in the year 2000, instead of 2007. There is an old saying: "timing is everything." Well, timing may not be everything, but it's certainly something! Something worth considering.

Those who base their decisions on proper and reasonable analysis will typically fare better than those who do not.

The Tradeoff

There are certainly many factors involved in making a good decision. Timeliness and Quality are the two most important. We all desire high quality decisions and we are all constrained by time. Although the relationship between time and quality are neither direct nor precise, these two elements are essential. It is important to note that a greater expenditure of time does not necessarily result in a superior decision, and a short decision-making process may not yield an inferior or unworkable one.

One thing to avoid is the "paralysis by analysis" syndrome where problems are overanalyzed and important decisions are deferred or never made. Some managers are so fearful of making a mistake that they end up in this situation. "Just do it" is a saying that comes to mind. And certainly this approach is attractive. But errors can prove costly and a balance between expediency and results must be struck.

The Equation

There may not be a simple equation to discern the BEST decision-making paradigm, and the timeliest outcome. We may actually have to resort to qualitative judgments. If the impact of the decision is greater than the importance of the timeliness, we will want to give this factor greater weight. On the other hand, if it's important to make a decision quickly we will give greater weight to this. For example:

>value of outcome = < value of timeliness

>value of timeliness = < value of outcome

In other words, when not so much is at stake, we can appropriately make our decision faster. However, when there is a potential for significant loss we may want to take our time. This is not to say that FAST and ACCURATE are mutually exclusive, only that a more thorough analysis will typically produce higher quality results.

We may intuitively recognize this relationship, and we may, in fact, apply it to our decision-making processes. However, we can further refine the equation to weight the values by utilizing a methodology somewhat more refined than a "guesstimate." Assigning a percentage value to each side of our equation will further refine the process, and should enhance its utility. For example:

80% outcome value vs. 20% timeliness value.

In this example the importance of accuracy/quality of the outcome is more important than being timely with our decision by a factor of 4. It is four times more important to be accurate than it is to be timely, so we would be prudent to err on the side of caution rather than rushing our decision-making process. Of course the opposite could be true, as well.

An Example

The textbook example of this dilemma is the *"Challenger"* space shuttle disaster (January 28, 1986). Typically, this monumental error is used as an example of *"groupthink,"* and that is certainly the case. The scientists, engineers, and project managers did not adequately challenge one another in the decision making process. But the *Challenger* disaster demonstrates another decision-making flaw. Namely, the decision equation was screwed up. Had the safety of the crew been weighted at 99%, and the time "window" (for launch) assigned a value of 1%, the decision to proceed with liftoff would have undoubtedly been deferred, and several lives would have been saved.

Some Tips

Despite the real risks in decision-making, paralysis is undoubtedly an even less attractive outcome. Here are some tips to help you in the process:

--Assess the importance of the decision (Is it worth considerable time and effort, or not; do a cost-benefit analysis)

--Focus on the outcome (it's easy to get sidetracked)

--Don't be overwhelmed by the size or complexity of your decision (remember the KISS principle ["keep it simple, stupid!"])

--Break down your BIG decisions into component parts (it's easier when you deconstruct into smaller, more digestible, pieces)

--Use data in your analysis (but limit to pertinent, relevant, essential items)

--Remember the Time/Quality tradeoff (don't shortchange the decision-making process, nor unnecessarily prolong it)

--AVOID PARALYSIS BY ANALYSIS (remember, the objective is to make the decision, and your fears, or perfection desires, can interfere)

ALMOST EVERYTHING IS NEGOTIABLE

With a few exceptions - like gravity, and death - everything is negotiable, even taxes. First, you need to believe it. Second you need to practice it.

Value and Pricing

Is there such a thing as a "fixed price"? Probably not. According to economic theory, the law of "supply and demand" governs pricing. And while this may be basically true, there are many other factors which enter into the equation. Furthermore, many of these factors are subjective. This means that there is room for negotiation.

The "fair market value" concept comes into play as well. Pricing is supposed to be the result of what a willing buyer will pay to a willing seller. In other words, subjective, emotional and psychological considerations may be in operation. Perhaps the best examples of the application of this principle are in real estate transactions. What you may be willing to pay for a house may be significantly discrepant from what I may be willing to sell it for, or vice versa. The same concept holds true for property appraisers. These experts determine a value based comparable properties, features of the property, and their experience and education. However, their value may be influenced by an "offer" price and perhaps even lender guidelines, neighborhood trends, etc.

Think about the last time you purchased a used vehicle, or a new automobile, for that matter. A friend of mine was a top salesman. He always said he liked to sell used cars because nobody knew the "true" value. Frequently the emotional component (i.e., "I love the car" or it "suits my image"), or the terms of the sale, override good judgment. This discussion demonstrates that value and pricing, like beauty, are in the eyes of the beholder. And, the beholder will certainly be influenced by his position (buyer or seller), and by psychological factors.

Negotiation

Negotiation is the process of bargaining. Donald Trump fancies himself as an extraordinary negotiator, and wrote a best-selling book on the topic *"The Art of the Deal."* However, it was his attorney and corporate V.P., George Ross (of *"Apprentice"* fame) who made the techniques more concrete. In *Trump Style Negotiation (Wiley & Sons, 2006)* he offers "Winning Negotiation Strategies from *Donald Trump's*

Right-Hand Man." Techniques such as "building trust, friendship, and satisfaction with the other side." are discussed. Determining "what the other side wants," then ascertaining their weaknesses are also covered. Weaknesses can be such things as pride, lack of cash, need, etc. Offering solutions to your "adversary's" problems is important, and so is convincing people that they got "more than they ever expected." Such mundane, but important issues such as controlling the place and pace of negotiations can also be used to one's advantage.

It's a Mindset

I maintain that just about everything is negotiable, and that you need to believe it and practice it! Many people are afraid to negotiate or inept at the process. Just ask. You may find that the other party is willing to deal. These principles aren't limited to your business life; they extend into all aspects of your life, whenever price, or terms, is a factor.

Next time you visit your supplier, mechanic, roofer, tailor, department store, barber, dentist, restaurant, etc., ask if they can cut their price, or make you a deal. Do they offer discounts? Do they offer low cost financing? Do they offer better terms? Do they stand behind their product? Will they offer extended service or replacement provisions? Just ask. Indicate that you are a serious and savvy buyer, cognizant of value, and that you are looking to build a "relationship" with them. You may be surprised at how often you will gain concessions. Remember, almost everything is negotiable.

THE DANGER OF SHORT-SIGHTED MANAGEMENT

Great leaders build great organizations and position them for a long-enduring future. However there seems to be a paucity of great leaders. Most leaders are so busy looking after themselves that they have insufficient time to devote to the future of their businesses.

Unselfish, excellent, future-focused management is becoming like the dodo bird----extinct.

So Little Substance

Managers are now more about image. Managers are concerned about their "brand." The priority seems to be "looking good," not doing good. Perceptions are everything as the "cult of personality" trumps the principle of "character." Managers will all too readily "throw their employees under the bus," rather than guide or mentor them when they have a problem.

Common wisdom suggests the manager needs to be perceived as assertive, in charge, and decisive. This is particularly true in times of economic downturn. Frequently the "best" manager in difficult times is thought to be the one who cuts the most the fastest, even when those actions may be jeopardizing the company's future.

It's important for the leader to nurture a long-term perspective rather than one aimed exclusively at short term profitability. The decisions made by management to attain more immediate objectives must be consistent with the mission and enduring objectives and values of the enterprise. This temptation to yield to current pressures instead of having the future as a top priority has resulted in the decline or dissolution of many organizations.

It's certainly difficult to focus on the long-term when the current problems seem so overwhelming. However, try an analogy. If you ran your life without regard to the long term viability of your personal enterprise, you might be tempted to get rid of your kids or wife as excess expenses. You might sell your house, or refinance everything to raise cash. And, yes, there are families that are compelled to take drastic actions to survive. But most of us have a long term view, because we know we will have to live with the consequences of our impulsive decisions. Oftentimes this is not the case in the business world, where managerial performance is based on current results. This short-sighted view results in many poor or counter-productive decisions.

Frequently managers do not have to live with the consequences of their decisions as their performance is based on quarterly or monthly results. By the time the damage is done, they're long gone. In fact, they're generally positioning themselves for the next career move from day one! Very few top managers spend their lives with one company; most probably only invest a few years. Accordingly, their objective, unfortunately, might lean more towards short-term success, rather than the long-enduring variety. With attitudes like these, the current generation of corporations may be in jeopardy over the long-term.

Building for the Future

A very influential management book titled *"Built to Last,"* (Jerry Poras, 2004) heralded the practices of some major corporations that employed and nurtured a culture and practice that allowed them to survive, adapt, and prosper over many decades, or even longer.

Another excellent book titled *"Good to Great"* (2001) by Jim Collins was based on studies that showed second-tier companies could make the leap to greatness through excellent management. Interestingly, in his study, a counter-intuitive finding about leaders was identified. Namely, the most effective leaders are "humble and strong-willed, not outgoing." Why would this be? Think about it. Jack Welch may be an extrovert, but is Bill Gates or Warren Buffet? And, how about the "Google Boys?" Of course, one could argue that the aforementioned are more entrepreneurial than managerial, and this argument seems to have merit. However, these individuals transitioned into management leaders as their businesses grew.

The point here is that leaders of successful companies are certainly there for the long-term. They're less concerned about their personal image, or next quarter's results, and more concerned about the future of their organizations. Perhaps if we were able to inculcate this kind of mentality in the non-founder leaders we would see more organizational permanence.

CHANGE IS THE HARDEST THING YOU'LL EVER DO

Change is the hardest thing you'll ever do. What's the hardest thing you'll ever do? CHANGE!

Why is Change so Difficult?

People and organizations (combinations of people) strive for homeostasis. Living organisms strive for a balance, and equilibrium. This is a survival mechanism and a protective strategy. Change involves risk and loss. You risk implementing a unsuccessful strategy and have to give up one that works. Of course the current behaviors might not work so well, but they may be preferable to change.

We are creatures of habit who employ practices, methodologies, and lifestyles which suffice. For confirmation of this, just look around at people you know. Some stay in abusive or unsatisfying relationships because they are fearful or unwilling to make a major change. Others stay in menial jobs or live in places they can't stand. It's uncomfortable and risky to leave our "comfort zones."

Apply this change-resistant mentality to the business world and you find businesses that are risk-aversive, unwilling or unable to adapt, and those that refuse to evolve. Evolution, progress and adaptation are necessary for the success, even survival of businesses. A prime example is U.S. automobile manufacturers like *Ford* and *General Motors*. These firms have resisted change, clung to out-of-date practices and failed to adapt to changes in the buying preferences of American customers. They shelved new technologies, such as electric automobiles, and persisted in their self-defeating practices. While gas prices escalated they continued to manufacture gas hogging SUV's, trucks and luxury cars. This persisted for years while consumers increasingly purchased smaller, more fuel-efficient foreign brands. Only faced with bankruptcy or extinction did they make the necessary changes.

The Environment

What is the target, and primary force, for change? It's the environment. People and businesses need to adapt to the environment. In order to adapt they must understand the environment and know what changes are required to be compatible, synchronized, and synergistic. A poor fit with the environment will cause all sorts of problems. You must know the requirements to survive, even thrive, in the general environment, and even more, the specific environment in which you find yourself. It would be even more helpful if you could see the direction of the environment, detect little changes, anticipate environmental changes and determine adaptive strategies.

Some organizations are large enough to impact the environment. Countries and large conglomerates come to mind. Because of their size, influence and power they can actually, to a limited degree, influence the general environment, and induce environmental change. The U.S. Government, for example, can impact the credit markets by making money available, reducing interest rates, and implementing more favorable tax laws. Companies can impact buyer preferences and purchasing practices by expending huge amounts of money on marketing and advertising campaigns. However, these interventions typically have little long term effects, and may prove futile when confronted with the enormity of the general environment. And, the business environment has expanded exponentially over the past several decades as markets, economies, and corporations have increasingly become internationalized.

Adaptation and Change

The change process is not easy. Every graduate student knows that *"resistance to change"* must be addressed in their theses and dissertations involving human subjects. And, every manager has experienced resistance when changing subordinates' duties, responsibilities or work processes.

It frequently takes something dramatic for us to change established habits and ways of behaving. Being diagnosed with diabetes or heart disease may provoke dietary changes. Losing a job may result in budget-tightening or lifestyle changes. But if it is so difficult for a person to change you can multiply this difficulty for corporations. You're not just changing one person, but perhaps scores, hundreds or even thousands of people; their roles, job requirements, evaluation, performance, expectations, etc. Sure you will encounter resistance, so be prepared. Because of this, many companies like to "spring" major changes on their employees. They wait too long, don't want employees to become discouraged, or less productive, and fail to keep employees in the "loop."

The change models and theories don't help too much either. But one practice seems to prove effective in most change situations. That is: Communication and Participation. Effectively communicating challenges, problems and opportunities helps. Employees feel dis-empowered and betrayed when they are not informed. They may even feel worse if they are not invited to participate in the change process.

Strategies for Change

Since change is ubiquitous, constant, inexorable, pervasive and frightening, what are the best practices for managers and executives?

FIRST, understand that change is inevitable.

SECOND, continually "sense" the environment so that you will be aware of trends, opportunities and threats.

THIRD, embrace change (as it is inevitable anyway) and look for ways to anticipate, adapt and benefit.

FOURTH, ascertain the "match" between your organization, it's industry-specific environment, the general environment, and your organization's internal environment. How's the "fit"? Is it compatible and complementary, or are improvements required?

FIFTH, work on your organization to capitalize on and develop its strengths, and reduce its weak areas.

SIXTH, determine your strategy. Do you need to act immediately, or can you implement a well-planned change process? Remember that immediacy can often provide the "spark" to gain workforce support.

SEVENTH, involve your leadership team, middle and first-line managers, and the workforce by effectively communicating with them and inviting their participation in the change process. Remember: "Everyone is smarter than anyone." And, you will need their support and involvement to successfully change.

EIGHTH, be a leader. This will be your prime opportunity to demonstrate your leadership skills. Leaders provide encouragement and motivation.

NINTH, managers often use consultants to give them credibility, an excuse, or as a "foil" to provide them with leverage to make change. Use this if it helps.

TENTH, try to incorporate the change(s) into the corporate culture. Do this through meetings, policies, change "slogans," revised procedures and continual reinforcement.

ELEVENTH, enlist "change agents" among your employees and managers to make sure your change "sticks"-- but not too much. You should be aiming for semi-permanent change as you will never make the perfect adaptation and you will always have a need or desire to make more change. Try to continually improve and adapt.

TWELFTH, become more expert at change, so that you can recognize the need early on and become more proficient at the process. This way your organization will become more forward-thinking, adaptive and successful.

DOES BAD MANAGEMENT PAY?

Sometimes poor management can pay off. While one should never aim for sub-par management, the law of unintended consequences, the unpredictability of financial conditions and government intervention may reward sub-par management performance. As this book is being written, the United States is in the midst of its worst financial crisis since the Great Depression. Many large corporations, particularly financial institutions, have lost boatloads of money and are in dire financial straits. Government "bailout" programs are in place to purchase "troubled assets" and to help businesses survive. "Uncle Sam" and the U.S. taxpayer have come to the rescue.

Bad Management

Good management requires an astute evaluation of the "risk-reward" equation. Businesses have to take risks to obtain rewards. Big risks often result in big rewards. However, the risks must be "calculated risks." Miscalculations can spell trouble, even bankruptcy, for corporations, and sanctions for their management team.

Peculiar Times

Under normal circumstances poorly run companies would fail, top executives fired, and shareholders lose their investment. But these are not normal times, and the established rules don't apply. With the help of the Government, and the unwitting complicity of the taxpayers, companies are not failing, that should fail, and executives are insulated from the realities of the business world. Take a look at *AIG Corp., Citigroup, Fannie Mae, Freddie Mac, Bear Stearns,* etc. And the list grows by the day, with many assets and much assistance provided by TARP *(Troubled Asset Relief Program)*.

The "Free Market"

The capitalistic free market may be dead or at least on life-support. Decisions used to have consequences, either positive or negative. Of course, these conditions do not apply if you're the "little guy." Thousands of small businesses have failed during this profound economic downturn. They take the risk, and sometimes it doesn't work out. Of course, some large businesses have gone "belly up" too. But the "too big to fail" axiom comes to mind. The logic for protecting the "big guys" is that they provide large numbers of jobs and their political and economic impact is too considerable to allow them to close. However, economists and business people know that small businesses, not large ones, employ most of the workers in this country.

We Need to Protect the "Little Guy"

The problem is, how do we protect the small business owner from the economic downturn caused by the poor decisions of the largest institutions, both public and private? The government, understandably, is more interested in big business. Big businesses have more influence. They employ lobbyists and have friends in the Administration and Congress. They contribute to political campaigns, and their large numbers of employees have some ability to sway policymakers' decisions. However, our economy will not be restored to health unless, and until, a proactive policy to assist small business owners is established and maintained.

In the meantime, don't "hold your breath." And make sure your business has the best possible management.

THE CHANGING NATURE OF LEADERSHIP

Perhaps you've worked for one of them. Or several, or even many like them... The tough, no-nonsense, "don't let 'em see you sweat," type of boss. The type that lets you know she's in charge; the robotic, unfeeling, "strictly business" persona. Well, fortunately, that image, the unemotional, always in control type, is on the wane.

From Mega-Billionaires to the Ordinary Guy

Just look around, and you will see that management has a new "face." When you watch "YouTube" and see the second (was the first, maybe now the third...but always in the top three) richest man in the world "cutting up," you realize management is different. Yes, that is Warren Buffet acting the part of a "rock star" with the long hair wig, singing (sort of), moving to the groove, and promoting his *GEICO* brand. And, he seemed to be having fun. At least he's a good sport. But if you meet Buffet in person, as I was fortunate to do, he shows charm, humility, wit, etc.-- a very personable guy. Yes, you remember he's a uber-wealthy tycoon, but one who doesn't distance himself by acting the part.

When you watch Microsoft's Bill Gates dress up as *Star Trek's* "Dr. Spock," or see the CEO of a multi-billion dollar firm cry on national TV when hearing about his employees' travails, you begin to realize that the image of business leadership has forever changed.

Even the President has his moments. President Obama is the type who demonstrates an ability to adapt to many roles and expectations. He looks and acts human. He dresses "down," relates exceptionally well with audiences, jokes, and yet can be tough when required. But are we ready for this more casual image? Well, a series of prior Presidents helped prepare us: Lyndon Johnson was perhaps a little too "down home," Reagan was friendly, congenial, and adaptable, George "W" Bush, was kind of a "class clown" (whether intentionally or inadvertently).

Is this a Change for the Better?

Do you want to see your boss acting like a "clown," or blubbering like a sissy? Or would you prefer the hard-nosed, "in control" approach, like British Royalty, above the fray; proper and dignified? Which approach engenders more respect, support, admiration...confidence...?

What is Expected of Leadership?

In order to be a leader you must have followers. So the leader, obviously, must engage in behaviors that will encourage, inspire, impel, require, or motivate followership. It is, of course, preferable to have willing followers. Not that they're less maintenance, but they are generally more loyal, dependable, and committed. Certain leaders "demand" respect, but as we've frequently heard: respect must be earned. There are some notable examples of this principle, but perhaps the best is General George S. Patton. During much of World War II, General Patton was considered perhaps our best (although quite eccentric) military leader. However, a seemingly minor incident, when he slapped a hospitalized soldier with battle fatigue - and called him a coward - contributed to his downfall. The perception of the General as an effective, gifted and noble leader was immediately questioned, and he was relieved of his command. Abuse of power and authority and disregard of those you lead is, in most cases, a recipe for disaster.

Leadership is demanding and burdensome. However, the rewards for the effective leader, and for the organization she leads, can be profound.

WHAT TO CONTROL

Without being a "control freak" what can the manager do to ensure that necessary controls are in place? An uncontrolled business is like a runaway train. It rapidly keeps going toward an uncertain future with an almost certainty that it will go off track.

How to Control

In the beginning of this discussion we referred to "control freaks." You know the type. They want to know everything, make sure they are involved in everything, even the most mundane or trivial. How can this type of manager be effective, without going nuts? The answer is, of course, a manager cannot possibly be effective and successful trying to control everything, except for a very short period of time and for a limited number of variables. Modern business are far too complex, and the environment way too unpredictable to accommodate "control freaks." This doesn't mean you should give up on trying to control what happens in your business. Far from it. Control is essential. The manager just needs to be selective, disciplined and creative.

What to Control

Start by analyzing what are the most important "success factors" for your business. Those areas that are most critical to your enterprise's survival and progress. Typical examples are: sales, costs, personnel, customer responsiveness, etc.

The list should be developed collaboratively with participants from key areas. Managers who are responsible for certain functional areas will typically be pleased by having the opportunity to participate in the process. They want to know and understand the criteria by which their performance will be measured. How else can they improve their performance?

Who and When?

The person(s) responsible for controlling certain aspects of business performance are those having responsibility for the function or task. Whether it is Accounting, Sales, Marketing, Production, etc., the assigned manager is the one who must implement and monitor the control mechanisms. Accountability is another consideration. While the manager can delegate "responsibility," he must retain "accountability."

The manager, ultimately, is the individual who is accountable for what takes place in his area,

Time frames are also important. Some factors require daily (or even more frequent) monitoring; others can be tracked weekly or monthly, perhaps even quarterly. Just consider the potential impact on the business and the monitoring time cycle will be apparent. While some expenditures, or income categories can bankrupt the firm quickly (i.e., days or weeks), others might be less critical. The "critical few" must be identified, selected and incorporated into the control and information reporting systems. The parameters for tolerable performance in these areas must also be decided and implemented.

Get started

Don't procrastinate. When it comes to control, information is essential. Actions must be taken promptly when things get off track, so that the course can be corrected.

Realistic control systems and procedures will be a significant advance in securing a bright, profitable, and more certain business future.

BUSINESS ON A SCALE OF 1 TO 10

Control is one of the more challenging management responsibilities. In order to control you must first measure. Without valid, meaningful and accurate measurements, control is just about impossible, i.e., "you can't control what you can't measure."

Estimating

As a beginning point, and sometimes even an end-point, estimating is the first step in the measurement process. It provides more substance and objectivity than just a "wild guess." People who estimate do so with standards and benchmarks in mind, and use their expertise and experience to make value judgments. For example, when you go to the auto mechanic, or consider a contractor for a home improvement job, you will invariably "ask for an estimate." "How much will it cost" is an important question.

So it is in management, we constantly want "time and cost" estimates and calculations. These numbers are an important component of the decision-making process. But more subjective measurements may be valuable too.

Subjective information

At one point in my career I had a boss who would begin most of our conversations with a question: "On a scale of One to Ten..." For example, he would ask: On a scale of one to ten how would you rate product X, or performance Y, or your speech to the regional managers, or... At first I thought it was interesting, or cute, or sometimes annoying, but I quickly realized this was his way of gaining information: Qualitative, evaluative information. Assessments, if you will, of various factors important to him or the organization.

Significance

My boss's approach was not a bad one. Sure, it had its limitations, but it had value as well. The technique was "quick and dirty," but a rapid numerical evaluation that helped him form a concept of what was going on, and how the organization was performing.

Organizations, politicians, marketing firms, etc., use this approach all the time. And, in colleges, particularly in the Social Sciences, "Attitude Surveys" are de rigueur for data gathering concerning public opinion.

The value of this type of data-gathering may range from fast subjective opinion to the basis for more serious research. It can provide the basis for further study, and more rigorous, objective analysis.

Application

Start using the "scale of one to ten" question in less important settings at first. When you go out to dinner with your spouse or "significant other" ask: On a scale of one to ten, "how would you rate the food"? Then, perhaps, and "how would you rate the service"? How about the "ambience?"

You get the idea.

When you try it at work, you'll be surprised at the results. Generally, people will be close in their assessment. However, sometimes you or someone else may be "off base." You will learn who has the "best" judgment and who does not. You will discover who likes to "play it safe," and who will emphatically stand by their evaluations. In any event, you may find this to be a useful opinion gathering mechanism, and perhaps a rudimentary measurement technique.

Remember, you can't control what you can't measure, and the first step may be a one to ten opinion.

TIME IS MONEY (AND RESPECT)

Disregard for punctuality is widespread. In business this can be a costly, inconsiderate, and inappropriate practice.

Bad Habits

Being late to work, meetings, events, or appointments can easily become a habit. Just like any other bad habit, if there are not consequences, or if it's easier to do the wrong thing, than it is to do right, the bad habit will persist.

Excuses, Excuses...

When an employee, manager, or business associate is late, you will seldom hear sincerity. You typically won't hear: "I didn't pay attention to the time!" or "I don't manage time well," or, "I didn't think your time was that important." Instead, what is generally heard is an apology or excuse, or both. Sometimes it's silence.

People are very skilled at excusing themselves, and justifying their behavior. Often, they'll make a quick "Sorry I'm late" comment or blame delays on the "traffic."

Annoyance

It can be annoying for employees to be frequently, chronically, or always late. More than an annoyance, the behavior can be an indicator of disrespect, or uncaring. If the employee doesn't consider their own time important, they should certainly value the time of their colleagues, boss, or customers. Managers, in particular, will appreciate the arrival of staff, as scheduled, and the respect, and professionalism these practices convey.

Costly Practices

It should be apparent that lateness can be costly. It isn't just the culprit that incurs the cost, but the entire organization. When a meeting doesn't start on time, it's the cost of the salaries of all participants. This multiplier effect can be devastating to productivity and budgets.

If a project doesn't start on time, the business doesn't open as scheduled -and revenue is lost- it's costly.

In tough times like these, when every dollar counts, managers have a right; indeed an obligation, to request and require promptness.

Organization Culture

Managers and executives would do well by promoting a culture of timeliness, a sense of urgency, respect for others, and personal accountability. A business-like culture and attitude will convey a reassuring perception of dependability, efficiency and performance that is important in dealing with customers, partners, suppliers, etc. A reputation like this is exceptionally valuable. It's nice to hear: "You can count on them!" "They're the best!" "If they said it, it will be done!" and, "They will be there when you need them!"

Some Steps Toward Improving Timeliness and Punctuality

--Be a role model for dependability and punctuality

--Emphasize the importance and value of showing up as scheduled

--Calculate the costs associated with delays

--Discuss the importance of stakeholder perceptions

--Don't let constant tardiness slide

--Connect the dots, so employees can appreciate the value of changing their behaviors

--Recognize and show appreciation for dependability

THE IMPORTANCE OF "COUNTING THE BEANS"

They call accountants "bean counters." Well, the total number of beans, whether they're available, increasing or decreasing, and if they're of high quality all matter to the viability and future of your business. Yes, accountants can make or break your business. Sales are important, so is customer relations and product, too. There is no denying it, successful businesses rely on many factors. Everything from strategic planning, to marketing, and more, contribute to success. But accurate, objective accounting is paramount.

The Entrepreneur

It is well known that poor management is the primary reason for business failure. Entrepreneurs are often the "idea people," and typically not very good at business details. Experienced mangers know that you must hire people who have strengths that you lack.

Accounting

Nothing may be more important to business success than bean counting. Accounting for, and knowing with accuracy and confidence, your financial standing is arguably the most critical determinant between success and failure. How can you possibly make sound business decisions without knowing, with confidence, your financial situation and the fiscal risks and potential rewards associated with your plans?

Cost accounting, cash flow accounting, accrual accounting, tax accounting, etc., may all seem incredibly complex, even incomprehensible, to many business owners. Yet when there are insufficient funds for a business expansion, relocation or acquisition, reality hits home. Poor cash management can cause or contribute to the demise of your enterprise, very quickly.

What Should You be Concerned With?

Cash management is probably the most important measurement. You need to know how much money you have on hand, whether it's increasing or decreasing, when your cash needs may increase (or decrease), how and where to obtain more cash, etc. What we all want is "positive cash flow" (i.e., more $$$ coming in than going out). If this is not the case, you need to be concerned and proactive, especially when it's not a temporary circumstance.

How do You Find an Accountant?

First, you must decide if you need a full-time accountant. Small businesses frequently rely on local *CPA*'s, and/or contract auditors and public accountants. Whatever your approach, the selection of an accountant is a task of import and consequence. The Yellow Pages won't do.

Ask other business owners, check with your *Chamber of Commerce*, obtain referrals, and/or check with the *American Institute of Certified Public Accountants*. On the Institute's website you can limit your search by city and state, or search your state's chapter resource. Because of the importance of this decision, take your time, perform due diligence, and consider several individuals and options. It has to be someone you're comfortable with. After all, your accountant will know intimate details of your business.

You will certainly want competence, experience, expertise, loyalty, confidentiality, good judgment and honesty. You will also want an individual who takes a personal and serious interest in your business; its success and growth. And you need someone who will go beyond the numbers and provide input to you so that you can achieve your goals and dreams.

CUT YOUR BUSINESS EXPENSES INTELLIGENTLY

With the possible exception of *American Banknote Company*, businesses are not able to print money. Because of this simple fact managers must effectively control resources, especially cash, so that they are able to weather business downturns.

Capital Shortage

It turns out that in the early 2000's some banks were loaning 30X their capital reserve. The folly of this tremendous leverage soon became apparent, with an economic downturn precipitated by the "housing crisis." When mortgages "went south" many financial institutions could not cover their outstanding obligations. So they curtailed lending in order to conserve cash and began a difficult, self-defeating spiral of credit shortage - reduced consumer and business spending - reduced income - further reductions, etc. And, although the downturn began with the housing sector, it quickly spread to other segments of the economy. Then, we found that many other companies (automobiles, retailers, etc.) also had substantial debt, and had based their sales projections on ever-expanding consumer purchasing assumptions. Even massive federal intervention could not stem the downward spiral. As a result of these circumstances everyone learned the perils of debt and over-spending. Plus they found that underfunded companies were vulnerable and unable to exploit business opportunities when credit dried up.

A Common Theme

The common theme here is that companies used debt as an expansion or operations tool while failing to build cash reserves to tide them over uncertain times. One thing is certain: change will happen. Cycles will occur, unanticipated events will take place, consumer sentiment will not remain static, and purchasing patterns will alter. This is particularly true in an economy such as ours, which is 80% consumer-driven. With mass media influence, consumer sentiment and purchasing plans can be influenced with rapidity and profound consequences.

In prior eras, and a diverse manufacturing/exporting economy, many factors would have to conspire to create an economic "perfect storm." Purchasers in diverse sectors and countries would have to curtail expenditures simultaneously.   No longer. With a national consumer-based economy and overwhelming mass media influence, consumer sentiment and purchasing plans can be influenced with rapidity and profound consequences.

Money is the "Lifeblood" of Business

Business owners, Boards of Directors, and company executives would be wise to adopt a philosophy and practice of sound financial management, perhaps even frugality. Executive compensation is one of the areas to examine. Almost every day we learn of some corporate executive or investment banker with a salary and bonus structure amounting to $100 million or more. This is absurd. While executives should be compensated in accordance with their contribution to the company, outlandish packages are counterproductive. How much in sales will be required to generate the amounts necessary to pay these overcompensated characters?

Yes, there are transformational leaders who can make a "sea change" of difference in corporate earnings. But these individuals are few, and far between. Bloated salaries more often go to marginal contributors who have cozy relationships with the Board's compensation committee. Structured compensation plans targeted to incentivize particular performance results, along with realistic total compensation "caps" would be better. Then, costs would be contained, while attainment of strategic financial goals is rewarded.

Cozy relationships with suppliers, consultants, and others can also hurt the bottom-line. We have all suspected or known of such deal-making. Certain vendors seem to have an "in" with management. And while the "low bidder" may not offer the best overall deal, it is certainly responsible to promote a competitive atmosphere.

The biggest savings usually accrue from the minutia. The little costs, as they say add up. In government, the joke is: "a few billion here, a few billion there, and pretty soon we're talking real money!" Saving a nickel on an item that you use thousands of will help the bottom line.

Recommendations

--Re-examine all cost items. Scrutinize them rigorously and identify potential cost reductions.

--Reward employees with incentive for identifying savings. Rewards should be based on a percentage of the cost-savings realized over a reasonable period of time, say first quarter actual savings or projected amount based on a trial period.

--Perform a compensation review, especially executive compensation, to make sure your salaries are in line with comparable companies, particularly the competition.

--Examine your pricing structure and ascertain if it is competitive, or too high or low.

--Negotiate with your suppliers, the landlords, everyone that you pay money to, and see if you can get a better deal. Negotiate, negotiate, and negotiate.

--Don't use a "meat axe" approach to cutting costs; use a scalpel instead! Across-the-board cuts only work over a short, emergency, period. Besides, it penalizes the most effective and conservative units in the organization.

--Develop a "cost consciousness" among your employees. This starts with the executive ranks, but is required of everyone in the organization. Wasteful mentalities cannot be tolerated in today's economic climate.

PRODUCTIVITY IMPROVEMENT - WHAT A MANAGER CAN DO

Getting the job done with fewer resources improves organizational performance and profitability. Productivity is a simple ratio of output to input. (i.e., P= O/I) The higher the ratio, the better the productivity.

The manager can have a profound impact on productivity by implementing a few simple practices. The following is a useful process, along with tips to improve productivity.

1. **Develop some basic measures of baseline performance.** The old axiom- "You can't improve what you can't measure" - holds true here. Establish baselines for output such as: Number of "widgets" produced, reports completed, sales closed, revenue, etc.

2. **Perform a similar process for inputs:** E.g., raw material consumed, dollars spent, time expended, etc.

3. **Be sure to measure what is truly important to the success and profitability of your organization** (e.g., the "critical few."). Measuring performance which is not critical (e.g., reports and analyses) wastes time and money and can deceive the manager about the real performance of the organization.

4. **Begin recording the numbers from steps 1 and 2**. Your first month, week, hour, quarter, will be your "baseline". Then you can track improvement (or deterioration) from there by comparing like periods to your baseline.

5. **Examine methods and procedures to ascertain where improvements can be made.** Be sure to involve the people actually doing the work as they will understand the process better than anyone else. Frequently the same employees, who have been underperforming because of outmoded or inefficient procedures and processes, will welcome the opportunity to make recommendations. Often, they have never been asked.

6. **Although the process doesn't require a Consultant, oftentimes dramatic and lasting improvements can be effected through the use of an outside analyst.** There is value to someone's opinion that is not immersed in the day-to-day process. Consultants or facilitators have an advantage of perspective, as they operate from the "catbird seat of objectivity."

7. **Provide incentives for improved performance.** These do not necessarily have to be monetary, but need to be valued by the employee, such as: Recognition, increased responsibility, variation in routine, time off, flextime, etc.

8. **Involve the entire organization in the process.** Show how improvements will benefit the employees. Celebrate success.

9. **Continuous improvement is another consideration.** Obviously, if you're content to "rest on your laurels" your organization will not achieve its full potential. Examine and reexamine your performance and processes to gain ongoing performance improvement.

10. **Make productivity improvement a personal and organizational priority.** Demonstrate your interest, concern, and willingness to invest the time, energy and resources to accomplish productivity goals.

PRODUCTIVITY IMPROVEMENT FOR TOUGH TIMES

One solution in tough economic times is to "do more with less." That's what productivity improvement is all about. They used to call it "more bang for the buck." And with fewer bucks to go around, managers are looking to productivity improvement to help them cope.

A Question

Would you rather have twenty employees producing 1,000 "widgets" a day or ten workers producing seven hundred and fifty? The answer is pretty clear. While the twenty employees are making 50 units each, the ten employees output, at 75, is 50% greater! This can mean the difference between loss and profitability; between survival and failure.

The Formula

The productivity formula is a simple one: **P=O/I**. Productivity = Output divided by Input. The more input required to produce something, the lower the productivity. Conversely, more output realized from the same or lower input results in greater productivity.

Measurement

The first key to productivity is measurement. The manager must know what the employees are doing. What are they supposed to be producing? Admittedly, this can be more difficult than it seems. Employees produce something. Is it reports, customer contacts, completed service calls, product sales, etc.? Frequently it is several outcomes/deliverables. Determine the basic outputs for each employee. This will require some analysis and thought, as what the employee is currently producing may not be what they should be producing.

Standards

The second key is establishing "standards." Once we know what the employee should be producing, how much of it should they be producing, and in what time-frame? Establishing standards is essential and will enable some measure of control and evaluation.

Benchmarking

Can you compare what your employees are doing with what other employees are doing in similar companies within your industry? If so, your task is easier. You will be able to make comparisons. This factor alone will provide some objectivity to the process. Sometimes these reports cover only a few types of jobs, and do not take into account all of the unique factors of your particular environment. In any event, adjustments will be required. However, you will have meaningful starting point for this part of your analysis, and industry comparisons provide useful leverage in dealing with employees.

Evaluation

The data which you have secured thus far must be analyzed. Tweaking the criteria, measurements, standards, data collection procedures and reporting will be necessary. If the outcome is not what you expect or need and it cannot be adequately explained by system deficiencies or measurement difficulties, then you must take action. For example, if your workers are 15% below the industry average, why? If they're twenty percent above, why? If they're "right on," why? Your analysis should include what you may be doing "right," as well as areas that cry for improvement.

Improvement Targets

When your monitoring system is in place, and you're satisfied that you're measuring the right things, measuring them accurately, and you have an ongoing capability to do this-it's time to consider improvement targets. The concept of "continuous improvement" is based on the premise that "nothing is perfect," and there is always room for improvement. You will need to establish moderate, realistic, attainable targets. Remember the *S.M.A.R.T.* goal-setting criteria. Goals need to be: **S**pecific, **M**easureable, **A**ttainable, **R**ealistic, and **T**imely.

Consistency

You're not done yet. Successful organizations not only implement the above steps, they consistently apply these principles, techniques, procedures, analyses, and processes aimed at creating a more productive enterprise.

Don't Forget Quality

Yes, productivity is important, but not at the cost of sacrificing quality. Shortcuts can be taken, processes streamlined, more "widgets" produced, but quality standards must be maintained.

A reputation for low quality will quickly negate any cost efficiencies realized through productivity gains.

Why is this Important?

Productivity improvement may be more important at this time than at any point in recent history. Current economic conditions necessitate cost reduction to maintain profitability. However, many companies are using a "meat axe" approach to the problem. They are cutting the payrolls by laying off employees. Sure this reduces costs, but without a more methodical approach, any long-lasting gains may prove elusive.

Tough times call for tough measures, but productivity management is simply a good business practice that is more important now than ever.

INFORMATION INFUSION

Business people are fond of talking about "Information Overload." However, is this really the problem? The availability and accessibility of pertinent, quality, timely and useful information is an essential condition for business survival, success and progress.

The Proliferation of Data

Of course data is important. Collecting data; numbers, if you will, is only a preliminary step. Knowing what you need and want to measure are decisions of consequence. You will certainly need financial data, sales data, inventory data, etc. You will probably also need data about payroll, personnel, customers, competition, etc., and much more.

Computers can churn out data so fast that it's impossible for anyone, or everyone for that matter, to keep up.

All of this data can be a bit overwhelming. Managers frequently complain that they are drowning under the weight of too much data. Technology has, of course, contributed to this groundswell. Just check your email, or in-box, or files, or... Remember when paper files were going to be eliminated, and replaced with electronic files? Well, if it happened I missed it, and so did the vast majority of businesses.

Information vs. Data

Data can be useful only through transformation. Although we constantly ask for data (i.e., "show me the data!"), most often we mean "provide me with the information!" In most elemental forms data is of little value (i.e., "raw" data). To be of value, it needs to be analyzed and transformed into useful information. This transformation process requires that decisions be made concerning which information will be essential to the success of the enterprise and those reports which afford critical planning and trend insights.

Designing Your Information System

Where to begin is always the question. Well, begin at the end! The final output that you need will dictate all aspects of your company's information system. So start identifying, listing, and defining what you need in your business reports. These requirements will determine the data elements that need to be captured. If you require sales information you will probably want to capture total sales volume and revenue, perhaps by item, then maybe broken down into categories (e.g., high profit items, types, brands or styles, by customer or type of customer, etc.). More sophisticated systems will provide analytical information and decision-making support.

Buy or Build?

The classic choice has been between buying an existing information system and building one custom-made to meet your needs. Of course there may be a huge cost differential. But there is a third path. You can purchase an Information Systems package and modify it to accommodate your unique requirements. However, you may need professional help to accomplish this.

Here again, you will have choices. You can find an Information Systems consultant or you can find a vendor that will make the changes to their existing package.

Whatever you decide, consider the following:

--Carefully determine your information needs.

--Start at the end--- your data output requirements.

--Look closely at what other companies (as similar as possible to your own) are doing.

--Consider "packaged systems," "custom systems," and modified package systems.

--Meet with vendors, consultants, etc.

--Get recommendations from friends, fellow business owners, Chamber of Commerce and Professional Business Association members, etc.

--Don't rush your decision. Remember that your decision is an important one, and take your time. The right system can enhance your business, control costs, identify opportunities, insure compliance with regulatory requirements, and make management, reporting and tax filing easier. The wrong system can be a nightmare.

INCREMENTALISM: ONE PATH TO CHANGE

Business people are enamored with change, and it makes sense. To stand still in the face of environmental and competitive change is a sure recipe for failure. New ways and new products must constantly be invented and implemented to survive and make progress in the marketplace.

Change Theory

The elements of change are quite simple; you merely modify what your organization is doing either incrementally or radically. The process seems rather straightforward but the process is far from easy or inconsequential. One of the most important aspects of installing change is the inevitability of resistance. When people are a part of the change process they will typically resist, even though they may appear to be embracing the new way of doing things.

This resistance must be anticipated, planned for, and dealt with. It is easier said than done.

Communication and Participation

There are two important keys to facilitating change. The first is COMMUNICATION and the second is PARTICIPATION. People react better when they know what's happening. Fear of the unknown will make even the most stable individual a little anxious, maybe even irrational. Even in this era of rapid change people tend to cling to the familiar. And perhaps it is because of the rapidity of change and it's unpredictability that people resist even more. Also change is frequently equated with loss. In the workplace there are always winners and losers. Every change brings with it opportunities (for advancement, challenge, etc.) and potential negatives, such as loss of familiarity, position, status, competence, even money.

Bosses are encouraged, or compelled, to put a "happy face" on change so that employees will "buy in." This is often an unrealistic expectation. How do you measure "buy in" or support? How do you know when employees are feigning?

Of course employees sometimes welcome change, particularly when the benefits have been communicated, observed, anticipated or realized. And, being a party to the change, helping install or make the change also promotes "buy in."

The Boiling Frog

Many have heard the story of the "boiling frog." The story goes something like this: A frog is placed in a pot of water. The water temperature is gradually increased until it is boiling. What happens to the frog? Because the temperature is increased so slowly the frog does not react. He suffers high temperature demise. What if we would have thrown the frog into the boiling water? He would have immediately jumped out. The assault on his senses would have been too great to bear. (This story is not to be construed that in any way I have a tolerance for animal cruelty. It is merely provided to illustrate the point)

Incremental change is tolerated far better than radical change. Think about inflation, gas prices, technology... Gradual change is more acceptable, or at least will meet with less resistance, than radical, complete, or instant change.

Lessons to be Learned

There are several lessons to be learned in implementing the change process:

First, change is often necessary, inevitable and/or desirable.

Second, the manager must be prepared for RESISTANCE.

Third, COMMUNICATION and PARTICIPATION will mitigate the resistance.

Fourth, benefits of the change must be identified and clearly communicated to those involved in the change.

Fifth, employees want to succeed, and will accommodate, adapt, and support change when it is handled correctly.

Sixth, people are resilient and capable of adapting.

Seventh, incremental change will be tolerated better, be less disruptive, and more likely to persist.

Eighth, sometimes radical, immediate change is necessary, and other times a more gradual approach may work just fine.

CRISIS MANAGEMENT

In business, crisis management is practically unavoidable. Mistakes will be made. Accidents will happen. Products will be flawed. Acts of God will continue.

Since you can't avoid crises, you'd better prepare for their inevitable eventuality, and: act promptly, intelligently, decisively, strategically, politically, sensitively, honestly, and with a genuine effort to resolve the issue and prevent further harm and recurrence.

Background

As a reminder, some major crises include: *Johnson & Johnson* (Tylenol); *Proctor & Gamble* (Tampon/ toxic shock); *Union Carbide* (Toxic Chemicals); Three Mile Island (Nuclear); Hurricane Katrina; *Exxon* (Valdez/ Oil Spill); the 2008 Financial Meltdown (as well as many prior Market crashes), and most recently, the *BP* (Oil Spill).

The BP Crisis

This part was written on around day 45 of the Gulf (of Mexico) Oil Spill Crisis. *BP* (British Petroleum) was under siege with public relations, environmental, and financial problems, as a consequence of a disastrous, deadly, contaminating, incident of unprecedented proportion. This infamous event began in late April, 2010 when an explosion destroyed the surface drilling platform, (with 11 platform worker fatalities), and shut-off devices failed to turn off the gusher of oil spewing from a severed pipe at the bottom of the sea, one mile deep.

Various strategies were tried to stem the daily multi-thousand barrel flow of pollution from the wrecked installation. Robots were placed to handle repairs at the high pressures, great depth, and poor visibility, on the seabed. The U.S. Government mobilized it's resources (*Coast Guard*, *FEMA*, various federal agencies, *National Guard*, etc,), but were largely ineffective and responsiveness appeared to be "too little; too late." BP tried multiple approaches to capping the well and stopping the oil flow. Approaches termed: "Top Kill,""riser package cap," "replacing a 'blowout' preventer," and a longer term "relief well" is in progress ("*BP* Begins...New Strategy..."*Bloomberg.com*, May 30, 2010). Nothing worked, and perhaps irreversible damage is being done to precious wetlands, beaches, and habitats for marine life, birds, animals, and birds. What a mess! Finally, the oil leak was stopped after about three months of leakage.

The Management Perspective

"Crisis Management" is a leadership specialty, and reputations and fortunes of individuals, governments, and private companies can be severely, perhaps irreparably, damaged if the event, public perception, and restorative actions are mishandled. The classic strategies for these types of events were largely ignored, or conspicuously fumbled. The President of *BP* looked bad, as did the President of the United States. Ineptness appeared to rule the day and the government; along with one of the largest energy corporations in the world, were unable to control, or resolve the event.

Crisis Management

Although there is no consensus about how a crisis should be handled, there are a number of common themes. The basics are:

--CRISIS PREVENTION

The most important activity which can be taken is to take action(s) to prevent a crisis from occurring in the first place!

--CRISIS PLANNING

Should a crisis occur, despite all your good preventative efforts, have plans in place to deal with likely, unlikely, and forecastable occurrences. Appropriate planning, prior to the inevitable disaster, will help focus efforts, limit delays, and mitigate the damage. It provides a level of reassurance for all stakeholders.

--CRISIS INTERVENTION

Initiate timely, forceful, and focused actions to limit the scope and duration of the crisis.

--CRISIS MANAGEMENT

Management consists of planning, organizing, leading and controlling. In a crisis, the leadership must be clear, respected, visible, and trustworthy. Coordination and resource management are essential; project management skills are required.

--CRISIS COMMUNICATION

Honesty, transparency, and frequency of communication are important.

Deception, minimization, hiding, or avoidance are deadly. Trust will be lost when lies or misrepresentation are discovered. The press needs access, and will become hostile if spokespersons are not forthright.

--CRISIS ETHICS and CRISIS HUMANITY

The crisis needs to be handled in an ethical fashion. It is essential that morality supersede financial considerations.

The emotions, health, feelings; personal and financial impact on individuals are paramount considerations. Leaders need to sincerely demonstrate their compassion, sensitivity, and empathy for those adversely impacted. The human side of crisis will undoubtedly require immediate, continuing, and genuine support.

Back to Our Example...

The *BP* incident appears to have been mishandled on so many levels that it will surely be a case study on how crises should NOT be managed. *BP* has suffered billions in stock losses, and probable financial liabilities. The damage to business and government reputations and trust is yet to be determined, although it is appears major destruction has been done in this arena, as well as to the environment and economy.

With the high stakes implicit in major crises, managers would be smart to consider the aforementioned points; update, review, and revise their Crisis Management Policies and Plans, and be prepared. You don't want to be in the news for your mismanagement in a crisis.

ESCAPING FROM THE "CORRIDOR OF CRISIS"

Have you ever worked in a chaotic organization? We already know the answer!

All organizations experience crisis at one time or another. It's not whether you're in crisis, but how the organization deals with the crisis that counts.

The Corridor of Crisis

Sometimes the situation is described as a "corridor" of crisis, meaning that it feels like walking down a fearful, chaotic hallway or tunnel in which you cannot predict what will happen next, but you're pretty sure it will not be good. Organizations in crisis do not make rational plans. The leaders are too busy "putting out fires" to formulate good decisions and strategies. They are in a reactive mode, rather than a proactive one, and therefore the circumstances control them, rather than vice-versa. Organizations in crisis are "pressure cookers" and stress is pervasive. Managers and employees suffering from stress make more mistakes, jump to conclusions, "finger-point" and blame. They contribute to the problems rather than address them. The Corridor of Crisis is a very unpleasant place to be.

Diagnosis

Consultants are fond of saying "the problem is NEVER the problem". And, so it is with crisis. The problem is not the crisis, but the crisis is a symptom of a real problem/problems.

Leaders need to begin the process of identifying the REAL problem(s) as opposed to the PRESENTING problem(s) which is/are undoubtedly a symptom(s).

Just like in your physician's office the diagnosis begins with "what's bothering you? And "do you have any pain, discomfort/ irregularities", etc. Then the process of ruling out causes, to come up with the treatable diagnosis begins. In the business scenario, is it procedures, processes, structure, culture, or a combination of factors?

In your organization the diagnostic process should be done with the consultation of outside experts (consultants) and/or internal parties. While the objectivity and experience of an outside party cannot be disputed, the stakeholders have a vested interest in problem resolution, and a powerful incentive to correct the situation.

Formulating a Plan of Action

The diagnosis/analysis process, described above, should have the result of confirming that management is serious about improving the situation, and the invitation of employees/managers to participate in the improvement process will gain buy-in.

Once you have identified the real problem(s), the treatment plan can be developed, implemented and evaluated. Generally, the manager's first priority should be to "slow things down". Leadership's primary responsibility is plan for the future. The future of the organization will be predicated on how well the organization functions, and adapts to its environment. Dysfunctional organizations will have challenges in adapting to environmental change and securing a successful future.

Slowing things down means that instead of reacting to the small crises the organization's leadership deliberately chooses to focus on identifying and resolving the main problems.

It's like "time out" in conflict situations. Just stepping back to examine what's taking place has some value. The perception that someone is taking charge and truly attempting to bring order out of chaos will in itself jump-start the change process.

Change

Leaving the Corridor of Crisis is not an easy process. There are many models of change; however, all are in agreement that the process is difficult. But not more difficult than remaining in the "corridor." All change models recognize that COMMUNICATION and PARTICIPATION are essential. Simply mandating change, while it may result in some temporary improvement, will not result in enduring improvement, and more than likely the organization will soon revert to crisis.

Social Psychologist and management change theorist Kurt Lewin developed a three-stage model of change implementation. The first stage is "unfreezing." This means taking aggressive action to break old, dysfunctional patterns. The next step is "movement" away from the old patterns and towards the desired new condition. The final step is to "refreeze" the new process/procedure(s)/system(s) into a state of permanency.

Escape

Managers will recognize that nothing is ever permanent and everything is constantly changing. So, the illusion that whatever steps you take will forever resolve your problems must be discarded. Instead, vow to revisit your improvements periodically to assess their level of functioning and to reinstitute the change process as necessary. This will promote a climate which is not as susceptible to crisis and a mood that is more anticipatory.

The adaptability, flexibility and sensitivity of management along with a willingness to experiment with and confront change will ultimately define organizational success.

CULTIVATE AN ORGANIC ORGANIZATION

Is your company alive or dead?

Most businesses are still organized in a "mechanistic" fashion. This model developed in the 1800's during the Industrial Revolution when machines were viewed as King. And, the design has held up well. The "One Best Way" philosophy led to *Frederick Taylor's* "time and motion" studies and efforts to turn employees into extensions of machines; predictable and efficient. (*Principles of Scientific Management,* Taylor, 1911). The organization, as a "well-oiled" machine is a view that continues to this day.

The quest for optimal organizational structure and functioning continued with *Max Weber's* concept of the "Ideal Bureaucracy" (*The Theory of Social and Economic Organization,* Weber, 1947). During this period, functionality, structure, hierarchy, reporting relationships, division of labor, job descriptions, etc., were all standardized to produce greater efficiency.

The machine model began to be reexamined in the second half of the twentieth century as its limitations in a rapidly changing world became obvious.

Organic vs. Mechanistic

Machines are not alive; organisms are.

Machines do not adapt well to environmental changes, they just continue to function in a predictable fashion no matter what changes are going on around them. Organisms, on the other hand, interact, adapt and evolve to meet environmental requirements. The survivability of organisms depends on their ability to adapt to environmental changes.

Organizations are, importantly, social systems as well as business systems. The social and human-interactive nature of these entities results in many changes in the way they function and adapt. This human component, while making them more adaptable, also makes them less controllable and less predictable. Whereas command and control are the essential elements of the mechanistic organization.

New machines can be developed to meet new requirements, although this is a time-consuming and futile process. Obsolescence is pervasive and unavoidable.

Of course, in the final analysis, organizations are not alive whether they are mechanistic or organic but we can appreciate the difference between a relatively static mechanism and an evolving, changing entity.

Organic is "healthier"

Whether in the Boardroom or the Supermarket, organic is healthier! The poisonous nature of a stagnant, outmoded, unresponsive, difficult to change, business organization is apparent to those immersed in one. There is an inertia, partly as a result of "resistance to change," largely due to "vested interests," and to some extent the delusion that there is, in fact, "one best way."

Having the characteristics of a living organism, the organic organization seeks the best and most synergistic "match" between itself and its environmental conditions.

Organizational health is largely dependent on the model in place.

How do we make the transition from mechanistic to organic?

Let's be up-front. This is not an easy task. There is over one hundred years of history, organization theory and practice supporting the existing structures. The inertia is huge, and there is always a fear of, and resistance to, change. Of course, it can be accomplished.

The mindset must be changed. In order to do this the leader must "cultivate" the growth of the "organism." How is this done?

To continue with the "cultivation" analogy, the leader begins by:

First, select an area that's fertile. Find an area that's fertile to plant "change". Start with a small garden. In many businesses this will be the research, product development or marketing areas.

Second, begin tilling the soil in preparation for planting. The tilling is "stirring up" the status quo, and preparing the selected area for growth. The old patterns must be deconstructed before movement toward the new can begin.

Third, plant the seeds of change and growth. The leader plants seeds (ideas) of change. Then once a few take root, he protects the fragile plants (change initiatives) with careful care and attention. As anyone who has grown a garden knows this is challenging.

Fourth, nurture and promote the plantings by using fertilizer, pulling "weeds", etc. Fertilize the new crop of ideas and relationships with support, praise, attention, feedback and caring. When the "weeds" of doubt or dissatisfaction appear, pull them out with participation, trust and communication.

Fifth, then: as the growth and change mature, harvest the crop. The rewards of the process will become apparent. The outcome should be productive, yielding valuable results; improved organization function, improved communication, teamwork, appreciation for individual talents and contribution, reduced territorialism, better adaptability to the environment.

Put it all together

Recognize if your formal, traditional, hierarchical organization is doing the job for you. In some industries it works better than others. If you decide you want to change the way you operate, consider a more organic form. Try the "cultivation" model described above.

Modern times require new approaches suited to rapidly changing conditions, better able to deal with more intense and broader competition, and more conducive to the sociology of the enterprise. Breaking down the artificial barriers of rigid organization structure, well-suited to a prior, more stable context may be your best solution.

SHAKE-UP YOUR ORGANIZATION

Just like people, organizations have a tendency to become complacent and lethargic. Once in a while it's important to re-energize your staff by initiating change. Now, you're probably thinking: "Everything is already changing so fast!" The problem is, most of these changes come from "outside" not "inside." External mandates don't carry the same weight. They're done because they have to be done; they're *reactive,* not *proactive. And, your staff knows it.*

Reaction to Change

The first human reaction to change is generally RESISTANCE. People prefer the status quo; it gives them a sense of comfort, security, and predictability. Change is difficult, it requires effort, leaning, adjusting and a whole lot of unpleasant activities.

In our society we're taught to welcome change, embrace it, and enjoy it. But the dirty little secret is: most employees know they're supposed to be enthusiastic, so they "fake it."

Managers know how to facilitate change and that most employees want to be regarded as "team players." They use participation and communication, invent slogans and acronyms; unveil change dramatically and in a positive light, and use the old "rah, rah" technique.

Making Meaningful Change

To be meaningful, change must be productive and useful; it must be welcome, purposeful, and doable. Management must be convinced of its value. The endless stream of procedural changes, policy updates, and new systems are viewed as an annoyance -- a cost and necessity of doing business. It's difficult to be enthusiastic about every change coming along. You'd have to be an adrenalin junkie or mentally compromised. People need to make sense of change; to understand its meaning. Psychologist Viktor Frankl (*Man's Search for Meaning*, Beacon Press, 2006) described this search for meaning (and purpose) as a basic human need. And, even though day-to-day business matters are comparatively insignificant, we still want to know why we need to do something, and what the purpose/intent is.

Obviously plausible explanations for major changes need to be provided. The benefits and compelling reasons for the change must be clear to achieve staff buy-in and support.

Initiating Change

As a manager it's your responsibility to successfully implement mandated change. It's part of your job requirements and position description. But as a manager it's also important to be a change initiator as well as a facilitator. So, what kinds of things should you change?

You may want to look at the match between sk lls, abilities and temperament, and employee assignments. Oftentimes there are mismatches that can be corrected through reassignment, job enlargement, job enrichment, or team responsibility. Pay inequities should also be addressed. Managers have a responsibility to ensure that compensation is fair and appropriate. Employee location, offices, work areas, equipment and so forth, are prime avenues for change. Working conditions, hours, schedules, etc. are also opportunities. Team assignments and responsibilities are frequent targets for change as are workload considerations. Re-examining work-low, streamlining processes, eliminating redundancies are also possibilities.

There are plenty of things to change and if done right it will be viewed by your staff as an indication that you know and you care. Signaling to your employees that you have their "best interests" in mind will build loyalty and garner support.

Think about it: What are you going to change?

THE WRITTEN WORD IN BUSINESS

Business writing is important, whether it is good, well-constructed, clear and effective communication, or not. While verbal communications are generally fleeting, written communications endure.

The Good, Bad, and Ugly

Over the years writing has become de-emphasized or neglected. If you have the opportunity, examine old letters, business communications or official documents. Writers typically spent time and effort in their writing, making certain it was elegant and effective. Even handwritten communications reflected a type of care which extended to penmanship, layout, and stationery selection. Somewhere along the way, as a gradual process, and probably as a result of time considerations and technology, beautiful writing (in all aspects of the word) became all but obsolete.

The Importance of Writing

Your writing conveys an impression. Many subtleties are conveyed, impressing the reader, and providing images and non-verbal clues. Your writing can leave the reader with the impression the writer is: Intelligent, caring, concerned, competent, careful, considerate, attentive to details, creative, humorous, organized, customer-focused, stable, etc. On the other hand, the correspondence may convey the impression that the writer is: Careless, unconcerned, incompetent, unknowledgeable, superficial, unintelligent, etc. We've all seen examples of careless writing, and we have all drawn conclusions about the writer, his or her intent, and the effectiveness of the communication. Let's convey a good impression and effective communication whenever possible.

A Simple Technique

A boss of mine once said: "Identify the villain before the end of the story." In other words, don't leave your reader with a mystery, or "clueless." In business communication you're not writing a story; directness and conciseness count. So, a simple, straightforward opening is often best.

An effective and expedient approach is to begin by writing: "The purpose of this letter (or memo, report, etc.) is..." This way your audience (the reader) is immediately aware of your reason for writing. Then, you can go on to explain the background, circumstances, reasons and/or support. Likewise, at the end of your correspondence you can easily state: "In conclusion..." Although this may not be the most elegant way to end, it is unambiguous and effective. Be sure to include what you want the reader to do with the information you provide. For example, are you recommending action, requesting approval, presenting alternatives, or merely being informative?

The Real World

Have you ever heard the responses by Congressional leaders regarding whether they have read an important Bill before they vote on it? Sometimes they will candidly admit that they haven't even read it, or that their staff has reviewed it. This is reality.

Even with important matters, sometimes we just don't have the time. In the business world many memos, letters or reports are not thoroughly reviewed. Although you may consider it your "masterpiece," frequently executives and managers are too busy to donate a great deal of time to reading your treatise.

A standard "busy executive" technique is to read the first paragraph, to see if it is something worthy of their attention. Subsequently the exec might review the last paragraph for any summary, conclusions, and recommendation(s). Finally, if the matter involves a weighty decision, the executive may delve into the body of your paper to gain more detailed information. This is the real world. Don't dismay, just adapt.

The Key Points

We started by stressing the importance of effective business communication through writing. Now let's use some of our recommended strategies:

The purpose of this document is to emphasize the importance of written communication and provide some useful tips. Background information and advice is presented to underscore this purpose, and explain the approaches. In conclusion, written business communication can be improved by adopting some simple strategies. It is recommended that you consider using this information to improve the quality and effectiveness of your business writing.

REINVENTION IS AN ONGOING PROCESS

Companies may have been created as a result of an invention, or new creation, but to survive they must keep the process going. This doesn't mean "tinkering" with minor components, systems, or procedures. It means an original creative process aimed at discovery. Discoveries are a product of the imagination. However, once a novel idea or approach has resulted in the creation of a business or product, to keep the thing going does not allow for complacency.

Reinvention is the process by which organizations regain that initial "spark" of creativity, enthusiasm and innovation that allows them to reverse the "decline" period of the business life-cycle, and begin re-building and growing again.

What is Our Business?

Rethinking what business you are in is a good place to start. "What business are we in?" may seem to be a ridiculous question with an obvious answer. However, it is neither! For example, it may appear you are in the auto repair business, but you may actually be in the transportation business. Your service is designed to facilitate the transport of individuals and families from point "A" to point "B." There are many ways to make the trip. Public transportation, rental car, taxi, or a replacement vehicle (new or used), are all options. Many repair shops recognize this simple fact and either provide transport to the person's residence or workplace, or provide a convenient rental car agency service, or even a loaner car. For some auto repair shops this service is the deciding factor for their customers, and without it they would not be as successful.

If you were starting your business today, would it look the same? With changes in technologies, business practices, consumer preferences, economic conditions, etc., few business owners or executives would create a business that looks the same, even after only a few years. We need to "step back" and take a periodic, and objective, look at not only what business we're in, but also the way in which we conduct business.

Some Examples

When *Disney* Corporation, looks at their business they do so intently and passionately. *Disney* executives use the term "re-imagineering," stressing the part that imagination plays in the process. The corporation is not satisfied with the status quo, and constantly seeks to provide a more exciting, rewarding and satisfying entertainment experience for its customers. This attitude has paid off, during good times and bad.

A regional corporation, *Taco Bell*, with less than a half-billion $ in sales has grown to a multi-billion dollar business by focusing on delivering value to their customers. This focus led to cost-cutting initiatives in all aspects of the business, new location sites and strategies, new marketing approaches, improved controls and technologies, and, interestingly, a reduction in the size of the kitchens at local outlets, through more off-site food preparation.

Hallmark Cards was faced with possible extinction as a result of competition, e-mail delivery methods, and a variety of other factors. The company joined the technological revolution, and successfully competed in this arena. But perhaps their most significant accomplishment was to reduce the cycle-time for development of new products to delivery to the marketplace. A new line of cards took two to three years from inception to marketability. After reengineering it only took eight months!

Corinthian Colleges, parent of *Everest Colleges*, *Everest Institutes*, *Everest Universities*, and *WyoTech* schools, redefined their business as "Changing Students Lives." Instead of narrowly focusing on the educational aspect common to all educational institutions, they broadened their mission to incorporate the whole person (student). This involved the development of a "full service" model centering on servicing and supporting all students throughout their educational process and well into their career placement. In order to "change lives," you have to get students into an appropriate program and keep them there until graduation and beyond. This is not as easy as it sounds. Students, especially many of the non-traditional types who come to *Everest*, have constant challenges, barriers, obstacles and setbacks. This requires that Everest employees; faculty, admissions, student finance planners, and career services go out of their way to help students succeed. This is a *Corinthian* expectation and requirement, and has resulted in, not only student success, but corporate growth and profitability.

Don't Wait for a Crisis

The "Big 3" automobile manufacturers are frantically trying to reinvent themselves. For even the least sophisticated business observer this has been a long time coming. It seems that the major automobile companies were frozen in the '60's, when gas prices were not a concern, and foreign competition was not as fierce. They continued to produce big "gas guzzlers" while customers clamored for fuel efficiency during the oil crisis. Their dealership network was overblown, as were the UAW (*United Auto Workers*) benefits and paychecks. The economic downturn in 2008 pointed out all of these deficiencies in dramatic fashion. What was the industrial and manufacturing mainstay for the economy quickly withered and fell into crisis, requiring government bailouts and executive changes. The industry was considered "too big to fail," and required major intervention.

For the sake of the national economy, the autoworkers, and all of the related or subsidiary businesses, let's hope their reinvention efforts are successful.

Reinvention is a Mindset and an Ongoing Process

Constant environmental change necessitates constant adaptation. The social Darwinist "survival of the fittest" model comes to mind. Organisms that don't evolve, don't survive-simple as that. The forces of entropy and homeostasis are always at work. These forces favor non-adaptation and resistance to change. The leader with foresight will recognize this and force change.

Oftentimes re-invention is necessary as a result of environmental, technological, or competitive situations requiring bold and immediate action. Frequently a decrease in "market share," profitability, or competitive edge, will provide the impetus.

Of course constant reinvention would wear out even the most optimistic, and motivated, among us. Therefore periodic review should be instituted as an ongoing practice. Perhaps an annual "Reinvention Retreat" is a good idea. (Some don't like the term "retreat" because of the implication of going backwards - so call it something else.) This should be a "no-holds-barred" brainstorming session at which the current and projected business environment is examined, along with possible adaptive responses and forward-thinking initiatives.

Episodic reassessments and looking at your business with "fresh eyes" can have many rewards. Some executives I know of periodically become a "mystery shopper" at their own business to regain a customer's perspective of the process. Others walk through processes as though they were an "order" or "complaint" to gain insights concerning the effectiveness and efficiency of the functions, and assigned personnel.

Many organizations form task forces or teams to rethink organizational purposes, processes and outcomes. This can be revealing and insightful. Often the synergy and variety of perspectives afforded by a group expert will quickly identify weaknesses, barriers, and opportunities.

Some companies require, or request, the help cf a facilitator or consultant. This provides a certain reassurance, and often a more objective assessment. It's frequently faster, too. However, the "buy-in" of key employees and management is essential. If it's viewed as the "Consultant's Idea" the project will fail. Commitment and participation from all levels is essential.

Whatever approach you use to initiate reinvention, remember:

--To recognize that reinvention is a necessity

- Business purposes and processes need to be periodically re-visited

--The same inquisitiveness, creativity and energy that helped start the business will help it continue to grow and prosper

--There is more risk associated with doing nothing than there is with trying actions that are risky

TREAT THE CUSTOMER SPECIAL – BECAUSE HE IS SPECIAL!

Customer Service stinks! How often have you heard that recently? No business can survive without customers for its products (goods or services) yet many businesses ignore or shortchange this simple fact.

The Customer is Always Right

Well, maybe not; however, satisfying the customer needs to be your top priority. If you don't satisfy your customers, someone else will. The competition!

Neglecting the Customer

Many businesses are now neglecting their customers as a business strategy. The cost of providing quality, personalized customer service is high. It generally requires prompt human intervention whether in-person, by telephone, or electronically (e.g., instant messaging).

Part of the prevailing strategy involves using customer service as a marketing tool. The longer they can keep you on the phone the more advertisements for additional products and services you will hear. Likewise, your billing statement will include more ad inserts.

We've all heard the "horror stories" of customers caught up in endless telephone menus, interminable delays, or speaking with call-center representatives in foreign lands with limited English proficiency and/or inadequate training. Others report an inability to even locate a phone number for the company, or to locate a salesclerk in a department store. Almost everyone has experienced first-hand these problems and others. Sure, the company achieves some cost-avoidance by employing the various customer neglect and delay practices, but at what cost?

The 80/20 Rule

Most have heard of the *80/20 Rule.* The premise is that most human interactions are subject to certain proportional propensities. In other words, the minority of events has disproportionately greater impact than the majority of events - by a longshot. The rule, called *Pareto's Law,* was named after a nineteenth century Italian economist. When applied to business, the theoretical outcome is, for example: 20% of your customers buy 80% of your goods. Or, 20% of your sales contribute

80% of your profits. Or, 20% of your customers make 80% of the complaints, whereas the remaining 80% complain quite infrequently (the "satisfied" [or indifferent] customers). You get the point.

Aware of this general theory, businesses have decided that it is not in the best interest of their bottom-line to provide excellent and costly customer service to everyone. After all 80% (or 75%, or 90%, or whatever the real percentage is) of their profit comes from a relatively small percentage of customers, and chances are they are not the complainers. However, what if you are one of those individuals who really wants, or needs, service?

Consequences

In general, service is so bad everywhere that the customer has few options. He can move from one product to another or one service or company to another. But chances are there will be no service improvement because quality, timely, knowledgeable customer service is such a rarity these days. The customer can also attempt to gain satisfaction by trying to speak with a higher authority i.e., "let me speak to your supervisor." Even legal recourse or reports to regulatory agencies is an increasingly used avenue.

"The Hall of Shame"

MSN Money conducted a poll, (reported 4/26/07), that identified American companies with the worst customer service. Their study reported that *Sprint-Nextel* had the worst reputation, with *Bank of America* coming in second, followed by *Comcast*, *Time-Warner* Cable, *AT&T*, *Citibank*, *WalMart*, *Verizon*, *Wells Fargo*, and *Direct TV*. Subsequent studies have reported similar results, although the top offenders have, in many cases, made significant efforts to improve the situation.

It should be noted that the aforementioned firms would be expected to have more complaints, as they are larger and have more customers. What really matters is the percentage of complaints in the total population of customers.

Whether measured by anecdotal reports, or survey data, it is clear that; overall, the deterioration in customer service has been rapid and pervasive.

What Should be Done

Notice that the heading doesn't say what can be done. Obviously much can be done to improve customer service. However, minor fixes will not resolve the underlying problem. There are some fundamental paradigms that require changing. Here are examples of what should be done, and it requires a change in mindset and business philosophy.

--First, an appreciation for the customer (and recognition that they are valuable).

--Second, realization that "Total Quality" means the entire process including sales and service.

--Third, respect for customers' time, opinions and needs.

--Fourth, realization that the customer can exercise their right to choose between various suppliers.

--Fifth, acknowledgement that negative customer reactions and opinions can destroy a firm's reputation.

--Sixth, a willingness to invest time and money in improving customer service.

--Seventh, an understanding that shortchanging customer service will ultimately result in reduced sales and lower profits.

--Eighth, designation of executive-level management with the responsibility and authority to oversee the customer service function and initiate improvements.

Finally...

The same companies that are providing such inadequate customer service, ironically, demand top performance from their suppliers and partners. A paradigm shift is required, one that harkens to the moral, time-tested business practices of yesterday. Without these attitude changes specific improvements will not, and cannot be implemented.

BE YOUR OWN CONSULTANT

Most business owners and managers use a "crisis" style, where they react to a problem, formulate a solution ("fix"), and then pat themselves on the back for a job well done. Wouldn't it be preferable to take a more "proactive" approach? To identify problems before they emerge as crises, develop plans and contingencies to deal with these issues, and minimize resultant disruption to the enterprise?

The popular concept of viewing problems as "opportunities" in disguise is hogwash! Problems are problems. They are the wolves in wolf attire, not dressed up as an innocent sheep, or a kindly grandmother. We can be grateful for this, as disguised problems are undoubtedly harder to identify and resolve. Moreover, we can be lulled into complacency when we believe that problems are either non-existent, or if they do exist, they will open up new and more profitable horizons.

Gathering Intelligence

Just like a cop or an espionage agent, you will need to gather intelligence. It's a shame, but many executives don't really know what's going on. They may be removed from the core business, preoccupied with meetings or reports, or receive thoroughly "filtered" information from their key subordinates. We all know that employees hide many things from the boss. This is particularly true when the boss is critical, fault-finding, or unapproachable. So, one item the leader may consider is to be more open and receptive. By no means does this imply being naive. It does, however, require genuine support and a desire to enlist cooperation in identifying problems and working together to resolve them.

Recently there has been a spate of CEO's who have gone "undercover" in their organizations to discover what is really going on. Fortunately their detective work has been filmed and televised for all to see. Whether the business is trash disposal, transportation, or fast food, the results are similar. The execs discovered things about their companies, mid-managers, processes, and employees, which they would have otherwise not learned. And, it has a bigger impact because they performed the "grunt" work, and know, first-hand, the impacts of their policies and decisions.

You Can't Fix "Invisible" Problems

The lessons learned from intelligence gathering will surface heretofore unidentified risks and problems which can negatively impact your business. This is essential to problem resolution, and to creating and maintaining an effective, efficient, profitable enterprise.

Don't Treat the Symptoms

Remember, just like the unsuspecting "Little Miss Riding Hood" alluded to earlier; with our "blinders," or "rose colored glasses" on, we can miss the obvious.

Physicians are trained to distinguish between symptoms and underlying disease or conditions.

A good rule of thumb here is to ask yourself: "Is this really the problem?" Understand that the first answer will seldom be "Yes." You will have to do some "digging." Unearthing the real problem will require inquisitiveness, skepticism, time, and effort. Consultants often recommend asking "is this really the problem" at least three times. For example, if poor quality is the problem, why? Because of poor manufacturing processes? If so, why? It may be lack of training is the root cause. Even here, the cause for inadequate training must be investigated. The point is, all along the way there are problems. Finding the "real," basic, root problem will take effort.

Always "Bounce" Your Feeling Off Others

No matter how smart we may think we are, it's always wise to solicit input. Other people have different, perhaps unique, perspectives and may see something we do not. Once you have this validation or disagreement you can formulate a course of action. It may be the problem requires more investigation, or analysis.

Plan, Implement, Review, and Correct

Once you're aware of the real problem(s) you're 90% home. The plans to resolve the difficulty(ies) will need to be developed, implemented, reviewed, and corrections/adjustments made as necessary. You will probably need to designate a change "champion" to see the process through to a successful conclusion. Of course you will still need to be heavily involved.

3

MANAGING YOUR EMPLOYEES

WHO ARE THE BEST MANAGERS, MEN OR WOMEN?

Who makes the better manager, men or women? Of course, like most questions the answer is not definitive. However, certain female characteristics may provide women with some advantages.

Management

The basic job of a manager is often described as performing the functions of: Planning, Organizing, Leading and Controlling, or better yet P.O.L.I.C.E. Who is better at this? Of course, men have dominated management jobs for decades, centuries, even millennia. Men naturally assumed working roles because of their size and strength, when most jobs required these attributes. And, just as naturally they progressed to management roles. For much of recent history, women did not enjoy a significant presence in the workforce. However, during World War II, women were needed to assume manufacturing and other jobs, while men went off to war. Still, following the war a sentiment of "a woman's place is in the home" reemerged.

For the past several decades women have re-entered the workforce in large numbers so that now the male/female worker percentages are not too far from parity. While men still occupy most top positions, the number of women serving as managers and executives continues to increase.

Evolving Job Requirements for Managers

As the nature of work has evolved so has the job of management. Far from requiring physical prowess, managerial positions now require such abilities as: mental agility, communications skills, technical and computer savvy, writing ability, analytical skills, etc. Most of our work is now cerebral, not physical. Higher level skills generally require more education.

Who's Better Suited to Today's Demands?

Interestingly enough, women college students now outnumber men. And, with more professional jobs in the employment market, women have the "edge." Women also have the temperament and communications abilities employers value so much. With these educational, emotional and verbal advantages they are tough contenders for management positions. However, not all women are "talkers." and not all men are the "strong silent type." Most of the differences between the sexes can be attributed to parenting and socialization. So, there are wide variations.

There have been several recent studies that support the hypothesis that women may be more capable managers than men. Ratings by peers, superiors and subordinates show higher scores for women on a wide range of measures-- everything from decision-making, to idea generation, to motivation and encouragement, goal-setting, quality of work, mentoring and staff development, etc. Various studies, as reported in *Business Week* (Online edition, Nov. 20, 2000), uniformly found women managers exceeded the performance of their male counterparts. Several of these studies were not industry-specific, and some were quite comprehensive. One involved a sample of 58,000 mangers.

There is an interesting caveat with all of this data. Evaluations of managers by their bosses (only) found less difference between men and women managers. Part of this may be due to stereotypes, and the fact that more males occupy the top positions.

The Basic Determination

Yes, in fact, women may be better-suited to succeed in management in contemporary work environments. And not considering women for top management slots would be a huge mistake. But we must not be simplistic in concluding they are the best managers. Although women have strengths, so do men. And, not all women, or men, have the same strengths or weaknesses. To definitively conclude that one sex is better than the other would result in the error of unwarranted generalization. Furthermore we want to avoid the stereotyping that has characterized the assessment of people for far too long. And, we must consider how well that individuals talents match with those needed in the specific position. **In the final analysis each individual must be evaluated on their particular merits.**

HIRING EMPLOYEES WITH AN ATTITUDE!

With the employment market tightening and jobs scarce, employers seek employees with the "right" attitude. Identifying these candidates can be a little "tricky," as the selection process is almost invariably not designed to measure these attributes.

Before discussing the hiring matter, we need to examine the underlying reasons for the hiring need in the first place, along with a framework for dealing with them.

New Employees are Costly

Employers hate employee turnover. If the turnover rate is high the company will notice a negative impact on the "bottom line." The costs of recruitment, selection, hiring and training new employees are high. And, depending on the complexity of the job, lower productivity, while new employees gain necessary experience, is another costly factor. Experienced employees lost to the competition are an even greater threat. These employees may know business philosophies, practices, techniques, trade secrets, and strategies which could strengthen your competition. Considering all of these negatives, savvy management does it's best to retain their valued staff.

Keeping Valued Employees

Experienced, qualified and productive employees are an asset, but keeping them can be challenging. Loyalty to employers hasn't been the norm for many years. Of course companies can do a number of things to keep the good ones.

Many years ago a researcher named Frederick Herzberg (*The Motivation to Work*, 1959) developed a theory that divided job satisfaction into two major components: Motivational factors and Hygiene factors; with the motivational factors such as interesting work, challenge, recognition, and variety being, by far, the more powerful. On the other hand, the job features we all expect, such as pay and benefits or working conditions are nowhere near as important, except to serve as potential causes for dissatisfaction. These findings may be counter-intuitive, but as we all know, we will spend hours doing the things we like to do, with people we like to do them with. Conversely, unchallenging tasks, or work performed in a non-supportive, or uninteresting environment, will typically not evoke our best efforts

So making your workplace a challenging, exciting, and supportive place will greatly help in reducing or limiting avoidable turnover. As an important added benefit the customers will have a better relationship with a motivated, helpful, satisfied workforce.

Now that we've examined the background, let's look at hiring new employees. While it's obvious that it is best to retain employees, turnover will occur, and businesses may grow. This being the case, a superior recruitment plan is essential, as it will help accomplish several things: hire the "best," have a good fit between employee and job, lessen the need for discipline or discharge, reduce turnover, and provide a competitive edge.

The "Right Stuff"

Employers tell us that the most important characteristic to look for in a new employee is the "right" attitude. What is the right attitude and how do we hire people with it? The right attitude, according to most employers, consists of several qualities:

- Positivity (doesn't focus on negatives)
 - Open-mindedness
- Flexibility
- Superior interpersonal skills / a liking of people
- Desire to learn
- Willingness to work, (and work hard)
- Dependability
- Desire to accept challenges
- Team player

With these characteristics the employee should exhibt a "good attitude" toward his employer, fellow employees and your customers.

Finding and Hiring Employees with the "Right Attitude""

Considering the attributes listed above, be serious about your hiring process, as you know the headaches resulting from poor decisions. Here are some suggestions:

--Identify the essential characteristics required for success on the job.

--Incorporate behavioral and attitudinal qualities into your selection criteria.

--Include these requirements in your job bulletins, advertising, employment agency, requisitions, etc.

--Carefully examine employment, educational and personal history (to the extent permitted by the law).

--Conduct a background check on candidates.

THE FRIENDLY MANAGER

Should a manager be friends with his staff? Should she visit her employees' homes, socialize with her subordinates and discuss details of her, and their, personal life? Or should she remain aloof and detached? Well, as in most decisions, the answer is probably somewhere in between.

The Age-Old Question

Fraternization with the "troops" has long been frowned on in the military. Actually, more than frowned on, forbidden by the *Uniform Code of Military Justice.* The officers have their "Officers Club" and the enlisted men, and women, have theirs. The thinking behind this is that it is difficult to lead, make tough decisions, and discipline subordinates when the lives of the leaders and followers are personally intertwined. Therefore, a strict hierarchy is well-established, observed, and promoted. Of course there is merit to this thinking particularly when it comes to war, but there may also be some applicability in the civilian workplace. The practice reduces perceptions of favoritism, and keeps things "business-like." Business is supposed to be somewhat logical and rational, rather than arbitrary and personal.

Keep Your Business and Personal Life Separate

New managers are frequently advised to keep their business and personal lives separate. Not because managers are engaging in kinky or illicit activities, although some may, but rather to encourage business-like behavior in the office and indulge in restorative activities while away from work.

Employees can use information about the manager to gain favor or manipulate the boss. Remember *"How to Succeed in Business..."* when the ambitious new employee took up knitting because the boss had that pastime? Most attempts at gaining favor are far more innocent than that example, as we all want to be viewed favorably by our superiors.

A Respectful Distance

Perhaps the notion that managers should maintain a professional, rather than personal, relationship with their employees is outmoded. Undoubtedly times have changed. Maybe mixing business and personal lives is acceptable, even desirable. However, it's important to recognize the downside and act accordingly.

Responsible behavior has limits, and standards should be observed. You probably should not become "best friends" with your staff assistant or secretary. And you probably should not share your insecurities, or "spill your guts" about your love life, or personal problems. Particularly resist the impulse to criticize or complain about the firm, its management, policies, or particular individuals.

In today's environment we often spend more time at work than at home (excluding sleeping, of course). The temptation is to treat those in the workplace as "extended family," or friends, rather than business associates and employees.

Some organizations have policies which discourage or prohibit nepotism, or related activities. And, it is easy to see how conflicts of interest may arise among intimate partners, married couples, and the like. Professional judgment can be compromised, and the advantage gained by one or more of the participants in such a situation can be unfair and demoralizing. Furthermore, a falling-out between the parties in an emotionally-charged relationship can easily spill over into the workplace with undesired consequences.

A respectful distance will promote healthy, productive, and constructive workplace relationships.

FOCUS YOUR ATTENTION

In today's fast-moving society it's easy to get scattered in focus and effort. The result is under performance and missed opportunities. As a manager you can achieve better results when you focus your attention.

Multi-Tasking is Over-Rated

Managers need to focus their attention in a few high priority areas. The "critical few," essential to management success, are the areas to concentrate on, if you want results.

Watch children at play; they can do several things at once (and have the attention span of a "gnat"). Easily distracted, kids will yell, and talk, and spin and run and play games and make up stories and chase other children-- all within a matter of minutes. But we live in an adult world where managers cannot afford to be torn in multiple directions simultaneously.

Management is Difficult, and it Requires Concentration

Leaders who understand management select a few priorities and then expend vast amounts of energy on them. No matter what your politics, a good example of focusing attention on a few priorities was during Ronald Reagan's presidential administration. *President Reagan* had a few top priorities: end the "cold war," increase "patriotism," and improve the economy. Because he focused on these few "big ticket" items he enjoyed a successful presidency.

Select Your Priorities

What is critical to the success of your business (or your segment of the business)? Peter Drucker was the man who invented the term "management." Drucker felt that planning should be the top priority and that managers should focus on the external environment. He also felt marketing should be high on the list. Pick a few high "payoff" areas to concentrate on rather than spending time and energy on scores of relatively insignificant matters.

Communicate Your Priorities

You can't do it all by yourself, and you shouldn't try. Management is all about "getting things done through other people." If you clearly communicate your priorities to your staff, and follow-up with high levels of attention paid to those areas, you should see results. If your priorities are unclear, unimportant, or constantly changing, you will surely fail.

Measure Your Progress

How are you going to determine your progress if you don't measure results? The answer is obvious, you can't! What should you measure? How often? And, how will you set up a process? How can you be sure you are measuring the right things?

Select those areas which are essential to the growth and profitability of the enterprise, then rigorously examine them. Have your staff provide input to this process. This will help them in focusing on your, and the business, priorities so that everyone is contributing to the organization's mission and goals. Benchmark your progress by including factors which other businesses in your industry most commonly measure and report. Some things need to be constantly measured, while others can be measured less frequently. Take a look at the "cycle" for each of your measurements -from start to finish- to establish the proper timeframe for each factor. Then simplify the measurement and reporting process so that it isn't too burdensome, otherwise it will fall into disuse.

Remember, managers, --focus your attention!

OVERWORKED, OVERLOADED, and FRUSTRATED

Delegation is the Manager's Salvation. In fact the definition of a manager is someone who "gets things done through other people." We're witnessing not only a transformation in technology, organizational structure, but a profound change in the way we manage. Whereas we used to talk about "span of control," and limits on the ability of managers to effectively lead and control large numbers of subordinates, this discussion appears to have diminished in favor of increasing managerial workload. Not too many years ago first line supervisors were limited to approximately five to ten "direct reports." It was widely believed that larger numbers of employees could not be effectively managed by one boss. All this has changed, and not so much as a result of new research, management theory, or human resources requirements, but because of cost containment imperatives. Modern technologies also permit an expansion of span of control as computer systems perform more of the monitoring of employee activities, performance, and results.

The New Management Model

Actually, there is no new management model. And, if there was one it would be a contingency-based one, focused on "whatever works." Management theory is lagging management practice. Experimentation is the norm, and top executives and senior managers are "pushing the envelope" insofar as the limits on human capacity to perform meaningful work are concerned. Expectations for employees continue to increase without much regard for practical limitations. Only a few years ago, although it seems like an eternity, employees were seeking work/life "balance." They wanted to avoid all-consuming work, so that they could enjoy a reasonable degree of family and personal time. This is rapidly changing as general economic conditions deteriorate, foreign and domestic competition accelerates, and unemployment increases.

It's a "buyer's market" for employees and employers know it. Employees are willing to spend much more time and effort making a living than previously as the "law of supply and demand" requires that they do so. Nowhere is this truer than for the ranks of "middle management." Already pressured by technology, they are now confronted with upward delegation of tasks by overloaded employees, downward delegation of increased responsibilities by senior management, increased "bottom line" requirements, and a whole range of other factors. With the degree of "fat" present in previous periods they had more ability to delegate more of their workload. But managers are increasingly viewed as "super" employees; employees who can not only manage others but perform significantly more of the work themselves. Besides, they are salaried so their working hours can be expanded without a corresponding increase in payroll costs.

Is There a Solution?

There is always a solution.

Short Term Considerations

With the redefinition of management, job descriptions will have to be rewritten to reflect the actual requirements. In many cases this will entail requirements for inclusion of what would have previously been called "technical skills." Additionally it will probably require expansion of "span of control" considerations and increases in the range of "numbers of employees supervised."

Different types of management employees will have to be recruited with a stronger mix of both technical and management abilities. Capacity to perform the work as well as manage the performance of the work will have increasing value in management employee selection, especially at the first-line and middle levels. People skills may have to be weighted less than technical considerations in the management selection equation.

Multi-tasking and capacity for dealing with increased pressure and responsibility will also have to be taken into account when selecting middle managers.

What about the Long-Term?

Nobody knows the impact on managers, employers, society, or organizations. It is difficult to compete on a cost basis in an international competitive environment when workers with similar qualifications and productivity can be compensated at a fraction of the U.S. pay scale. The manager has picked up much of the slack in this competitive, demanding environment. How much longer this can be the case remains to be seen.

LET'S FIRE THE INCOMPETENT EMPLOYEE

We've all seen the incompetent employee: The employee who just can't seem to effectively handle their responsibilities; the one who doesn't contribute much to the organization. Although we may recognize this individual, typically the employee continues to work, or work too long.

Why is it so Difficult?

Incompetent employees are employed by most companies, large or small. They seem to be tolerated or indulged and not called to task. It's much easier to dismiss the employee who doesn't come to work, is disloyal, or disruptive, a substance abuser, a thief or a cheat. I suppose it's human nature.

Efforts at Rehabilitation

What's wrong with rehabilitating the incompetent employee? Can't we help him, or her, improve their level of performance to an acceptable level? Of course we should try. The poor performer may need additional training, remedial education, a new assignment, etc. Perhaps there is a mismatch between the person's abilities and skills and the position to which they are assigned, and a reassignment may be warranted. It's worth it to give the problem employee every chance. Maybe he or she will surprise you!

Of course training may not correct the problem, re-education may not suffice and there may not be a suitable position to which the employee can successfully be reassigned. What do we do then?

Documentation

Hopefully the employee is a participant in the MBO (*Management by Objectives*) program. If so, has the manager been forthright in evaluating the employee's performance? If not, this is the time to rectify that problem. Employees should be held to realistic, and reasonable, performance standards. These standards should be included in Position Description and Position Expectation documents, made available to, and agreed to by the employee.

Employees need to have periodic reviews, which are documented and discussed with the employee so that the employee has fair opportunity to improve. The time frame needs to be fair, and the support and monitoring rigorous. The time and effort to create and document all aspects of the *Performance Improvement Plan* must be invested if the employer doesn't want to run afoul of the labor laws. The plan and outcome must not be perceived as unfair, discriminatory or punitive. The outcome must be appropriate and warranted.

The HR (Human Resources) department will be the most important resource throughout this entire process, especially when it comes to the next steps. They will have policies that pertain to *"Progressive Discipline"* and be aware of requirements to avoid *"wrongful termination"* suits. They will make sure everything is in order, justifiable, and legal.

Here's the Unpleasant Part

Let's say that despite all of the manager's (and perhaps the employee's) best efforts, improvement is not achieved. Then, the discharge process must be initiated. Up to now it has all been positive and constructive, but this is the time to look out for the organization's best interests. After all, it's a money-making enterprise and feelings and compassion must take a backseat to business purpose. This is not "tough love," it's just tough.

The employee needs to be warned about the possibility of discharge, the exact reasons why, and the fact that management has unsuccessfully tried to rehabilitate, retrain, and/or improve the employees performance. The employee should also be provided with adequate notice of termination or allowed to resign with dignity. A suitable severance package may be in order, particularly for an employee with tenure. As the process may be extremely difficult for the incumbent offers of transitional assistance, help in finding a new position, etc., may be required or desired.

Hopefully you won't, as a manager, find yourself in this dilemma, but if you do, the approaches and actions described here will help you through the process.

A MORE RESPONSIBLE HIRING APPROACH:
CONTRACT FOR SERVICES

How can managers improve their "batting average" in the employee selection, hiring, evaluation, retention and discipline processes?

Selection, Hiring, and Evaluation

The employee selection process can be abbreviated due to pressing staffing issues or truncated because of hiring priorities, a limited applicant pool, unsound evaluation processes, or any of a number of reasons. The standard process results in businesses hiring and retaining certain employees that they should not have.

Businesses generally hire employees, and then give them a probationary period of from six months to a year. During the probationary period employees can be released without much fuss or fanfare as long as State and Federal regulations are observed. However, unsatisfactory employees often get through this probationary period due to managerial neglect, ineptitude, or conflicting priorities. Managers, caught up in their day-to-day work responsibilities, oftentimes fail to:

1) adequately monitor and evaluate the performance of new employees,

2) document unsatisfactory performance, and/or

3) submit the required paperwork on time.

In addition, there is a perception problem. New hires (probationers) are viewed as permanent employees by their colleagues, management and themselves. Furthermore, the new employees become ensconced in the organization and its social network even if they are not high-quality.

Retention/ Discipline Issues

As indicated, the standard process results in businesses hiring and retaining employees that they should not have. This, in turn, causes training and discipline hassles and expenditures, while prohibiting the company from having the competitive advantage of the best available talent. This environment can also "contaminate" other members of the workforce, particularly as they observe the behaviors and performance of the under-performers.

A Better Approach

A reasonable and realistic remedy is DON'T HIRE THE EMPLOYEE in the first place. Instead, make new employees Contact workers.

Hiring on a Contract basis for a defined period gives the employee the opportunity to demonstrate their abilities, while providing management with the time to observe their performance (WITHOUT HAVING THEM ON THE EMPLOYEE PAYROLL). Then, following the contract period, if there are any doubts, just don't renew the contract. This is a much simpler, straightforward and less risky process. Following expiration of the contract, management will have the flexibility to renew the contract, not renew the contract, or perhaps (and, best of all), hire the employee.

A caveat

As with everything it is not as simple as it appears. While this approach has attractive features, there are some potential drawbacks. The best employees may not wish to be hired as "only" a contractor.

And, there is the sticky matter of Employee Benefits.

Despite these issues, the realities of employee selection and hiring make the Contract Employee approach a better one.

COMPETENCIES – RECOGNITION, DEVELOPMENT, AND PRESERVATION

Every organization has employees with a variety of skills and specialized knowledge. However, many organizations either do not recognize these talents, or fail to fully capitalize on this knowledge and experience base. Organizations also need to preserve these competencies by reducing employee turnover.

Human Capital

Companies would be wise to consider the human component of their organization as capital, equally or more valuable than tangible physical resources like plants, equipment and inventory. The employee knowledge base can provide stability in the organization, a "competitive edge" in the marketplace, may result in more effective and efficient customer service, and allow the company to transition more smoothly to changing conditions.

The impact of an experienced and knowledgeable workforce will be felt in all areas of performance. How many times have you contacted one, several, or many companies with a problem and been dissatisfied with the level of knowledge, expert analysis of the problem, and identification of workable solutions? In these "throwaway" times the value of experienced, capable employees is frequently underestimated or ignored. The "if you don't like it here, there's the door!" mentality can prove extremely costly and counterproductive.

One key to developing organizational competence is to identify these competencies in the first place.

Cost Factors

Failure to recognize the expense associated with employee turnover and inadequate employee training will prove costly. In a highly specialized position the lower productivity of a new employee can impact revenue, costs, customer loyalty and goodwill. Recruitment costs may include advertising, recruitment agencies, the costs of temporary agency replacements (if applicable), etc. The cost of training a new employee in a complex job can easily exceed their first year's salary. This cost is calculated by combining reduced productivity with the cost of training. The time away from the job can be considerable, and associated negative impacts can be reasonably anticipated. So, even replacing an underperformer can be a costly proposition for the company.

Morale Factors

Constant changeover in staff can also have broader implications on employee morale. Workplaces are also human networks of friends, associates and colleagues. Disruption in these inter-relationships can result in decreased morale and adversely impact overall productivity. Employees will waste time gossiping about the personnel actions, perhaps grieve the loss of their associate/friend, spend time developing new relationships, and do all of those things we expect in human societies.

"Bottom Line"

The ability to recruit, develop, and retain competent staff is a critically important business practice. There are several steps management can take to identify competencies, share and promote these competencies, and retain competent individuals. Cross-training would be an important first step, so that competencies can be shared. The transfer of knowledge among members of the work team will provide depth, and ensure that business can be conducted seamlessly when critical members are unavailable.

It is often surprising how little employers know about their workforce. Typically there are "hidden" talents among the employee base. Employees may have interests, talents, abilities and skills that management is unaware of. For example: Mary may be an amateur artist; Steve may be a backyard mechanic; Delores could be a computer "techie;" or Harry, an accomplished writer. Identification of these competencies could prove beneficial, even essential, at some juncture. Once employee competencies have been identified, whether they are specifically job related (to the present position) or not, these skills and abilities can prove to be a valuable, (previously hidden) resource. The development of a company-wide employee competency inventory is a logical outcome.

Finally, keeping your competent and valued, multi-talented workforce is a major competitive advantage. You could be allowing employees with hidden talents to go out the door. Worse yet, they could walk in the door of a competitor.

CAN YOU PLEEEZE HELP ME?

Asking for favors or help can be awkward or difficult. However, in business we have to do it all the time. Whether we're requesting better service, a lower price, or negotiating an agreement or contract - we typically need help.

Various Business Strategies and Viewpoints

I've learned a lot from many bosses, associates, colleagues and friends. One early manager focused only on the product and taught me the importance of believing in what you're selling. Another, with an accounting background emphasized: "follow the money." One supervisor in a public service agency showed me the critical importance of empathy with the client. A lifelong friend was one of the top ten automobile salesmen in the country. His "thing" was motivation and incentives, and he would give the: "*My friends are dead Presidents*" speech to new salesmen. Yet another constantly "sensed" the organization by taking informal, impromptu "attitude surveys."

Can You PLEEEEZE Help Me?

A friend and neighbor of mine, is a salesman, and, a good one at that. He is also a primo negotiator.

Listen carefully to him and you will hear him say "can you please"... (with an emphasis on **pleeeze**) help us, or me? He usually uses the plural, and asks if they can help **us** because he believes it's more effective that way. But sometimes he just asks "can you help me"? His point is, people want to help. Also, it sometimes shows how much clout, authority, or good will they have when they are able to grant your request. It's a good strategy, and a sincere one. I observed the man negotiate with an insurance company. He has this "down home" friendly attitude and demeanor. It's genuine and disarming. The Insurance Adjusters were willing to help their new found friend when he requested their assistance.

We're All Human

People relate on a human level. They interact with each other primarily in a positive fashion. They typically evidence empathy or at least some degree of caring. Of course there are exceptions, and certainly there are ruthless individuals. But the wheels of business continue to grind based on some degree of trust, confidence, and goodwill. Sure, some will view your request for help as a sign of weakness, however, many more will extend a hand to help. Some years ago a book was published titled "*The Givers and the Takers*" (Evatt and Feld, 1983). The authors concluded that the vast majority of Americans are "givers." The point is, if you ask for help you stand a reasonable chance of getting it.

Put it Into Practice

The conclusion is: Don't be afraid to ask for help. The likelihood of your gaining concessions, or assistance, in business is probably better than you think.

SMOOTH SAILING WITH LEADERship

Thinking about what it takes to be a Business Leader, the Captain of a ship comes to mind. Although this analogy may have its flaws, the basic tenets are valid.

The Ship Captain

The Captain of a ship must perform the basic management functions of: Planning, Organizing, Leading, Informing, Controlling, and Enhancing. The Captain must define the destination and chart the course. The Captain is responsible for ensuring that all hands are doing their job. The Captain must provide leadership, inspiration and motivation to the crew. And, the Captain must identify if corrections (such as course, speed, etc.) are required, and implement corrections as necessary.

The Captain must be an experienced seaman. He must know, understand, and be prepared for, the vagaries and cruelties of the sea. He must a leader in the true sense of the word, leading his ship, its' cargo and its' crew safely to their destination. Modern captains use modern technologies, such as radar, sonar, navigation systems, communications systems, electronic chart display, automatic pilots, fathometers (depth finders), etc.

The Captain must know and understand human behavior. He must know how to motivate people, discipline them as necessary (no keel hauling though), organize, mentor, inspire, and control them.

He must know and follow the law - in this case maritime rules.

The Captain must know the competition. Think of the recent and immensely popular, "*Deadliest Catch*" series on *PBS* where each ship is competing for the fastest arrival at the best areas in which to set their crab traps and harvest their catch.

So, the Captain must use all of the resources available at his command to be successful. And, although most captains are honest and hardworking, some captains are pirates (think *Enron*).

The "Captain of Industry"

Captain of Industry is a term coined by Thomas Carlyle and was used to describe the "heroes" of capitalism in the mid-1800's. Incidentally, there were pirates, too - called the "Robber Barons."

Captains of Industry were held in high esteem as builders of the economy and producers of wealth. This notion continues to this day as we idolize successful business people and celebrate their success. The *Forbes 500* and the Billionaire edition are popular renditions of the score-keeping associated with business.

Here's to the Captain

We salute the Captain. Whether he be a seafarer or desk bound. We admire the adventure, risk, skill, talent, knowledge, ability, responsibility, and tenacity required to succeed in these professions. And, whenever you as a manager decide that you're ready for this role, think of LeaderSHIP.

Here's to your smooth sailing!

TOUGH AND TENDER: THE IDEAL BOSS

Some will say the ideal boss is tough-minded, forceful and driven, while others appreciate an understanding, caring, supportive, manager. The best bosses may have a combination of these attributes, and more.

The View from the Top

Top executives want results. They appreciate managers who can deliver those results. After all, business is about the money! Managers who focus on results and delivering profitability are most valued in the corporate world. But does executive management care what styles or approaches are utilized to get those results? Probably not, unless extreme, dishonest, or ultimately non-productive tactics are employed.

Petty "tyrants" evolve when managers become impressed with their own power and position. But these individuals generally do more harm than good. Their tactics typically decrease employee morale, contribute to absenteeism, and increase employee turnover.

"Results oriented" bosses tend to place numbers over people in their priorities. This can have a short term benefit, particularly at quarter, or year-end, or when bringing in a project. This is not to say that results oriented managers disregard their people as individuals, as some derive exceptional efforts from individuals and teams.

What Works

Managers develop their own style, partly as a result of their unique personalities, sometimes as a result of management education or training, partly to meet the expectations of their employer, frequently in reaction to their employees, and generally as a combination of factors they are comfortable with and/or believe works best.

Effective management is a challenge. It's a big responsibility. Managers have obligations to themselves, their employer, and their employees. And, while some styles are more effective than others, any style can achieve results.

The important factor is to balance the management equation with consideration for task along with consideration for people. This was pointed out in a study by Blake and Mouton, back in the 1960's. These researchers found that a combination of a concern for people combined with a concern for production is the most effective "style." When managers had a concern for neither, the researchers found the management was "Impoverished." Not a positive outcome by any measure. When the concern for production dominated, it was called "Produce or Perish" (or, authoritarian). And, when managers focused exclusively on "people" rather than production the result was a "Country Club" atmosphere. Certainly not the results that CEO's or shareholders desire (unless, of course, it is a COUNTRY CLUB).

So, as in most cases, a balanced approach seems to work best. The concern for people as well as production engenders an "espirit de corps," a kind of teamwork oriented approach to work, and a results focus, as well. Like the best of worlds, motivated employees, producing results and getting consideration and recognition for their efforts.

Some observations

--Tough, production-focused bosses with a genuine concern for their employees - tough, yet tender - probably yield the highest results on a variety of measures.

--As a manager you must strive for balance

--Short-term results may require disproportionate attention to productivity and outcomes and consideration may have to temporarily take a back seat

--As a manager, you cannot afford to disregard the human factors; people are not machines to be used and discarded

--You will promote loyalty and goodwill through your human-centered actions and attitudes

--Empowered employees are more productive and gain a sense of responsibility

--The "bottom-line" is essential but not one-dimensional

--Communicate with your employees constantly, to get everyone moving in the same direction

--Committed employees can make a huge difference in overall results and company profitability

The stress and demands of the workplace can cause managers to lose sight of their humanity. It's easy to become abrupt, inconsiderate, even uncaring. The ultimate test of our society and our business enterprises is that we provide people with not only an income, but self-respect and fulfillment too. Make an effort to objectively evaluate yourself and your management focus, and, if it's too one sided, make necessary change.

MANAGERS: SHOW YOUR FACE!

Much too frequently employees toil on projects or assignments without seeing their boss - except at the beginning and the end. While managers can be extremely busy, their primary function is "leadership." Without leadership there are no "followers," and managers rely on followers to get things done.

The "Big Project"

At one point in my career I had close to one hundred employees working on a "special project" over the weekend. There was an audit finding that required immediate resolution, and necessitated examination of thousands of individual files. After the project initiation, explaining the purpose, defining the parameters, designating project managers, deadlines, responsibilities, deliverables, etc., I was ready for the weekend. This was early in my management career and I thought I had done a terrific job of organizing this major effort. It was when *my* supervisor asked if I had planned to visit the staff over the weekend, that I replied, "No, I have plans," but "everything's under control." However, that comment made me realize that I needed to be there. And, so I was.

I showed up early Saturday morning with donuts and coffee, and said "hi" to everyone, spoke with the team leaders and the project managers and thanked them for their dedication. This was the first of three visits that weekend. Did it make a difference? You bet!

The employees maintained their enthusiasm and productivity, knowing that the "Big Boss" was giving up his weekend, as well.

Importance of "Showing Your Face"

We all know that the manager's presence is not sufficient to cause exceptional effort among employees. But it is one of many factors that help. Good Project Management is a study in itself, and the design and controls which are put in place are essential to a timely, effective, completion. However, the "personal touch" does make a difference.

Some Tips

There are several things you can do to make the most of your "power of presence."

--Recognize the "power" of your visit, the judgments that may be made about *you*, and your opportunity to have a positive impact on your employees

--Don't always schedule your appearances; sometimes unannounced or unanticipated visits have a greater impact

--Personalize your visit. Try to see everyone, not just the managers and supervisors

--Use your meetings with managers to support, verify, or gain clarification of your impressions

--Maintain a positive, supportive attitude during your visit; avoid the impression that you're "checking up" on them

--Ask questions, but don't conduct an "interrogation"

RECOGNITION – A TERRIFIC WAY TO MOTIVATE EMPLOYEES

Executives and managers seeking an effective, low cost way to motivate their employees don't have to look too far. Often overlooked and dismissed as an ineffective or short-term fix is "employee recognition."

The Rationale

It must be understood that people don't work for money alone. Yes, there's no denying that the principal reason for going to work is to earn a living. But there are many ways to earn a living, and many places to satisfy that requirement. Plus, we want people to excel, not just do the minimum. So, obviously, we need to be creative in our approach to gain that "extra effort."

Although motivational theories abound, and everything from pay to "perks," to "Theory X" controls and prodding has been tried, simple recognition of desired behavior and accomplishment is a powerful incentive. Leaders seeking performance improvement must rely on "soft skills," essentially human interactions, to advance their agenda. This generally translates into meeting your employees' needs through a variety of approaches which increase the incumbent's **desire** to perform. Only when both sets of needs - the employer's and the employee's - are met does the employment "contract" make sense.

There are many obvious and compelling advantages to recognition as a means to reinforce superior employee performance. First, it is straightforward: You show appreciation for the efforts and results you like to see. Second, it is inexpensive. It can be practiced at no cost or little cost. Simple comments, commendations, public accolade, and the like, are effective. Third, it is consistent with motivational theories (e.g., Maslow's *"Hierarchy of Needs,"* B. F. Skinner's *"Reinforcement Theory,"* Goal Theory, Equity Theory, etc.)

Many companies have formal employee recognition programs and/or policies, but some do not. However, there are always opportunities to show appreciation and recognize high performers.

Practical Approaches

There's an old song called *"Fifty Ways to Leave Your Lover,"* (by Paul Simon, 1975) -- and there are probably many more. Likewise, there are lots of ways to recognize your employees. Here's a few for your consideration:

Formal commendations, plaques, certificates, awards, "pat's on the back," public praise, lunch, luncheons or dinners, donuts or bagels in the morning, letters of appreciation, time off, reserved parking spaces, employee of the month or year designation, appreciative comments, gift cards, parties, bonuses, pay increases, performance evaluations, promotions, cards, observations of significant occasions, "we missed you" comments, genuine smiles and enthusiasm, special projects or choice assignments, a chance to "shine," small gifts, introductions to key individuals, spending time with the employee, encouragement, positive feedback, conference attendance, workshops, training, celebrations, etc.

Good managers are a reflection of high caliber, motivated employees, and vice-versa. So go ahead and apply some, or all of these techniques, and perhaps you already do. Just make sure that what you do is deserved and consistent. Unfair treatment and undeserved recognition may, in some cases be worse than no recognition at all, and can have a demoralizing effect on other employees. Get started-- practice employee recognition techniques skillfully and frequently to develop a happy and motivated workforce.

COMMUNICATION: THE BIGGEST PROBLEM IN BUSINESS

The biggest problem in most organizations is communication. How can you, as a manager, get what you want, need, or expect from people who don't understand those requirements? Just look at the user manuals for simple electronic devices, like your cell phone. Can you figure it out? Do you want to pore over complicated instructions and details to use the thing? Why is everything so complicated?

Communicating

Communication involves transmission of information from one person to another. It sounds simple enough. However, the sender of the message (whether verbal or written) needs to take care in developing, conveying, and verifying that the intended message is accurate, has been received and understood, and acted upon appropriately. So, prepare and organize your written or verbal message. This does not have to be a lengthy process. Sometimes just a few moments of reflection, and jotting down some notes will suffice.

Purpose

Readers and participants should not be confused or left to wonder what correspondence or meetings are about. Nor should time be wasted in trying to analyze, decipher, ascertain or engage in conjecture about the purpose, meaning, significance or reason for communicating. The purpose of the communication should be clear and direct. Oftentimes I have used the technique of beginning a memo or letter by simply stating: "The purpose of this memo (letter) is..." The same technique can be used in meetings, e.g., "the purpose of this meeting is..."

Clarity and Brevity

Business communications are best when they are kept brief and to the point. Rambling discourse and lengthy memos only serve to get people lost and confused. Use clear, unambiguous, direct, concise, and emphatic terminology. E.g., "the reason for these instructions is..." Put yourself in the readers place, if you were in their circumstance, with their level of comprehension, would you understand the message? Clarify unclear messages ASAP.

Brevity is quite important when dealing with managers and executives.

These are busy people with lots of correspondence to review. Many executives practice a reading style that pays attent on only to the first and last paragraphs, while ignoring the discussion in between. This way they learn the essence of the correspondence by reading the statements concerning the problem or issue (the purpose) and the summary and recommendation(s).

Accuracy

Make sure your message is accurate, that it fully and honestly describes the issue(s), and that it is consistent with reality. It is insulting to the reader and/or embarrassing to the writer if inaccuracies are present. The same applies to verbal communication. You do not want to compromise your credibility by providing questionable, or downright incorrect information.

Watch Your Language

Messages can be compromised or even ridiculed if they are replete with errors like misspellings, improper grammar, and the like. For written messages, have someone proofread your work, particularly if you know that you're prone to mistakes. Even good writers make mistakes, so take care in this area. Likewise, the language should match the circumstances in both written and verbal communications. A formal speech will require more attention to wording and structure than an informal staff meeting will. Remember, you will be judged by what you say or write.

Timeliness

In order to be of value communications must be timely. Most messages lose their impact and relevance when delayed. Circumstances change; what is so important today may not matter much four months from now. And, change is so rapid in the business world that delays can cost money.

Feedback

Pay attention to, encourage, and welcome feedback, whether positive or negative. If feedback indicates support and compliance, that's obviously good. If, on the other hand the feedback is negative, view this as an opportunity to improve the message, and perhaps revise the policies or requirements it conveys.

Improve Your Communications

The importance, and value, of improving your communications ability, and performance, is difficult to overestimate. The manager is responsible for getting things done through the efforts of others. Any confusion or delays in this area can result in misspent resources and unrealized objectives.

REDUNDANCY IS THE KEY TO COMMUNICATION

What is the key to communication? REDUNDANCY!

What is redundancy?

According to *Meriam-Webster Dictionary*, redundancy is: "superfluity," "profusion," "abundance," "needless repetition," etc. Although some of these definitions may have negative connotations, I will argue that a manager needs to be redundant to get his message across. Whatever a manager communicates frequently, forcefully, and repetitively will make an impression on those in the organization. The message is clear: If the manager says: "Quality," more "Quality," improved "Quality," better "Quality," etc., it won't be long before the staff will get the message. QUALITY IS IMPORTANT.

The same can be done with Mission Statements, slogans, goals, targets, etc.

THE CUSTOMER IS IMPORTANT, THE CUSTOMER IS IMPORTANT, THE CUSTOMER IS IMPORTANT. Pretty soon even the biggest dolt in the corporation will understand the importance of the customer.

Why redundancy is required

Human behavior experts understand how people process information. Single, random events are viewed differently than regularly encountered situations. And experiences having a great deal of power or significance are also more important. Reinforcement Theory underscores the impact of regular feedback, as do many other approaches to motivation. Repetitive experiences reinforce patterns of thinking and behaving.

Therefore, if as a manager, you want your subordinates to remember and practice certain ideas, concepts or behaviors, you will need to keep reminding them.

The importance of feedback

Communication is a two-way process. It requires a "sender" and a "receiver."

Someone to deliver the message and another to receive, interpret and react to it. Feedback will help you reassess if the communication is accurate and acted upon.

Messages that are delivered at the appropriate time, place, and in an effective manner will have the most impact. However, one message is never enough. Even if you go through the process of verifying receipt of the communication, and that the purpose or intent was understood, you will need to reinforce the message.

The "Bottom Line"

Remember the common refrain of parents? They seem to constantly ask their children "Did you hear me?" Well, they may not have been listening. Or, they may have heard you, but not understood you. Or they may have heard you, and understood you, but did not ACCEPT your message.

And just like the family, so it is, with your employees, in the workplace.

The bottom line is: Keep telling them! Then, tell them again! Maybe one more time! Perhaps they didn't hear you, so you better repeat yourself. Do they understand me? Did they understand the message? Did they *UNDERSTAND* and *ACCEPT* the message?

Once they've heard you, understood you, and accepted your message, they may do as you indicated or instructed. This is the key to communication.

WHAT MANAGERS CAN LEARN FROM U.S. PRESIDENTS

The essence of management is getting other people to support you: your policies, direction, and leadership. Although there may be considerable differences between political leaders and business leaders, the similarities are more significant. Perhaps we can learn from the top executive with the greatest responsibilities on this planet-- our President.

What qualities and behaviors make the Chief Executive of the most powerful country on earth successful? Let's limit our examination to recent office-holders-- the one's we're most familiar with, or at least, have some modicum of knowledge about. We can begin with the current President, and move backwards in time. Here we go...

Barack Obama - President Obama is an excellent communicator, possesses a fine intellect, is persuasive, and well spoken. He is handsome and likable. He has an agenda. He surrounds himself with people of like views. He is a media person who recognizes the power of the Internet, Social Networks, T.V., and the like. The most technologically adroit of our Presidents he calls his *BlackBerry* a "Crackberry;" constantly at his side.

George "W" Bush - President Bush was somewhat of a "bumbler." He frequently made foibles and put his foot in his mouth. On the other hand, he was likable, good-looking, self-effacing, decisive, strong when necessary, and had trusted "right hand men," Dick Cheney and Carl Rove.

William Jefferson Clinton - President Clinton had charm, poise, and likability. He is intelligent, a gifted speaker, and has an equally ambitious wife (Hillary). Clinton was persuasive and able to relate effectively with the "common folk." His time in office was a period of prosperity.

George H.W, Bush - The father of "W," he gained experience in the Reagan White House, as V.P., and the C.I.A. (*Central Intelligence Agency*). He was knowledgeable about government operations and foreign affairs. He too, was tall and pleasant-looking, with an amiable manner.

Ronald Reagan - Called the "Great Communicator" Reagan brought theatre to the office. He had "movie star" looks (he was actually a former movie star), and presence. Reagan was supremely likable (he even charmed the Soviet leader to end the "Cold War"). Reagan had strength and resiliency, and was a complete patriot, who believed unfailingly in America. He was an accomplished delegator who recruited top talent to do the detail work while he concentrated on policy.

James Earl Carter - President Carter had a relatively ineffective term of office. He was a former Nuclear Engineer-- with an engineer's mentality. Extremely detail oriented, he focused more on inconsequential matters and neglected the "big picture." During his tenure the economy suffered with high interest rates stifling investments and business. His pedestrian appearance, shrill voice, and tentative demeanor did not help matters.

What are the Lessons?

The most effective Presidents have some common characteristics and styles. Although you may not be able to do much about your physical appearance or innate intelligence, you can certainly modify your leadership style. Yes, some are "born leaders," or "natural leaders." However, management leadership can be developed or enhanced. The Presidents referred to owe their success, in part to these "critical few":

Intelligence, Superior Communications Skills, Likability, Healthy Delegation, Selection of Loyal and Competent staff, Personal Strength, Decisiveness, Focusing on the "Big Picture," and Effective Prioritization.

So take a clue from the "top" leaders, and focus on enhancing these skills, characteristics and abilities. You could do a lot worse than using these leaders as examples.

IS A DIRTY DESK THE SIGN OF A DIRTY MIND?

Is a "clean desk" the sign of an efficient, well-organized, productive employee, or an indicator of something else? Many employees have work surfaces free of clutter. Others always have stacks of paperwork, telephone messages, and other assorted stuff. If a cluttered desktop is the sign of a cluttered mind, what is an empty desktop the sign of?

Conflicting Reports

There are several studies and considerable anecdotal information concerning the neatness of workplaces. Managers would like to have definitive answers concerning employee organizational practices, and which approaches work best. Unfortunately, as is the case with most human behavioral matters, clear-cut answers are elusive. The following is a sampling of some studies and expert opinions.

Staffing agency *Ajilon* reports that "just 11% of workers earning over $75,000 a year call themselves neat freaks, compared to 66% of those making $35,000 or less."(Mina Kimes, *Fortune*, October 8, 2008, *CNNMoney.com*.) So is neatness inversely correlated with income? Probably not. However, organization ability and styles vary considerably.

David Freedman, a self-appointed "mess analyst" and author, says the concept of organization is context-bound... "People do better when they're in their natural state - neat or messy." (Kimes, *Fortune*) This indicates that when you force people out of their comfort zone they may be less productive, even when their behavior is at odds with conventional or optimally desired practice.

Herman Miller, the office furniture supplier conducted a study of workplace organizational habits and found that "'filers' actually stored more useless information than their unkempt counterparts." They also identified a group of "'work masters,' particularly efficient employees, and reported that those employees were more inclined towards "piling than filing." (The Miller finding seems counter-intuitive, although "out of sight, out of mind" may apply here.)

On the other hand, some studies suggest that as much as fifteen percent of your time can be wasted with a messy desk, because you may be distracted by things or unable to easily find things.

And, many managers have learned to use technology to organize themselves. They are comfortable with having files, reports, and data on their desktop, laptop, or *BlackBerry / iPhone*.

Is it All Related to Individual Learning and Thinking Styles?

People have different learning styles, such as Visual, Auditory, or Kinesthetic, they like to See, Hear, or Touch. Some employees prefer to see their work, and use post-it notes, paperwork, postings on their cubicle walls, etc. Others prefer conversations, instructions, dialog, etc. Still others need to feel, touch and experience. How much these preferences translate into organizational characteristics, remains to be seen. It seems likely, however, that that those who like to touch will want their work around them, and those who like to see, may as well.

Another factor that may enter into the equation is the *"Right Brain/ Left Brain"* theory ("Left brain/right brain" *Science Weekly*, vol. 19, Issue 10, January 24, 2003. pp. 1-12). You will recall that left brained people are more organized, rational, methodical, and linear thinkers, while right brainers are more unconventional, random, intuitive, and creative. Guess which ones are likely to have the messiest desks?

Practical Analysis

Some managers equate clean work surfaces with well-organized, efficient, and productive employees, while others believe it's a sign of "too little to do."

It's probably simplistic to draw any conclusions about a person's capabilities, productivity, effectiveness, or personality from the appearance of their desk. So go ahead, mess up your desk, or make it tidy, either way you've got research to support your decision.

Some Useful Tips

Despite the conflicting data, an employee should consider these guidelines:

--Understand and respect your employer's expectations and policies

--When you're dealing with customers, or the public, the expectations for tidiness will probably be higher than if you're working in a back office

--Try using techniques and aids such as organizers, filing systems, in/ out baskets, labeling, handling papers only once, etc.

--If you're technologically inclined, you probably already use computer and smartphone calendars, reminders and digital data storage and retrieval systems

--Don't be too hard on yourself, your style may not be the same as most employees, although you may function effectively

--If organizational abilities are "hardwired" as a part of our personality or thinking style, it may be a struggle to change

--If you're hopelessly unorganized you may require the assistance of a professional organizer (consultant)

<u>TEAMWORK (the Miami Heat Example)</u>

Perhaps you've seen all of the excitement, hype, criticism, anger, dismay, hatred, joy, optimism, and other emotions surrounding the Miami Heat's signing of uber basketball star, LeBron James, for the 2010-2011 NBA season. Was it a business decision, a personal decision, or a little of both? There's a great story here, and some lessons to learned for all businesspeople.

Recruitment

LeBron was courted by several top franchises, including his home team the *Cleveland Cavaliers* who desperately wanted him to stay, as well as the *New York Knicks, New Jersey Nets, the Chicago Bulls*, and of course, *Miami*. Top talent is always in demand whether it's in sports or business. Of course professional sports is a HUGE business, and very much in the public eye, so the talent recruitment was big news, captivating the public's interest for weeks in advance of the announced decision. The Radio City Music Hall *Rockettes*, made a commercial, politicians sang, financial analysts (from New York) claimed he could be the first "athlete billionaire," if he would only sign with them.

Talk about high profile; a rap mogul (*Jay-Z*), the Governor of Ohio, the Mayor of New York, even the President of the United States tried to influence his decision.

The announcement was an event

The pressure, as you can imagine, must have been incredible. To make matters worse, or better, as the case may be, *ESPN* provided an entire "show" so that LeBron could tell, and explain, his decision to the public on on national cable TV. Coverage was also provided by *CNN* and other major networks. The stakeholders are many, and with the stakes so high, the interest so great, and the coverage so public, emotions ran high.

ESPN of course wanted the visibility, and to sell the advertising minutes. LeBron said he didn't want the money, and declared he would donate his share from the broadcast to the "Boys and Girls" Club. *ESPN* is trying to raise their profile, and what better way than by pandering to the massive public interest. Over 10 million viewers tuned in (including me)!

The fallout

With his announcement, and so many people disappointed, the reaction was immediate and powerful. Dan Gilbert, owner of the *Cavaliers*, wrote an open message, berating and disparaging, LeBron and his decision, calling him "heartless and callous" (and making some very unprofessional personal comments), and published it on the team's website. Cleveland fans burned James' jersey on the streets. Commentators said his decision was a mistake. Meanwhile, fans in Miami rejoiced. There were instant parties, a celebration at the *American Airlines Arena*, and loads of publicity, Season tickets immediately sold out, as did LeBron's no. 6 jersey.

It isn't about LeBron, it's about winning!

LeBron James made a courageous decision; some might say an unselfish one (although I wouldn't go that far). He wanted to win a championship. He wanted to play with teammates Dwayne Wade and Chris Bosh. He thought this would be the best chance to achieve his goals. So, when he saw this opportunity, he snatched it!

This is the most highly visible affirmation of the value of teamwork I've recently seen. Dwayne Wade is a superstar in his own right. So is Chris Bosh. So are many of the other team members in place, or still being recruited. Wade, James, and Bosh all took a pay-cut to make this happen. (Although when the numbers get that big I'm sure they're not hurting, especially with endorsements and such.) Many of the other players also contributed by accepting reduced compensation. Their willingness to sacrifice personal ego and glory, for the sake of teamwork, excellence, and winning, is commendable.

There are always variables

Even with the best talent you sometimes don't win. Even if the "chemistry" is good it's never 100% certain. But without the best talent you're doomed, especially in the sports business. It remains to be seen how this team will perform. Certainly the odds favor Miami.

Business lessons to be learned

You might say "it's only a game!" Yes it is, but it's a big business game, not dissimilar to other businesses. Risks must be taken. The right people need to be hired, and perform. The team must function effectively. The results must be achieved. Sometimes it requires sacrifice. People will be critical. It may mean going against popular opinion. It takes commitment and a lot of effort. Of course, in the end it's worth it to win a CHAMPIONSHIP, whether in the business of sports, or any other business.

THE ROBOTIC EMPLOYEE

Have you noticed the change in the working environment? If you've been in the workforce for over ten years, I'm sure you have. Conformity is now the norm. Individuality is no longer valued, at least in large organizations. There's increasing standardization of procedures, processes, attitudes, behaviors, appearance, etc. It's *"Scientific Management"* (Frederick Taylor's approach to work measurement and standardization) revisited. A resurgence of the belief that there is *"one best way"* for every work process is underway.

Workers, even managers, are treated like robots; robots that perform their duties in an unfeeling, machine-like fashion, for hour upon hour, with standardized efficiency.

It All Started With McDonald's

The evolution of management thought promoted and accommodated changes in the workplace. First it was Scientific Management that, in the early 1900's that resulted in the assembly line, then it was W.E. Demming's TQM (*Total Quality Management*), along with CQI (*Continuous Quality Improvement*), and further development of Business Process Management theories and practices.

Some would argue that *Henry Ford's* automobile assembly line was the beginning of standardization, and it was. However, the concept was advanced much further with *McDonald's* Corp. The standardization was extended to include work environment and layout, purchasing of supplies, timeliness and manner of customer service, employee apparel, preparation of consumables (*Big Mac's*, etc.), menus, design, architecture, advertising, supply chain management, and so forth.

WalMart, FedEx, Hewlett-Packard, IBM, General Electric and many more have embraced the Process Management concepts, and applied them with vigor, and positive results.

There are Benefits and Drawbacks

Rigid adherence to standards does improve efficiency, but at what cost? Remember that efficiency is only one part of the management and productivity paradigm. Effectiveness is even more important. And quality is yet another major consideration.

Perhaps most importantly, innovation may be stifled in a standardized, routinized, conforming workplace. Great leaps in productivity, significant inventions, new products or services, major transformations have not occurred as a result of incremental improvements made by process oriented employees and managers.

Another problem with rigid adherence to standardization is the compounding error when something goes wrong. By this I mean, should there be an error or misjudgment in the original process, the mistake will be carried throughout the organization.

Not too many years ago, managers were touting the value of *decentralization*, and the benefits of adapting an individual division, or location, of the company to the peculiar demands or needs of their particular environment. There were considerable advantages to this tactic but there was less overall conformity. The *"empowerment"* concepts also supported individuality and creativity. Now, the pendulum is swinging back to *"top down"* management with most, if not all, major decisions being made at headquarters and an expectation that policies and procedures will be carried out in "lock step." While this may entail certain efficiencies, the feeling among local managers is that they're being asked to forgo their ingenuity, even their "leave their brains at home."

Once employees become like machines, doing work in a robotic, mechanistic and repetitive fashion they tend to lose some of their spontaneity, humanness, and individualism. While this may be in synch with the company's objectives, it may prove dysfunctional for the employee; even dehumanizing. Furthermore, the organization loses out on the creativity, and different perspectives, of many individuals. This "dumbing down" of the workplace will have consequences.

The Challenge

Leadership involves foresight, motivation, and inspiration. The leader must take risks in order to achieve significant results. To be a leader means the identification of opportunity and the acceptance of challenge.

The challenge for many leaders is to:

--design work that is not demeaning, repetitive and unfulfilling, while still achieving company targets and goals for productivity and ultimate profitability

--value individuality, while recognizing that certain procedures must

be followed

--fully engage the employee and manager and welcome their critiques and recommendations.

--recognize the importance of diversity, and the multiplicity of backgrounds, experiences, and perspective this entails

--experiment with other organizational models instead of following like sheep or lemming

A final important consideration is to incorporate the new realities into business curricula, so that tomorrow's business leaders will be able to make informed decisions and judgments. It is clear that management paradigms do not continuously move forward in an ever-enlightened fashion, but they are much more reactive to competitive and economic exigencies. Constant re-evaluation of business imperatives along with essential human, individual, and social considerations will be required.

Only in these ways will the economic engine of the country spring back to life.

MOTIVATION: MY FRIENDS ARE "DEAD PRESIDENTS"

There is a long-standing argument about whether money is a motivator. Various researchers (most notably, Herzberg) indicate money is not really a motivator, but instead it is other factors such as: "Intrinsic value of the work," "meaningfulness," "sense of accomplishment," "responsibility," etc. The importance of this argument to managers, and Human Resources Departments, is simple. How do we create conditions which will encourage the employee(s) to be more productive, and satisfied? Compensation packages are designed to address this issue, along with Pay for Performance programs and other techniques. How to motivate each individual to contribute to the organization as much as they are capable of doing is genuinely a challenge worth pursuing.

The "Dead Presidents" Speech

A friend of mine was one of the top automobile salesmen in the country. He made lots of money and attributed his motivation to "chasing dollars." At one point he became a sales manager, and tried to motivate his employees the only way he knew how. Now, I'm certain many others have tried this technique as well, and he didn't claim it was original. But he shared his "Dead Presidents" sales meeting speech with me one time, and I never forgot it. In abbreviated form, it went something like this:

My friends are Dead Presidents. (At this point he would pull out a huge wad of $50 and $100 bills and show them to his audience.) These are my best friends and I like to keep them close to me. They never ask me for anything but they stand ready to help me in times of need. If I want something they will help me get it; whether it's a new car or a new house. If I get sick they will help me get treatment. If I have children they'll help me pay for their College education. Yes, my friends are Dead Presidents.

I will always cherish these friends and always try to have more just like them. And, you can be sure that if these friends were ever to leave me, some of my other friends might go too. Yes, my friends are Dead Presidents.

I suspect that you, too, might want to have Dead Presidents as friends.

And, if you do, you need to work to get and keep them. So, go out there and sell cars!

Was this a motivating talk to the salesmen? Did it appeal to their more mercenary instincts? Or should my friend have elevated his rhetoric to appeal to their more noble aspirations?

The Motivation Quandary

It is difficult to ascertain and then attempt to successfully meet the motivational needs of others. We're all individuals, and motivated by different things. Some crave recognition, while others desire challenge, or being on a team, or the opportunity for self-determination. But one commonality exists among all employees: We all work for the money. Take away our salary or commission and see how long we continue to work.

Now this "greed factor" may not be our primary motivation and to say so flies in the face of research, motivational theories and many expert opinions. As an academician, I am on "thin ice" to question the accepted rationales. However, question it, I do. As an undergraduate I recall behaviorist B.F.Skinner's *Reinforcement Theory*, and how the little rats would run mazes, jump moats, do tricks and difficult tasks to get cheese (their reward). Are we humans so evolved that we won't perform similarly?

The Question

Will humans, like rats, do all sorts of things to gain rewards? I believe we know the answer. Yes, we will. And since we know that money may help us attain the things we need, might we seek money? Again, I think we know the answer.

According to Abraham Maslow's *"Hierarchy of Needs"* we are first motivated to satisfy the lower level needs, like food, sex, shelter and security. Once these basic needs have been satisfied, then we can move on to higher levels like social, self-esteem and self-actualization needs. But the question is: Do the lower level needs continue to motivate us or not? Besides, a case can be made that money provides us with the means to satisfy needs at all ends of the spectrum. Perhaps "self-actualization" through money is too much to expect, but very few people reach that level anyway.

Further Research is Needed

The purpose of this discussion is not to propose some definitive, or comprehensive theory of motivation, (or more specifically, employee motivation), rather it is to question the current premises and invite further research. You are welcome to draw your own conclusions concerning the efficacy of money as a motivator. As for me, I'm leaning toward my friend's hypothesis and in favor of the "Dead Presidents" view.

Note: As you probably realize Ben Franklin on the $100 bill is not a former president - although, many people don't make that distinction.

MANAGEMENT BY OBJECTIONS! (No, this is not a misprint.)

How often have managers decided on a compromised course of actions due to objections from staff or management?

Consensus

The optimal decision cannot be made by consensus, even though research shows that groups make better decisions than individuals. (I.e.," everyone is smarter than anyone.") The problem is there are too many compromises which need to be made along the pathway to agreement.

Pros and Cons

The advantage of group decisions, or participative decisions, is they tend to identify problems and opportunities more effectively than those made by individuals. Decisions made in this fashion also gain the support of those who participated in the process.

The obvious strength of having multiple perspectives and experiences is undeniable. And, since decisions made in a particpative manner, or by consensus, have the advantage of participant buy-in, they should be easier to implement. This all seems good, but at what cost?

There are always tradeoffs. In the case of consensus, the result is extremely difficult to achieve and the process is time-consuming. These are also "watered-down" decisions because, in an effort to arrive at consensus, opinions from participants favor safety over risk, conservative over expansive. Additionally, there is the profound danger of "group think," typified by the *Challenger* Space Shuttle disaster, where the desire to conform and be supportive, overrides the nay-sayers sound advice. Consensus or even participative management may mean a path to the lowest common denominator, or possibly huge mistakes in decision making. The Japanese decision-making model favors decisions by consensus. Of course, this is more cultural than stylistic. American managers come from a more individualistic cultural context and consensus skills are not as well honed.

Objections

In any decision-making process the steps include: definition of the problem, fact-gathering, analysis, evaluation of alternatives, and selection of the "best" alternative. These steps may not adhere to to a strictly linear process but the elements are standard. At any point objections can be raised. This is a healthy process insofar as it raises issues and concerns which need to be addressed. However, some objections may fall into the categories of: trivial, meaningful but unessential, indirect delay, process problems, ego-driven, or tactical. Addressing these objections consumes valuable time and energy while not necessarily contributing to the outcome. This is a fine line which may test the manager's judgment and capabilities.

Decisions

All too frequently managers abdicate their role as decision-makers and become immobilized as a consequence. Nobody wants to make a mistake, particularly when the stakes are high. Yet making inferior decisions, or no decision, will ultimately result in mistakes of greater consequence. Also, risk taking is a part of management. So exercise your decision-making power, and get plenty of input. Just be sure that the extreme risks are not taken without due consideration of the consequences, and don't let those who object for the sake of finding fault cause you to be immobilized.

<u>YOU'RE THE BOSS! ACT LIKE ONE!</u>

Let the clerks, accountants, janitors, or messenger boy do their jobs.

Don't get bogged down in the trivial details. Your job is to provide leadership and direction. When the managers are spending their time on the day-to-day routine, who will provide the pathway to the future?

Management Myopia

Many bosses lose sight of their responsibilities and priorities. Some believe that "if you want the job done right, do it yourself!" Many are more comfortable doing work they were trained to do, expert at, or proficient with, during a previous part of their career. What they fail to realize, or have repressed the thought, is that they are shortchanging the company, themselves, and their employees.

Subordinates are deprived of opportunity for growth when managers perform tasks intended for lower levels of staff. Plus, top executives don't get their money's worth when their managers are spending the bulk of their workday doing work well below their pay scale. Furthermore, more important management tasks and responsibilities are undoubtedly being neglected.

A Little Advice

Managers must remain cognizant that their top priority is being a manager! That means delegating work to others. For high-level management, their direction should focus on leading the way to the future, and external relationships.

"Sensing" the external environment is a must. It's essential to be aware of changes in the organization's environment which could have beneficial or detrimental consequences - the "opportunities," and "threats." Will you identify those major unforeseen, perhaps knowable, dangers, or will you be: "Rearranging the deck chairs on the Titanic?"

What of "best practices" in your sphere of responsibility, could the competition be outpacing you? You obviously need to be aware of what is working, and what isn't, in your industry.

The manager has an obligation to perform her managerial

responsibilities: Planning, Organizing, Leading, Informing, Controlling, and Enhancing (*POLICE*). Being a "Super-Clerk" is not part of your responsibilities. Recognize this and adjust your priorities accordingly.

WHEN RUMORS RUN RAMPANT

Gossip and rumors are commonplace in almost every organization. The bigger the firm, the more rampant the rumors are. The more secretive the management, the more prolific the rumor-mill is. Also, greater conditions of change within the organization and/or more volatility in the external environment, all contribute to the creation, proliferation, and perpetuation of rumors.

Official vs. Unofficial Communication

The official lines of communication are based on the formal organization structure and the reporting lines of authority. However all organizations have an informal network of friends, colleagues, associates, etc. who participate in an informal network which is often equally as extensive as the formal structure, and frequently even more powerful. Personal relationships and affinities cross all organizational boundaries and include all levels of authority.

These unofficial communication channels are often very functional. They provide context, significance, a framework for understanding, and interpreting events. They also grease the often arbitrary barriers to efficiency within structured settings. For example, the official policy may be to have forms completed for each sales transaction and submitted to the shipping department. However, the salesman may have a good rapport with that department, and be able to efficiently transact business over the phone with documentation to follow later. This way the salesman can provide faster service to his customers, and keep them happy. Likewise, the Human Resources Office may use a cumbersome approach to hiring new employees which can be abbreviated, so that essential staffing requirements can be quickly satisfied, because of the rapport between the HR rep and the hiring manager.

The Human Need for Understanding

You have seen this many times. The victim of a nasty divorce will try to analyze and explain the reason for the failure of the marriage. The survivor of a plane crash may rationalize by attributing his good fortune by saying it is God's will, or "I have more work to do in this world." While the events in the work place may not be as profound, or shattering, as the aforementioned events, we humans still have a need to explain happenings.

When you combine the need for understanding, the search for meaning, and the vagaries of economic beings in an organization the result is predictable. In the absence of definitive information, employees will create explanations which may, or may not, bear any resemblance to objective reality. A large workplace is in some ways like a big, often dysfunctional, family.

Employees not only try to explain events in the workplace (e.g., why someone was fired, transferred or promoted) they also may start rumors to be malicious, appear "in the know" or merely to entertain or experience excitement. The reasons behind sometimes purely rational business decisions may be theorized as having subjective elements (e.g., "she's sleeping with the boss").

Functional Aspects of the Grapevine

Astute managers realize that rumors are rampant in the workplace and that these channels of communication are an alternative to the formal channels for disseminating information. Some managers actually "plant" rumors into the grapevine and know those individuals who can be "counted on" to gossip and spread rumors. Other managers recognize that quick, effective communications can counter the rumor mill. However, this approach requires a reputation for candor and honesty. Otherwise it will backfire, and may be viewed with suspicion or even an attempt at manipulation. The consequences of these reactions will ultimately prove detrimental to management's reputation and effectiveness.

Some tips:

--recognize the various channels of communication

--realize that the official channels may not be the most trusted sources

--"tap into" the grapevine by identifying major participants and contributors

--sense the internal environment by asking: "What have you heard about?"

--don't be afraid of the grapevine

--consider utilizing the grapevine to spread information

--minimize the dysfunctional aspects of the grapevine by confronting

mis-information promptly and directly

--remember, if insufficient information is provided, employees will fill the "vacuum"

CRITICISM IS SOMETIMES NECESSARY

Communication is essential in business. It represents the biggest obstacle, and the greatest potential for productivity and profit improvement. Communication can improve, maintain, or destroy morale. Poor communication can lead to mistrust, higher employee turnover, or strained employer-employee relations. Lack of communication can result in uncertainty and feed the rumor-mill.

Unfortunately, not all communication can be positive, nor should it be. However, even negative commentary can be framed in such a way as to make it more palatable, constructive, and results-enhancing.

Purpose

Criticism can be demoralizing-- particularly when the criticism is considered unnecessary, unwarranted, heavy-handed, or out-of-proportion. The manager needs to consider her intent when communicating negative comments. Is the communication intended to help the recipient of the message? Is the intent to correct the behavior of the employee? Is the message directed at improving the employee's attitude?

Sometimes the intent is not so pure. The manager may be attempting to exert their authority, overcome their own insecurities, or pick on employees who seem to be weak, or different. The intent may be to bolster the manager's reputation as a "tough guy," to "send a message," gain compliance from others, or even a consequence of the manager having a "bad day."

Time and Place

The time and place of the criticism should be strategic and planned, if possible. Occasionally, this cannot be accomplished. For example, when the employee's behavior is so egregious or dangerous, as to necessitate immediate action (such as an employee who is rude to a customer, or engages in reckless behavior like failing to clean up a spill, or leaves an unattended ladder in an aisle).

Generally, the manager can arrange a time and place to meet with the employee. Remember the saying: "Praise in public; criticize in private."? It's a good guideline. As a rule, the meeting to criticize the employee's conduct, attitude, or specific behavior should be done in private. A time convenient to the employee should be arranged. The meeting should take place within a reasonable period, following the incident. Don't wait until the annual performance evaluation, or the last Friday of the month. Timeliness is important to convey the significance, to not allow memories to fade, to promptly initiate corrective behavior, and to move forward on a positive basis.

Content

Should you use the "sandwich" approach? This involves a reassuring message first (the bread slice). For example, "Bill, you have a great reputation around here, and you're a valued employee...however, lately I've had some concerns about..." Secondly, comes the "meat." "On Tuesday last week, and again on Thursday...you left your workstation for over..." Then, the (other slice) with words like..."I know that you can correct this..."

Some business people do not like the sandwich approach. They feel it's too contrived, formulaic, and insincere. However, you be the judge. If it's comfortable, go for it. If you're inclined to use a more direct approach, that's fine too.

Whatever approach you use, make sure to focus on the issue, objectively. Don't personalize the problem. Also, emphasize the consequences of the employee's performance or attitude, AND, the consequences of failure to address the issue(s). Be objective, supportive, understanding, and business-like. Be FAIR. Set some objectives, a timetable for improvement (immediate, one week, measurable progress, etc.), and follow-up. Offer help and support as indicated.

Also, be sure to initiate the documentation process, although the first warning is typically a verbal one. You will, however, need to refer to this communication, should further, and more serious, corrective action be required in the future.

Results

If you're satisfied with your purpose, your intent, your actions, and the process, you've acted responsibly to address the problem. You have turned a potentially destructive communication interaction into an opportunity for correction and growth. Make sure you obtain the desired results. Has the employee's performance/attitude/behavior improved? Are you regularly following up?

As a manager, you will not enjoy the good fortune of having employees who always do what they're supposed to do, on time, in a quality fashion, with excellent results, while demonstrating a positive, can-do attitude. You will need to become more expert at correcting behavior, as well as rewarding excellence. You have an obligation to your company, your employees, your customers, and the shareholders. Don't shy away from warranted criticism; just perform the task in a direct, yet tactful, supportive, non-destructive, and results-producing way.

THE "WONDERFUL" EMPLOYEE

Self-esteem is a wonderful thing. If you have high self-esteem, you're a better person, right? Not necessarily! Self-esteem is our perception of ourselves. But what if your self-assessment bears no relationship to reality?

Some hold themselves in high-esteem, deservedly so. Others do not hold themselves in high regard even though an objective assessment would prove otherwise. With these types of disparities can we trust self esteem to be a good measure of our character and competencies?

Many organizations, including school districts, corporations, public entities, etc., developed initiatives based on the reasoning that higher individual self-esteem would benefit society. In California, the State legislature actually passed a Bill and enacted a law concerning self-esteem. (AB 3659 created the *California Task Force to Promote Self-Esteem...* authored by John Vasconcellos, 1995).

Does High Self-Esteem Result In Better Performance?

Self doubt is a terrible burden. Second guessing, always coming up short, feeling inferior, are symptoms of low self-esteem. It stands to reason if you are confident in your abilities you will act in a fashion consistent with that belief. The pioneering motivational theories (E.g., Maslow's *"Hierarchy of Needs,"*) supported the benefits of this characteristic.

We admire people with confidence, and envy them. However, does high self-esteem translate into high performance? The answer, although not completely clear, seems to be NO, it does not. An extensive study involved a review (meta-analysis) of all major studies (over 18,000 articles) on self esteem and concluded that high self-esteem has either weak, negative, or non-existent correlations to "school performance, job and task performance, interpersonal relations, happiness..." etc. (Elish, J., *"FSU Study Finds Self-Esteem Programs Don't Work,"* FSU. com, 2004, 03/01)

Additional research confirms the premise that high self esteem is not a good predictor of success, good behavior, or high performance. In fact, it may prove to be a contra-indicator in some of these areas. For example, violent criminals score higher on self-esteem measures than the more law-abiding (Baumeister, R., "Violent Pride," *Scientific American*, 2001, 284, No.4, pp.96-101).

Implications For The Workplace

It would seem that applicants with more self-esteem would have an advantage in the hiring process. After all, they would have a higher propensity to exude confidence, and tout their accomplishments. They would also have that "firm handshake," eye contact, and other attitudes and behaviors that recruiters like to see. Likewise, seasoned employees with that positive, "can do" attitude are appreciated by supervisors. But in the workplace, as in life, the real test is in *results*, not nice words or confidence. The research does not support the connection between self-esteem and job performance.

We've all seen the overconfident employee and may even think of them as a "blowhard." And, we have all seen the quiet person who just performs their work, efficiently and effectively. I'm not implying that all employees with high self-confidence are poor performers, nor am I indicating that those with low self-confidence will consistently outperform. The point is that one's self-confidence is not a good indicator of ability, value, or capacity to achieve results.

Substantial numbers of the "Generation 'Y'" employees who inhabit our workplaces today were raised in a positive self-esteem promoting environment. Many of these individuals enjoy a sense of confidence and ability which far exceeds their actual (objective) performance. They were consistent receivers of accolades, awards, and "at-a-boys," "good job," "you're the best," throughout their developmental years. No wonder they believe they're invincible. Frequently their confrontation with a realistic assessment is their first encounter with "harsh" reality.

Tips For Managers

--question your preconceived notions, and biases, concerning self-esteem

--don't overlook the shy ones that don't "toot their own horn"

--give the less demonstrative employees a chance to "shine"

--hold the "high esteem" employees accountable for results

--recognize that because someone is confident, doesn't necessarily mean they will be able to perform competently

--don't diminish or disregard employees who are reluctant to "join the bandwagon;" their reluctance may be warranted

--be political, strategic; perhaps even gentle when criticizing young employees with outsized egos - don't "burst their bubble" too quickly or forcefully

--provide honest, yet supportive feedback to employees concerning their performance

--value all individuals for their uniqueness and ability to perform.

THE CONTINGENT MANAGER

Which is better Theory X or Theory Y?   Is it best to practice a participative management (Y) style or a directive (X) one? Should you use an empowering approach or a controlling one? Well, the answer is, **it all depends**.

What if you were able to match your management style with the demands of each situation? Would you be a more effective manager? Wouldn't it be preferable to be able to switch your approach to meet changing requirements and priorities?

Successful Management

Successful management requires flexibility, adroitness, intelligence, and an understanding of the situation.

Some experts argue that a "steady hand" is what is needed during turbulent times. But often the "steady as she goes" approach won't work. What may be required is immediate, bold and decisive action, not the inclusive, participative, time-consuming, employee buy-in, strategies which may work so well under normal circumstances.

Whenever we lock ourselves into a *"one best way"* approach, as espoused by Frederick Taylor for line employees during the *"Scientific Management"* era, it won't work well, or it won't work well for long.

Management is an art, not a science and formula approaches are doomed to failure. What is required is the flexibility to modify approaches as required by the exigencies at hand.

The Contingent Manager

Warren Bennis may be the most highly regarded expert of our time in the field of leadership. *Bennis* believes that leaders are "made not born. In *"Leaders: The Strategies for Taking Charge"* he identifies four essential competencies:

-Forming a **Vision**
-**Communication** of that vision
-Building **Trust**
-Searching for **self-knowledge**

Although *Bennis'* research and theories differentiate between leaders and managers, I would argue that similar qualities may be required for success in each job. The most effective managers have superior communication skills, nurture trust in the workplace, and have developed a decent understanding of themselves. These seem to be requisite strengths for success. As for Vision formation, the manager generally has a role or input to the process, and even if not, the manager must interpret and convey the Vision to subordinates. Often the success of the entire entity depends on the adroitness with which the manager(s) handle(s) this responsibility. While it is clear that leaders emphasize the visionary, planning, and external environments, while managers do less of this, a comparison can be made. And, since good leaders engage in succession planning they would be wise to nurture these skills in their trusted and valued managers, as an investment in the future of their organization.

Contingent managers will not practice their craft by rote, instead they will endeavor to develop the abilities required for top leadership roles. This means that they will have to adapt and change.

Advice for Aspiring Managers and Leaders

Here are some tips:

-Practice the competencies that top leaders have
-Envision yourself at least one level above your current position and act accordingly
-Learn from your experience and contact with top leaders
-Emulate their qualities that you admire or find useful
-Spend time getting to "know yourself;" identify your strengths, and more importantly, your weaknesses
-Don't get stuck in a single style; try using different approaches
-Determine which approaches work best in specific situations
-Work on understanding yourself so that you know and understand your proclivities
-Assume additional responsibilities especially those tasks with high visibility
-Remember to be flexible, malleable, and adaptable; flexibility and adaptability are keys to success and progress
-Learn from your mistakes, and don't be afraid to make them

The most successful managers are on the track to leadership roles. It is essential to be a "contingent manager," one who can make the best of any situation or circumstance. One who adapts

to new demands and is a constant learner. Forget the "one best way" path to management and leadership, if it ever worked, it is not applicable to today's unpredictable and demanding work environment.

THE MOST AMAZING THING I'VE LEARNED AS A MANAGER

I've spent most of my working life managing people, and I've learned a lot. Probably the most amazing thing I've learned is a very basic concept: "Hire high quality people, motivate them, and let them make you look good!"

Yes, it's more complicated than this, but not too much. Quality employees will invariably exceed your expectations, if you just let them.

Motivation

Top performers are internally motivated. Sure, they expect to be paid fairly, but their basic motivation is intrinsic. They do their best because of the challenge and satisfaction they get from exceeding expectations, and doing a superb job. They resent, or at least do not react positively, to close supervision, tight controls, micro-management, over-direction or mistrust. They want to define their own job, to an extent. They value independence and creativity. If permitted, they will come up with new systems and better approaches.

The Smart Manager

If the manager is smart, she will recognize the advantages of the above described behaviors, even though she might feel uneasy about the process. If she's too insecure it won't work.

Smart managers are more concerned about results than process. They're eager to share the "glory." They are willing to take a chance on other smart people. They lead by example.

Guidelines

Consider the following when you're in management:

--Hire QUALITY PEOPLE

--Provide them with guidance, resources, and training

--Recognize the risk/reward potential of allowing more "free rein"

--Give your high performers additional responsibility and freedom

--Support, recognize, and motivate them

--Build loyalty (it's a two way street)

--Let them exceed your expectations

--Enjoy the fruits of your good management

4

 MANAGING YOURSELF

THE SINGLE MOST IMPORTANT LEADERSHIP ABILITY

The single most important LEADERSHIP ABILITY is the ability to influence people.

Over half a century ago Norman Vincent Peale wrote perhaps the most successful self-help book of all time. Its title: "*How to Win Friends and Influence People*." This book, through its immense popularity and widespread usage, influenced millions of people to this day. And, his advice was particularly applicable to the leadership role, with one minor exception. Leaders don't necessarily need friends, but their position requires an ability to influence.

Leadership

There are numerous theories of leadership, and many successful examples of leaders. Some believe that "leaders are born not made." Others feel that leadership can be dissected into its components. Most think that leaders are disciplined, charismatic, inspirational, motivated, "great thinkers," have vision, or some combination of qualities that elude most mortals.

Great Leaders

Think about it. Modern leaders in business, politics and religion have used their abilities to influence people, and in the process have: achieved success, accomplished their agenda(s), and gained fortune or fame. Likewise, the great leaders of the past have achieved similar results through identical ability and practice.

It does not really matter which leader you wish to examine. Whether it is some of the Presidents: *Lincoln, Reagan, Roosevelt*, or others; Religious leaders such as *Christ* or *Mohamed*. Great despots like *Hitler* or *Mussolini*. Social movement leaders like *Gandhi* or *Dr. King*. Or American business figures like *Bill Gates*, *Jack Welch*, *John Rockefeller* and *Andrew Carnegie*.

Motivation

Some may consider influence and motivation as the same. They're not. There is a long-standing argument whether we can really motivate others at all. Are we really capable of causing someone to attain a certain attitude, achieve a specified objective, or perform a particular task? Probably not. What we can do is influence an individual's attitude and behaviors by creating conditions which will be likely to result in the behaviors and attitudes we wish to promote. Most often these conditions will involve a set of rewards and/or punishments. These rewards or punishments will work best when they are personalized to meet the needs and desires of a specific individual or group.

The Natural Leader

Rare individuals seem blessed with a profound natural ability to influence others. These natural leaders may have great oratory skills, charisma, attractiveness, bearing, wisdom, or likability. Or a combination of these attributes. The natural leader can influence others to achieve his goal(s) and those goals or aspirations of the "followers" This ability can be used for good or bad purposes.

Improving Your Ability to Lead

Influencing others can be a learned skill. Some leaders feel more comfortable using their charm or personality, whereas others may be more comfortable exerting the strength of their character or will. Here are some considerations and approaches:

Diagnose your personal strengths and style. Be brutally honest in identifying your weaknesses. While some weaknesses are normal, you will probably want to address those which may be holding you back. Your strengths are another matter, and these assets will prove valuable to you.

Capitalize on your strengths. Once you have identified your strengths it will be essential to refine and hone them. If you're a good speaker, practice so that you can become a superb one. If you're a friendly individual become even more outgoing and attentive.

Work on your weaknesses. If you're a poor speaker join *Toastmasters*. If you're reclusive by nature try to become more outgoing by joining clubs, professional organizations, etc.

Cautiously gain feedback. Understand how you are perceived. Often we're blind to our faults. Ask trusted advisers to give you honest feedback about your performance and efforts to improve. Then act on it.

Select Role Models. Find people who exemplify the style you admire and seek, then try to emulate them.

Thoroughly understand your followers. It is essential to understand your followers. What needs do they have? What are their goals and ambitions? How can you better connect with them? It is far easier to influence followers who agree with you in at least some measure.

In conclusion, there are a few individuals who possess a remarkable ability to greatly influence others. Sometimes this appears to be innate. Others have a more limited capability. But it is fair to say we all have some abilities in this area. The important consideration for a leader, or for those aspiring to be one, is the possibility of change and improvement. Like anything else, it's easier if you are naturally blessed with these talents. However, the ability to influence people can be acquired and developed.

BECOMING A BOSS

Becoming a boss may be your goal. If it is, there are a few things you should know. First, it's not all that it's "cracked up to be." Second, it's probably better than you thought.

The Boss

What is a boss, anyway? Do you boss people around? If so, you probably won't be very effective. Do you like to motivate people? Achieve objectives? Get things done through other people? Team build? Develop people's abilities and skills? Then you're a good candidate. Do you like to have regular working hours? Do you dislike responsibility? If so, you will not like management.

What does it Take?

Effective managers are "people people," they enjoy being around others. They have self-discipline and are able to make effective decisions that are unbiased. They don't show favoritism, and if they feel it, they keep it to themselves. Effective managers don't like to be called boss. This has a connotation which is reminiscent of the Theory X managers of bygone times. Modern bosses aren't as hung up on the control and authority aspects of their position. Nor are they typically enamored with the status, prestige or accouterments of their position.

Effective managers are able to embrace the mission and goals of their organization, and become an advocate for the company. They like seeing everyone "on the same page," and value loyalty and dedication. Effective managers are cost conscious and not wasteful. They realize that contributing to the growth and profitability of their firm is a paramount objective. Effective managers gain satisfaction from achievement and progress. They take "ownership" of projects, tasks and responsibilities, and enjoy seeing successful conclusions.

Getting from Here to There

The challenge is to get from the non-supervisory position to first-line management (i.e., Supervision). In order to successfully navigate this transition, you will need to take several steps:

--Consider your reasons for wanting to become a manager. Make sure it is something you really want.

--Make sure you "stand out" from your peers in the non-management crowd. Sometimes just doing a little extra will make you a "star." This is because so many of your contemporaries are satisfied with doing the minimum to get by. You cannot afford to be mediocre if you want to advance.

--Let management know about your desire to advance. This will help you enter the "management track" and be considered for future openings.

--Emulate the successful managers in your company. Try to develop attitudes, habits and practices like them. Frequently if we practice behaviors they become ingrained and "second nature."

--Go to school, participate in staff development programs and training; take an interest in improving yourself.

--Take "ownership" of your job, projects, assignments, etc. This goes beyond responsibility, into true involvement and commitment. Learn all you can about your organization, especially its vision, mission, goals and objectives.

--Be seen. Go to holiday parties, birthday celebrations, etc. Participate in all company events. Attend all staff meetings.

--Be aware of paths to management. In some businesses it's the sales orginization, in others the manufacturing branch, and in some the staff side may have the edge. If appropriate, and available, try to maneuver your way into the "fast track" area.

--Be enthusiastic, and demonstrate a cheerful, positive attitude. Employers look for positive people not "naysayers."

In difficult economic times like today, companies can be more choosey about candidates for management positions and the competition is more intense. These factors are exacerbated by the overall decline in management positions as a result of technology, increases in the "span of control," and the imperative to reduce labor costs. So you must distinguish yourself.

You Decide

Management has its rewards, both monetary and non-financial. There can be a great satisfaction to leading a team to higher levels of performance and achievement. You will also have the opportunity to learn and participate more fully in the organization. Of course you will have enhanced career opportunities and increased potential. This all comes at a price. And the cost is usually longer hours, greater responsibility, and more pressure.

If, after all this, you are still interested in a management position, then "go for it"!

LOOK LIKE YOU MEAN BUSINESS!

The business world is not that different from the entertainment industry. In fact, entertainment is big business; a business that relies on image and believability. Actors use costumes to "fit the part" they're playing. Whatever role you're playing you need to dress the part.

Dress for Success

The "*Dress For Success*" (Malloy, John T., Warner, 1975) books were a mainstay for American business people for decades. They reflected the standards of their time and specified acceptable apparel protocol. The standard wardrobe for men included the obligatory Blue Blazer, business suit, black and brown dress shoes, appropriate ties, long-sleeved shirts, etc. Everything from belts to haircuts was specified. For women conservative pants or skirt and jacket were typical. These standards for business attire were rigidly observed and informally, or even formally, required.

The current, less rigid, work apparel for office dress, evolved gradually. "Casual Friday's" were implemented so employees could dress more comfortably. And, as employees "tested" the limits of tolerance in workplace attire, they experimented with new styles and increasingly informal wear.

Current Casual

Over the years dress standards for business people have relaxed considerably. It is now difficult to ascertain a person's position or status within an organization by the way they look. The CEO may be wearing a Polo shirt, while the Administrative Assistant sports a Sports Coat and slacks. In fact, sometimes executives confirm their status by not having to follow office dress codes.

So is the old *Dress For Success* model outmoded? Can we all come to work in tank tops, shorts and flip flops? Well, not yet. And, maybe never; although there are some notable exceptions.

In the high-tech industries a wide range of styles and apparel is tolerated, maybe even encouraged. Microsoft, for example, permits the programming, systems, and other staff to pretty much dress the way they please. Theoretically they can perform their duties in pajamas, or swimsuits as effectively, or better, than in standard office apparel. It is viewed as a "perk" and a necessity if a company wishes to attract and retain the best, most creative talent. Frequently, exceptionally creative people, refuse to follow arbitrary or rigid rules, or be forced into a "box." When you want people to "think out of the box" it may be best to not constrain them in superfluous areas.

At Microsoft, even sales staff can "dress down" while at headquarters, although they may be expected to dress up for business meetings, or when representing the company in other venues. Other companies having liberal dress codes include such diverse enterprises as *Proctor and Gamble*, *Ford Motor Company*, and *IBM*. In fact the vast majority (over 80%) of companies permits, or even encourages, "business casual" attire.

What Difference Does it Make

What difference does it make, anyway? Society has evolved, and so has office attire and practices. However, there are many reasons to dress the part:

--Business attire helps create an image of confidence.

--Much of business is about image. Your appearance is reflective of your self-image

--Dressing the part shows respect for the other party(ies). Appropriate business attire shows professionalism

--When dealing with other cultures, many are considerably more formal than ours

--You will feel more confident when you dress the part -People judge a person's status by their appearance

--People often treat you differently according to your dress

--It's easier to dress down than dress up (You can always take off a tie, and unbutton a shirt if appropriate.)

--You are the face of your business to customers and stakeholders

Obviously, you are the best judge of what to wear in a business setting. And, while business casual has certainly become a norm, consider what role you are playing, and what image you want to convey, and dress accordingly.

PRIORITIZE TIMES THREE

In business the manager must PRIORITIZE, PRIORITIZE, PRIORITIZE. Prioritize times three! There just isn't enough time in a day, week or month to get everything done. And, even if you're a proficient delegator, there are some tasks which are inappropriate to delegate.

The Need for Prioritization

Prioritization requires time and judgment. There is always a wide array of things to be done. Discriminating between those that are critical, those that are important, and those that would merely be nice to handle is the trick. The effectiveness of a manager will largely depend on her ability to distinguish among the various competing tasks, responsibilities, actions, etc. that need to be completed. Trying to do everything will merely result in frustration, inefficiencies, incomplete work, unnecessary stress, and disappointment.

Prioritization Strategies

1. Make a daily, weekly and monthly "to do" list.

2. Compare your list with the annual goals and targets for the organization. You must align your priorities with the organization priorities.

3. Include your personal business goals in the mix. Create your own list of priorities that will meet the company's objectives, satisfy your needs, and build the business. (If you neglect these "special" projects or goals YOU wish to accomplish you are likely to suffer from demotivation and discouragement.)

4. Focus on the "big picture." Whereas performing a large number of inconsequential tasks will keep you busy, it will not necessarily be productive in a larger context. Avoid busywork.

5. Maintain your perspective. Step back periodically to reflect on where you are and how far you've progressed.

6. Emphasize financial and customer related goals. After all, you're in business to make money, and without customers you won't. These areas deserve a higher priority than any others. So if your priority task does not contribute to the "bottom line," and/ or improve customer volume, service, or satisfaction it should be

reconsidered.

7. Concentrate on your top priorities. It is easy to get distracted, and some people find it very appealing to work on non-essentials.

8. Don't get overwhelmed by competing priorities, use the following step to deal with this.

9. Delegate. Delegation is an art. In order to complete the "picture" of your business you must be free to "paint the canvas." Your creative powers and time will be freed up by delegating those tasks and responsibilities which: 1) can be done better by someone else, 2) you find distasteful, or 3) interfere with your main responsibilities for planning and leading.

10. Have fun. Reward yourself. Enjoy your accomplishments. Although many of us gain satisfaction from completing an important task, too often we fail to experience the process in a positive manner. Recognize that accomplishments take time, effort, energy, sacrifice, etc. Be kind to yourself and provide yourself with the kind of recognition you like to get from others, or more importantly GIVE to others.

11. Don't let events determine your priorities. You must determine your priorities based on your analysis of what needs to be done and what its relative importance is. It's easy to get pushed around by constant changes and frequent crises if you don't have your priorities firmly in place.

12. Publicize your results. Let others know what has been accomplished. Be sure to recognize that it hasn't been a "one person show."

Prioritization is an essential and challenging management responsibility. The more adroit you become at it the more you will accomplish and the better you will feel about your outcomes. It is something that doesn't come naturally. We tend to focus on what seems important AT THE TIME rather than those things that will make real, enduring, and meaningful differences. Prioritization is perhaps the most critical aspect of your PLANNING process. So, take a deep breath, list everything you need to do, then, utilizing the strategies listed above, begin your prioritization process.

THE "HURRY SICKNESS" and SOME RECOMMENDED CURES

Ever notice how the pace of business has sped up and intensified? How you're never able to catch up and feel on top of things? That you constantly feel under stress and never relaxed? That work isn't as fulfilling as it once was? Well, living in a "pressure cooker" is no fun - even for the carrots and potatoes.

The Hurry Sickness

You've been there. Too much work, too many assignments, and deadlines that are too short. These pressures will ultimately take a toll on your happiness, and your physical and mental well-being, unless you can figure out a way to effectively deal with them.

Perhaps you remember hearing that "balance in life" is most important; that you should have some time for your family, your work, and yourself. Is this an outmoded concept, or a realistic objective? Is it attainable in today's world and business climate? If it is attainable, how do you go about it?

Management Solutions

Managers are experts at solving problems. We basically do this for a living. However something has gone awry. The same tools we use to solve our business problems, we are not applying to our careers and lives. What do managers do? What are their responsibilities? How do they become effective? The traditional model is: Planning, Organizing, Leading, and Controlling. If these functions, responsibilities and approaches work so well in performing our jobs, why can't they be applied in a broader context to us as total human beings and not just in the little "management box"? Of course they can.

Hurry Sickness Cures

PLAN-- Plan your day-each day! Of course there will be interruptions, and changing demands that you will have to handle. This level of planning is at the "Operational" level, the day-to-day plans that get you through the moment. The traditional "To Do" list is a helpful technique here. As far as the longer-term "Strategic" and "Tactical" plans, spend more time in developing and analyzing them, and less time focusing on the details.

ORGANIZE-- Prioritize your work. Everything is really not a "top" priority, and some things don't need to be done immediately, or even today. Organize your desk too. Clutter and disorganization will cause you to waste time finding things and increase your overall stress level. Break big projects into smaller more manageable components so that you can get a sense of accomplishment from finishing something (even if it is a piece).Managers typically try to control by "exception." That is, when measurements indicate a real concern to organization or project success. If the deviation from plan or schedule is minor, these variances typically don't need to be addressed or micro-managed.

LEAD-- As a manager you need to motivate and delegate. Providing leadership to your employees and constantly motivating them will result in many items not even reaching your desk. We all know how important it is to provide encouragement to others - but don't forget about YOU. You also need to inspire and motivate yourself; self-talk, exercise, providing little rewards or incentives to yourself all help. For example, giving yourself a "treat" or a break, or a "pat on the back" for accomplishments. Part of leading is collaborative so set your objectives and goals with those who are involved and impacted. They will not only appreciate your consideration, but because they participated in the process they will have more of a commitment.

CONTROL-- Setting realistic deadlines is important. Deadlines which are too short frequently result in missed due dates or slipshod work. Missed deadlines cause stress and aggravation, and some of this can be avoided. Be realistic and set your objectives and deadlines collaboratively with the people affected. Of course, be flexible and not too hard on yourself or others. Change deadlines when necessary. Just don't make a habit of it. If the deadlines have been set by someone else, don't wait until the last minute to get started, pace yourself, ask for help when necessary, and try to get the deadline changed if imperative. If the responsibility or task pertains to quotas, expectations or standards do the same thing. Revisit the requirement and see if it can be modified to more closely approximate reality in performance and expectations.

Finally...

Try implementing these approaches. Most of us already know these concepts and practices. Sometimes we just need a reminder. Take care of yourself. In the end "you're all you got". Fit in some leisure or diversion, even for brief periods. Laugh a lot. Researchers have discovered that laughing promotes health, reduces stress and even strengthens your immune system. If nothing else works: ESCAPE. Better to leave a position that is destroying your spirit, body and mind than endure and suffer the consequences.

IN BUSINESS, AND LIFE, TIME IS RELATIVE

Managers frequently feel the pressure of deadlines, and day-to-day concerns about "too much work" and "too little time." How much of this is REAL, and how much is perception?

Now here's a key concept: Time is Relative

You undoubtedly, perhaps vaguely, remember that *Einstein's Theory of Relativity* has something to do with time, mass, and velocity, and that these concepts are interrelated, not fixed. Well, Einstein was a Genius and he postulated (in the Special Theory) that time is relative to the observer. Now let's take this scientific concept and make some practical use of it (with appropriate apologies to Einstein for liberties taken).

Since time is relative to the observer, and you are the observer-- it stands to reason that time is not just this rote and unchangeable measurement of seconds, minutes, hours and days-- but rather, it is relative to your perspective.

A Practical Example

We can demonstrate the limited applicability of this relativity concept with the following:

When you were five years old, it seemed to take forever for Christmas or your Birthday to arrive. Yet, when you're fifty, holidays seem to fly by. Why? Let's examine this. When you're five, you've only experienced five birthdays and four or five Christmas's. However, when you're fifty you've been through at least forty-nine of these occasions. Thus, time being relative, it appears to go by faster in relation to your experience. When you're five, one year is one fifth (or, 20%) of your total life's experience. When you're fifty, one year is only one-fiftieth or 2% of your life. Time appears to go twice as fast at twenty than at ten, and three times as fast at sixty than at twenty.

So time appears to be going proportionately faster with increasing age. This is because we can judge its passage from an increasingly broader perspective, with each time unit representing a decreasing proportion of our total experience. If you are lamenting that "time flies" you are probably older not younger!

Think of it this way; how long will a 24 hour day seem when at age 30 you've already been through almost eleven thousand of them? Or, at age sixty-five when you have almost 23,000 under your belt?

What to do

Since we only have so much time, and since it always seems to be going by faster, the question becomes, what can we do to make the best use of our time? We all know that prioritization is one answer. There are tasks which really need to be done and others that would merely be nice to complete, and spending your time on insignificant matters is wasteful. A simple, yet effective, technique is to create a "to do" list in priority sequence. Another, more powerful technique is to DELEGATE. In effect, you spend someone else's time, not your own. Most readers are familiar with the concept that authority and responsibility can be delegated but accountability cannot. The delegator is accountable for outcomes and results no matter who is assigned responsibility for the task(s).

Many managers are poor at the task of delegation. They are reluctant to assign responsibility to others because they don't trust the employee's judgment, skills, or competence, or because of their own insecurities. We've all seen bosses who try to do everything themselves and end up frazzled or overwhelmed. So practice delegation, first with small tasks of minor consequence, gradually increasing the complexity and importance of assignments until the subordinate staff and you are comfortable with the process and outcomes. This will ultimately relieve stress and time pressures.

Finally...

The relativity of time is a useful concept. When you're doing things that are important to you time seems to go even faster, particularly when you enjoy what you're doing. This is especially important as you grow older and time seems to go faster because your past life is an increasing proportion of your total life. Your extensive experience may make it appear that the present is only a "blink."

Although we all have the same amount of time (hours and minutes), it appears to be going faster or slower depending on the individual, his/her age, the nature of the activity and our attitude. Since you can't modify your chronological age, try to change your attitude, and spend more time on the activities you enjoy. Devote your available time to your highest priorities, and

conserve your time through this practice, and by "spending other people's time" on things of less importance and consequence, or on tasks which are just plain unpleasant. In this way your time, however short, will have more quality.

THE TERRIFYING TASK OF PUBLIC SPEAKING

Almost all business managers and executives are called on, upon occasion, to give a public presentation. And most are terrified at the prospect. It makes no difference if you have experience, there is anxiety associated with public speaking. Even in the confines of a staff meeting or small group, many are reluctant to voice their opinion. I'm sure you've all heard that public speaking ranks so high on people's list of fears that in some cases it actually ranks higher than death! How can one learn to conquer their fears and move towards tolerating, perhaps even enjoying the opportunity to speak publicly?

The Speaker's Concerns

We often believe the stakes are higher than they really are. We worry about a faux pas, factual error, or other missteps. We worry about our voice, our appearance, our manner, etc. Sometimes this anxiety and nervousness translates into physical symptoms and impairments such as vocal changes, forgetting your "lines," or a "flight" impulse. In actuality, most members of your audience are so wrapped up in their own issues that they really are not intensely interested in yours.

Remember, the audience is generally sympathetic, or even supportive, to the presenter. People do not expect perfection from a presenter; generally they are just interested in obtaining information, opinion or entertainment.

Speakers at their Best

A few speakers actually revel in the spotlight. They often gravitate toward jobs in the media, religion, sales or politics. Some are so entrancing that their audience is almost mesmerized. Most politicians are effective in front of a crowd; if they weren't they wouldn't win elections.

One current example of a great speaker is our President, *Barack Obama*. President *Obama* is a likable and effective communicator; so were Presidents *Clinton* and *Reagan* (called the "Great Communicator"). All of these individuals enjoy a "likability" factor along with a gift for relating with their audience. It is reported that President *Obama* is aware of his skill and commented ("without a hint of braggadocio or conceit") to Congressman Harry Reid..."I have a gift." *(*Washington

Post, April 29, 2009)

Preachers are particularly good orators. Most have polished their skills in front of congregations for years. The best of all are the "TV Preachers." There is a lengthy list of TV preachers, several of whom have "fallen from grace." Here are a few popular preachers: *Oral Roberts, Jimmy Swaggert, Jan & Paul Crouch, Jim & Tammy Bakker, Creflo Dollar, Benny Hinn, T.D. Jakes, Joyce Meyer, Joel Osteen. (St. Louis Post-Dispatch, Nov. 18, 2003, and, Yahoo! Answers, Yahoo.com- Question Index: 20080321053715AA21tXY.)* They offer messages of faith, hope and redemption. They typically have unbounded energy, enthusiasm, and excellent public speaking techniques (e.g., voice, eye contact, body language, intonation, etc.). If you want to become a good motivational speaker, watch them.

Other speakers are on late night TV; the "pitchmen," often earning obscene amounts of money, they sell widgets, gadgets, products and services through "infomercials." *Ron Popeil, Billy Mays, Anthony Sullivan* and *Tony Robbins* are prime examples. They use likability, humor, body language (e.g., "nodding" in agreement with their own comments), motivational techniques, etc. (*CNNMoney.com as reported in Fortune Magazine, April 6, 2009.*)

You may not aspire to become a politician, evangelist or pitchman but you probably want to become more confident, persuasive, and effective at public speaking. Or you may just want to be able to stand up in front of a group without falling, or getting sick.

Lessons to be Learned

What can we learn from these professional, expert, and highly effective speakers? Several things come to mind.

First: **know your audience**. Are they sophisticated, or "regular folk"? Are they knowledgeable about your subject matter, looking for encouragement or consolation, action, or support? Are they men or women, religious, investors, scientists, seniors, schoolteachers, etc.? You must know who you're talking to in order to find a topic that is important to them, and to present it in a fashion that is most appropriate.

Second: **look the part**. Whether you're selling gadgets or ideas, promoting religion, or politics, you need to "dress to impress." You've seen politicians in shirtsleeves talking with union members, or in formal wear at State functions. In other words, dress in a manner appropriate to your role, and audience. Sometimes it's a suit and tie, other times you must dress down to relate to your audience.

Third: **be enthusiastic and animated**. Although there are some exceptions to this rule (e.g., eulogies), as is often said: "Enthusiasm is infectious."

Tips, Strategies, and Approaches

There is so much advice to speakers available on the Internet, in books, and articles. However, the best resource may be "Toastmasters." *Toastmasters* is an international organization with a specific mission to help people become better speakers. There are Toastmasters Chapters practically everywhere.

Toastmasters International offers advice to speakers, as well as support, and an opportunity to practice, learn techniques, gain feedback, and improve. Their advice can be summarized as: "know your material, practice, know the audience, know the room, relax, visualize..., realize that people 'want you to succeed,' don't apologize [for nervousness], concentrate on the message, and gain experience." For a more complete explanation, see: "*10 Tips for Public Speaking,*" at www.toastmasters.org. And, of course, there are numerous additional considerations and more strategies, approaches, and techniques to be learned.

A Personal Note

I confess. I've always been fearful of public speaking. - I often thought I was the only person to ever graduate from the University of Washington without saying a word! (Well, maybe one or two). Over the years this fear has dissipated somewhat and become more manageable. My personal advice is to confront the fear, make the speech, and attempt to get better at it. Try focusing on a few "friendly" faces in the audience to help you through the process. And, if you're so inclined, take a Public Speaking class, or join Toastmasters. You will be in good company and experience a sense of accomplishment.

GO AHEAD! COMPARE YOURSELF!

You've probably been told not to compare yourself to others. This admonishment is common in religions, many societies, and most families. The popular *Desiderata* advises: *"If you compare yourself with others, you may become vain and bitter; for there will always be greater and lesser persons than yourself."* Comparison is one of those things that "you're not supposed to" but "everyone does".

Comparison is Pervasive

In practice, it's almost impossible not to compare yourself with others. You see, hear, meet, observe, read about, and learn through the media how others are doing - their triumphs and failures, their joy and despair - constantly. This is particularly true now. Each day we are deluged, perhaps overwhelmed, with information: Public opinion polls, consumer sentiment, news events, rankings, etc.

In school our performance is compared (not only by grades), at work we're compared by performance, quotas, compensation, evaluations, etc. Our homes, automobiles, appearance, vacations, vocations, financial success, lifestyles, clothing, etc., are all topics of conversation and comparison. We frequently compare others to make evaluations or distinctions: E.g., "Sue's smarter than Annie," "Mary has a better personality than Fred," "George is better off than Bill," "Michelle is prettier than Zelda," "Sam's a better driver than Olaf."

Sports may be the most competitive and comparative field of all. With team standings, individual player and team "stats," media coverage, etc., it's impossible, counter-productive, and downright silly, not to make comparisons. After all, even *"Little League"* is not just for fun and sportsmanship, otherwise they'd stop keeping score.

Government makes comparisons all of the time: "Standard of living," "morbidity and mortality," "life expectancy," "home ownership," "income," "educational level," and so forth. Sure they're done in aggregate, but comparisons are cross-referenced by race/ethnicity, age, state and community, and between us and the rest of the world.

The business-world is exceptionally competitive. Firms compete for top talent, strategize to increase market share, maneuver to improve share price and innovate with new products. Businessmen and consumers alike, compare products, service, growth, earnings, and reputation. We almost invariably make purchases based on comparison - price, quality, utility, appearance, and value.

Comparison is Good

Comparison, even among and between individuals, may not be the villain it's often portrayed to be. Let's look at some of the positives.

Comparisons...

--permit us to make more informed distinctions and evaluations

--help us in making selections among choices

--may serve as a challenge or motivating force

--can stimulate us to excel

--may help us avoid impulsive behavior

--give us 'grounding' in fact and opinion

--can make you feel "better"

--assist us to make the best decision

So the next time you decide to compare your looks, values, ethics, appearance, financial and career success, or any of the remaining multitude of variables, remember that it's only human, and can be good. When you look at others, try not to be malicious, certainly don't be defensive, but see if there is any benefit that can accrue from setting new goals and standards, finding appreciation for what you have, enjoying your accomplishments, stimulating your competitive spirit, and motivating yourself!

DO YOU TAKE JOY IN OTHER PEOPLE'S MISERY?

The Germans have a word for it – "Schadenfreude." Taking joy in other people's misery is not an attractive trait. However, many business people cannot resist the inclination to revel in others misfortune. Some actually make their living by it, snapping up distressed properties, unprofitable businesses, bankruptcy assets, etc.

The Comparison Game

Individuals and organizations are accustomed to counting and comparing. Profits, growth, promotions, income, competitive advantages, new product releases, reputation, stock prices, etc., etc. How do we know when we're successful, if there are no standards or comparisons by which to measure?

With all this comparison going on, it is perhaps natural to keep score and to feel good when you're on top. On the other hand, feeling good when someone isn't doing well can be rewarding too, particularly when it's someone you envy or despise.

Competitiveness

Business is all about competition and money. Particularly in a free-market economy like ours, individuals get caught up with all kinds of competition. "Keeping up with the Jones'" is about competition, comparison, and perceived success. We typically learn to compete at an early age. Sports and games are competitive, so is school. Later, the competition often centers around houses, cars, jobs, and money. Competitiveness can be a positive influence in our personal and business lives when not carried to extremes.

Self-Esteem

Researchers believe that enjoyment from the misfortune of others may be related to the individual's perception of himself. Those with low self-esteem are used to coming up on the "short end of the stick." They do not feel good about themselves, and in a society where many people do, there is a discomfort and dissonance. A response to this discomfort, no matter how dysfunctional, may be to gain more happiness and satisfaction when their colleagues and "friends" are suffering.

Envy is a related emotion, and another unhealthy reaction is to be envious of those who seem to have better lives than we do.

Check Yourself

- Do you get more enjoyment from seeing others succeed or fail?
- Are you "crushed" when you experience difficulty or failure?
- Are you preoccupied with comparing yourself with others?
- Are you envious of those who you estimate to be happier or more successful than you?
- Can you help others succeed and gain genuine satisfaction from the experience?

Your answers to these questions will provide an indication of whether you embrace or reject Schadenfreude and if you have a healthy level of self-respect, self-esteem, and competitiveness.

THE "COMEBACK" MANAGER

It is often said: "it's not how many times you fall down, but how many times you get up!" And, in today's business climate it seems that people are falling more often. The loss of a job, demotion, reassignment, reduction in pay, diminished responsibility, change to part-time status, etc., can be a devastating blow to even the most confident individual.

Dealing with Job Loss

The job loss I am referring to can be any of the aforementioned circumstance. While some scenarios can be more hurtful than others, any negative action adversely impacting one's security, status or pay can range from annoying to devastating. In these times, and under these conditions, you should steel yourself for more setbacks than you may be accustomed to.

Although comeback stories are not too rare in sports, or even politics, the business world seems more unforgiving. And once you are "labeled," (as a reject, incompetent, "over-the-hill," terminated, inflexible, demoted manager, etc.) it's difficult to recover.

You Need to "Stay in the Game"

Serious employment setbacks may *put* you into a Kubler-Ross type of cycle. You know, the "Grief Cycle" in which you go through the various stages of: Denial, Anger, Bargaining, Depression, and Acceptance (Kubler-Ross, E., *On Grief and Grieving...,* [2005] Simon & Schuster). Only you don't have time for a long grieving process. You need to get back in the game and start healing along the way. If you wait until you're healed or "ready," it may be too late; too late for other negative impacts to occur, like family troubles, delinquent bills or foreclosure.

Keep working, even if you have to accept a less than optimal position. Go back to school, take courses, join clubs, become involved in your community, network with friends, business associates, former employers, professional organizations, etc

Most importantly, conduct a rigorous self-assessment and identify your strengths and weakness. It may be you have been in a field that is not a good match for you, if so, you may want to pursue a different direction altogether.

Attitude Counts

Although it's difficult to be upbeat in stressful times involving adverse job and career conditions, it's essential that you retain your spirit and motivation. If you look, act, or sometimes even feel dejected or defeated, this will likely be communicated to a prospective or current employer, either directly by words or actions, or in indirect ways like facial expressions or body language. So watch your attitude, use positive self-talk, and try to foster that up-beat, "can do" attitude and demeanor.

The Comeback

A successful "comeback" can be exhilarating and confirming. The fact that you're a survivor, and can conquer the most difficult of circumstances is personally empowering, and confirms that you have all of those great qualities that managers look for. The ability to adapt, the capacity to learn new things, a willingness to accept challenge, experience with handling adversity, a "bounce back" capability, to name a few.

So, as painful, discouraging and disheartening as employment reversals can be, they offer growth opportunities, and heretofore undiscovered possibilities.

IN BUSINESS "EVERYONE'S A POLITICIAN"

It's another election year and politicians are busy touting their ideas, wisdom, and qualifications. Well, **we're all politicians** - especially in management. Organizations are political as well as economic entities, and you better hone your political skills to thrive in the business environment.

The Environment

Organizations are political minefields for the naïve and uninitiated. Many careers have been abruptly or permanently derailed due to the political ineptness of the incumbent. It requires savvy, skillful human relations to move up the corporate ladder, and recognition of, and appreciation for, the political landscape.

Some organizations are more political than others, but they're all political. Government managers are often so close to the body politic (formal political structure) that they frequently cannot avoid becoming enmeshed in politics. Marketing firms, corporate law firms, media conglomerates, and public relations firms typically are also highly politicized, whereas highly technical and manufacturing firms may be lesser so. Of course, all of this can change in an instant. An *SEC* investigation, *FDA* ruling, auditor's opinion, union disagreement, newspaper article, or corporate scandal can politically charge the most stable, and ostensibly non-political, organization. And, much of what is described so far, can be considered external influences. Internal politics, and jockeying for positions, advantage, and favor is the norm in most enterprises.

Political vs. Rational Organizations

There is a continuum on which organizations can be placed: from rational to political. This continuum describes the decision-making processes of an organization. Those closer to the political pole of the continuum tend to make decisions based on **power and influence**, the primary ingredients of politics. Organizations which enjoy a more rational decision-making paradigm base their decisions primarily on logic and reason. Of course, in the real-world the completely rational organization does not exist, and neither does the 100% political organization.

Where does your organization fall on this continuum? Is it highly political, with most decisions based principally on power and influence? Or is it highly rational, where decisions are made using logic and reason, facts and data?

The "Bottom Line"

Recognize that all organizations are political, although to varying degrees. And, all managers must have political skills and knowledge to survive and advance. Analyze your organization and become aware of, and sensitized to, the political environment in which you operate. Whatever the circumstance, try to develop your political awareness and skills.

DON'T BE A "KISS ASS"

Everybody hates a "kiss ass." You know the type - always flattering the boss, spending excessive amount of time in her office, bringing gifts, expressing compliments, offering to run errands, etc.

Kiss Ass Strategies

Some people are so insecure, or so desperate, or so manipulative, or so ambitious that they will stoop to any level to get what they want or need. A "kiss ass" is someone who fawns over their boss, tries TOO HARD to please, perhaps agrees with everything the boss says, offers more praise than is warranted, deserved or reasonable, etc.

It's unflattering behavior, even though it may involve lots of flattery!

Motivation is the Key

Employees have various reasons for sideling up to the boss. Sometimes it's a sincere liking or admiration, but many times the motivation is not so pure. Employees all want to look good to their boss, and be in her favor. The boss generally is the "gate-keeper" for promotions or raises. In difficult times, the boss may also determine job security.

All individuals recognize the power of the boss in relation to their career, but self-serving employees attempt to gain advantage through insincere tactics.

Kiss Ass Strategies May Work

Some naïve or needy bosses may not recognize the nature of the "kiss ass" behavior. They may even think they deserve all of the favorable attention, and not detect the insincerity and self-serving motivation. Of course, most bosses will feel uncomfortable, try to diminish the behavior, and not react favorably.

"Kiss Assers" may win but they pay a price. They are reviled by their colleagues, perhaps detected by the target of their KA strategy, and may jeopardize their own self-esteem.

Check Yourself

You probably do not want to have a reputation as a "brown-nose," "ass kisser," "kiss-ass," or some other negative or derogatory label. If you don't:

-- Watch your behavior, and try to be genuine

-- Have some self-respect; don't yield to your baser behaviors

-- Recognize the reactions of your peers and colleagues

-- Offer genuine support and sincere compliments, as warranted

-- Strive for balance and integrity

If You're the Boss

If you're the boss, recognize the impact indulgence of KA behavior may have on your staff. Your reputation, as well as the KA perpetrator's, may suffer. You may even be accused of favoritism, or disparate/ unequal treatment. Your perception as a fair-minded person, who treats employees equally will also be jeopardized. And, you may inadvertently promote "kiss ass" behavior.

DON'T LOSE YOUR SANITY AT OFFICE FUNCTIONS

Office parties can be fun, but don't lose your wits by imbibing too much, careless comments, off-color jokes and the like. Remember it's still an *OFFICE* function, and there can be repercussions. Whenever you are partying with your office colleagues, bosses, peers, and subordinates it isn't just innocent fun. After all, this is where you earn a living, and there can be implications for your career and your reputation.

The Office Clown, the Drunk, and Other Assorted Characters

When you're kicking back with your drinking buddies, gossiping with your friends, or...you get the picture...you can pretty much be yourself. But an office event such as: Christmas Party, Fourth of July Picnic, after-work get-together, business lunch or dinner, has entirely different implications.

If you're the "*office clown*" you may limit your possibilities for promotion, because you may not be viewed as manager "material." Business is serious, and while we all need laughter and comic relief, managers are not generally viewed as "clowns," (although some may be, unintentionally). At office parties the tendency to "clown" and joke may be even more pronounced, due to the atmosphere, and the influence of alcohol.

The "*drunk*" can be downright unappealing. Slurring words, staggering, loud talking, and outlandish behaviors can be disgusting. With commonsense gone, the drunk may say or do entirely inappropriate things. The partygoers will all be talking about their boss (or subordinate) the next day, that is if he makes it home in one piece.

The "*complete ass*" is another problem. We've all heard about someone "making an ass of himself," and it happens at parties more frequently. With the constraints of normal business protocol and environment absent, good judgment may be absent, as well.

The "*too friendly*" associate is yet another issue. Partygoers may not observe reasonable boundaries, and may become way too familiar, and personal. This refection of poor judgment can harm the offender's reputation.

The "*argumentative*" individual is also uncomfortable to deal with. In some instances he could become belligerent, or worse.

The "*Lech*" or "*come-on*" may also be present. Sexual innuendos, lecherous behaviors, or other sexually charged behaviors are out of place, in the office or at company sponsored events. Beware.

There are many other problem "types" although I'm sure you will recognize at least several of the aforementioned.

Consequences

We teach our kids that "behaviors have consequences." Nowhere is this more apparent than with people we work with. The manager can lose some of his/her influence and stature by engaging in "problem" behavior in, or outside, the office. He may create enemies or generate malicious gossip. He certainly can jeopardize his chances for promotion; perhaps even his job. And, on top of it, there's no privacy anymore and your reputation-destroying issues, with compromising photos, may be posted on *YouTube*, *FaceBook*, or some other social networking venue. There can even be legal ramifications (e.g., sexual harassment, accidents, intoxication, etc.). The setting at office functions is clearly conducive to "letting it all hang out." Make sure to not "hang" yourself with the consequences.

The message is to be on "good" behavior, if not your "best" behavior at work, and in all functions related to work. This way you will ensure that you will be judged primarily on your performance and personality, and not your misdeeds.

A BASIC MANAGEMENT SKILL IS TYPING

Alright, so the title is a little "tongue in cheek," but if you want to succeed in management you had better learn to type. A manager's basic trade is thinking, acting and communicating. The manager, by definition, is someone who gets the work done through the efforts of others. Managers must inspire and motivate. It's difficult to accomplish this if you're spending a significant part of your day typing emails, letters, reports, etc.

Management in Transition

I'm an "old school" manager, who could delegate work and had secretaries who knew "*Gregg shorthand.*" I spent my time planning, organizing, leading, informing, controlling, and enhancing. I was not tethered to a computer keyboard. Those were the good old days. How could I have known that my most valuable high school class would prove to be, you guessed it – Typing. I look back on my naiveté as justified by the environment of that era. Now managers must type to survive! Of course I still type with my right index finger, envious of those who can type with two fingers.

How did we get to this situation? The "division of labor" seems almost non-existent when it comes to clerical duties. Now, we have executives making $200 an hour "hunting and pecking" their own emails, correspondence or text messages. Is this the most efficient and effective use of labor?

The Future

Typing seems here to stay. Voice-recognition software is still in its infancy and not yet ready for "prime time," but almost! That will be a happy day. In the meantime, there is software available to help the executive or manager improve their typing proficiency. Commonly referred to as "Typing Tutors," most of these "packages" can be purchased for a reasonable fee, although there is also freeware available; just *Google* it.

The objective of these programs is to assist the manager in increasing his typing speed. "Touch typing" is the ultimate goal so that you will not have to look at the keyboard when typing.

You probably spend more time than you want to entering data into your computer. To be more productive and relieve some of your stress, learn to improve your typing skills. Because it looks like managers will be performing those distasteful clerical tasks for the foreseeable future.

PREPARE FOR A "KNOCKOUT"

If you're a fight fan you know that the ultimate victory in a boxing match is a "knockout." This represents the decisive blow which results in winning the contest. It's the same in business. Knocking out the competition will result in your business winning the battle and claiming the prize.

The Analogy

A student of mine is a boxing fan. He says he often wondered how the "smaller guy could beat the bigger guy." Sometimes the bigger, stronger man will be defeated by a less impressive adversary. Why does this happen? And is there something to be learned that may be applicable to business?

Competition

We're all faced with competition, whether it's in the boxing ring, our business life, or our individual situation. How we perceive the situation, and more importantly, what we do to prepare ourselves will determine the outcome. Whether its victory or defeat it often has more to do with us, than the prowess of our competitor.

Preparation

A key factor in winning is **preparation.** This preparation must be both physical and mental. We must try to achieve the winning state of mind and develop an appropriate strategy. We must study our opponent; understand his strengths and tactics, but also his vulnerabilities. And we must prepare ourselves to confront this competition and prevail. We cannot leave the outcome of the contest to chance. If we do, we run the risk, even probability, of defeat.

Tips for a Winning Strategy:

--Know yourself. Be aware of your strengths and vulnerabilities. Do a SWOT analysis. Identify your STRENGTHS and WEAKNESSES.

--Know your opponent. The strengths and weaknesses of your opponent are equally as important as your own. The strengths and weaknesses of your adversary are in actuality OPPORTUNITIES and THREATS to you. This is the second half of the SWOT.

--**Develop a Plan.** Your planning can be considered a strategy. What will be your winning strategy? How will you capitalize on your strengths? How will you deal with, overcome, or protect yourself from your weaknesses? Conversely, how do you plan to exploit your opponent's weak areas and counter those areas in which he has superiority?

--**Prepare and Train**. Much of the outcome will be determined by your readiness. Preparation is essential. Work harder than your opponent. Dedicate more time and energy. If you're smaller, have a less stellar reputation, less experience, fewer resources, etc., you will need to double your efforts.

--**Execute your Plan**. Once you have spent the necessary time to get to know yourself and your opponent, the strengths, weaknesses, opportunities and threats associated with the situation, and trained and planned to prevail, you need to: **Get in the ring and battle it out.**

Whether it is personal competition, or company competition, in business knowledge, preparation, planning, strategies, and execution will help you succeed, prevail, and win!

KEEP THE FAITH BABY!

Business depends of faith and confidence. Without these attitudes the economy would grind to a halt. *"Keep the Faith, Baby"* is defined by *Dictionary.com* as "stay encouraged and positive." It has come into common usage over the forty-plus years (1966) since Brook Benton sang the song by that title.

Faith and Confidence

Confidence in the economic system, future business prospects, stability of the government, and fair and equitable treatment of the business community, is all essential to investment. Investment in business, employees, products, resources, buildings and materials requires faith that the future will be favorable, or at least neutral. When there is no confidence capital dries up. This is what is presently occurring in the U.S. economy. Businesses are reticent to invest capital. Even if they have faith in the economy, the banks and other financial institutions are fearful of the viability of their supply of capital to the business community and have reduced the availability of funds. The lenders don't think they will be repaid, or repaid on time. The borrowers must meet more stringent requirements and perhaps enjoy less favorable terms. As a consequence of all of this doubt, mistrust and suspicion, the economy is shrinking.

The Government's Role

The federal government - especially the *Treasury Department*, *Congress* and *Federal Reserve Board* have decided to improve the situation by infusing unbelievable amounts of cash into the financial system. Providing liquidity is their objective. However, despite trillions of dollars in government funds the economy remains stagnant, or in decline.

Everyone Seems "Tapped Out"

The *United States* has become a nation of debtors. We're addicted to borrowing, and the norm is to live beyond our means. Look around. A short time ago everyone seemed fine. Now it appears that the Government is broke, businesses are broke, and the people are broke! This may not be a reality, but it appears to be a strong perception. Corporate values are declining, household net worth is falling, and the government debt is expanding at unprecedented rates.

Correction Time

The imperative is to take immediate steps to restore confidence in the economy and the free enterprise system.

This is not only a government problem - it's a you and me problem. It's a problem that requires mindset changes and actions taken. Some of these changes are:

-- We must all learn to live within our means. This means the government sector and the private sector, agencies, business, and individuals.

-- Practicing thrift is a value worth restoring.

-- We need to remember that business cycles, and economic corrections are natural. However, the unpleasantness and pain of economic and business decline are real.

-- We need to be aware that economic interventions are a "double edged sword." On one side, they provide some stimulus, cushion and relief; on the other they pile up debt and cause distortion. All businesses are not impacted equally, some are rescued and others are not. Interference with the principles of "supply-demand," the concept of "risk," and perceptions of unfairness will prevail. Inefficient and poorly managed businesses may survive, while more deserving enterprises will be allowed to fail. It's a political process: largely determined by relationships, money, favors, power, and influence.

-- Government and businesses need to become more honest. In an era of public and private scandals, it is important that we not lose confidence in institutions and individuals. These are essential values. Customers need to feel confident that the products they buy will serve their intended purpose. They need to feel confident that they will be treated fairly and not taken advantage of. Investors must be assured that their money will be safe, and that they won't be lured into bad investments. Those who extend credit must have assurance that they will be appropriately repaid.

Yes, "keep the faith, baby" we'll get through this economic mess, and restore the values, practices and beliefs that made our free enterprise system the envy of the world.

MANAGERS: "POP YOUR BUBBLE"

Remember the *"Bubble Boy"*? This was the little boy back in the 1970's-80's whose immune system was so compromised that he needed to live in a specially built plastic "bubble" so that he would not be exposed to germs or viruses that could kill him. Well, some managers, especially executives, live in a sort of bubble too.

Examples of the "Bubble"

Presidents live in a "bubble" constructed to protect them from outside influences and dangers. A good example is the first President Bush. He was insulated from the world to such an extent that he didn't even understand the basics about shopping in a supermarket. At the 1992 *National Grocers Convention* he visited a mock supermarket and appeared to know nothing about the checkout process, barcode scanners, even how to pay for his purchases. (*New York Times*, Feb. 5, 1992) The man was insulated from the most mundane aspects of life. However, his image suffered when the "average Joe" realized that the President could not understand or relate to his problems and the challenges of everyday living.

During the 2008 Presidential campaign Presidential candidate John McCain committed a similar faux pas. When asked about the economy, he stated: "The fundamentals of the American economy are strong." (*Wall Street Journal*, Sept. 15, 2008) This made him seem "out of touch" when millions of Americans were struggling to pay their bills and keep their jobs during the greatest economic downturn since the "Great Depression."

Following the 2008 national election, the Presidents of the "big three" U.S. automobile manufacturers (*GM, Ford*, and *Chrysler*) went to Washington to ask the administration and Congress for billions of dollars in "bailout" money. But in all their arrogance and detachment they traveled to Washington, D.C. in SEPARATE private jets. (*Detroit Free Press*, Nov. 24, 2008) They didn't even have the sense to "jet pool." The irony, incongruity, and blatant insensitivity of this act was not lost on the press and the public, and Congress turned them down. Of course they were be back again, but with less hubris, a little more humility, and more modest transportation.

The "Bubble" at Work

Executives are frequently ensconced in a "bubble" largely of their own making. They're supposed to delegate, and they do. They relate with others in their "inner circle" and their experiences and knowledge are "filtered." How many times do you see the CEO of a large corporation utilizing the approach advocated by HP founders David Packard and Bill Hewlett: "Management by *Walking Around*"? And even if you do, are their interactions with subordinate managers and rank-and-file employees meaningful and serious?

This is a big problem. The "encapsulation" of top management, and their isolation from the "real world" can spell trouble for them and the organization. It's worth it to try and "pop" the "bubble."

"Popping the Bubble"

Top management must first recognize that they may be insulated from reality. Then, they need to take some definitive actions to change this:

--Start by self-reflection and analysis.

--Then, ask trusted advisers who you know will be honest, to provide an assessment of your degree of isolation. This can be tricky, and you don't want to ask "yes men."

--Start getting out of the office and relating with people of different levels and status.

--Don't just read trade journals, stock reports and company materials. Try and get some exposure to the "pop culture." A good resource (although with a conservative slant) and having a wide range of features, both serious and entertaining, is the "*Drudge Report*" (www.drudge.com).

--Try socializing with a broader range of people.

--Practice "environmental sensing" at all levels, both within the organization and outside. Go out, take off your "blinders" and experience many aspects of life. Interpret, and share your experiences (but not with the media, until you're comfortable with your evaluations).

--Consult you PR staff before making public appearance to understand "agendas" and avoid pitfalls.

--Have fun, and enjoy your new found experiences and perspectives.

THE ADD MANAGER

An employee with Attention-Deficit Disorder (or ADHD [Attention Deficit Hyperactivity Disorder]) may survive for years in the corporate world despite the handicap this condition entails. Many people are considered for, or promoted to managerial positions due to their ability to think and react quickly, and in today's fast-paced business environment, this is clearly an advantage. However, many of these same employees have difficulty in remaining focused on the task at hand, and have even more difficulty in completing their assignments.

Of course in business you need both the fast, short-term effort, and the longer-term perspective. Not every project enjoys the luxury of being long-range with periodic milestones, however, even with these assets, not all managers have the ability or interest in seeing these projects through to the end.

ADD

ADD, or *Attention-Deficit Disorder*, describes a set of behaviors characterized primarily by an inability to concentrate or focus. Frequently a level of hyperactivity and impulsivity is also present. Typically the ADD (or more accurately, ADHD [Attention Deficit Hyperactivity Disorder]) sufferer is easily distracted and has difficulty seeing a task through to completion.

Although many of these ADD managers are diagnosed, some are not. Some ADD Managers change jobs so often that their deficiencies cannot be recognized. Also, the short-term present day business environment makes it even more challenging to detect these individuals. "Get this done," "see that this is handled," or even "I need this yesterday!" are common refrains.

Although numbers of ADHD sufferers escape labeling, increasing numbers of children, young adults, and even mature adults are being diagnosed. What implications does this have for business?

The Structural Problem

While ADD Managers may be competent and valued within their organization, without help they typically are not Executive Management material. Even middle managers need to focus their attention on the tasks at hand, and plan, and organize at least for future timeframes. And, the further up the chain of command you go, the more long-range the perspective. Top management, when they are functioning most effectively, have a long-range, strategic mindset. They are responsible for organization survival, success and competitive advantage. They need to examine the external environment and be prepared to generate plans and directions which will lead the organization to an improved future. These tasks are not well accommodated by a person with an ADHD syndrome.

Potential Consequences

The ADD Manager, or particularly Executive, can wreak havoc on an organization. His inability to pay sufficient attention to the details, priorities and challenges of the business can increase risk and jeopardize the entity. Frequently there is a tacit recognition of these difficulties and key managers/employees or trusted subordinates will attempt to compensate for the ADD Manager's weaknesses.

What are the Solutions?

As in every behavioral concern, there are really only a limited number of practical options. Some of the most straightforward and effective are:

1) Be realistic in identifying behavioral issues/concerns.

2) Recognize and capitalize on the ADD Managers strengths (e.g., high energy and enthusiasm; perhaps creativity and intuitiveness).

3) Be careful not to "diagnose;" leave this to the experts.

4) Make realistic accommodations for the ADD Manager.

5) Consider surrounding the ADD Manager with a support group of individuals who can take over some of the most critical projects/ tasks.

6) Encourage delegation by the ADD Manager of certain tasks and responsibilities to competent subordinates.

7) Closely monitor the ADD Manager's performance and evaluate his sphere of influence in accordance with his extent of compromise/ limitations.

8) Assist the ADD Manager in obtaining therapy/ treatment, and/ or behavioral intervention to alleviate symptoms, where desired/ indicated, and as appropriate.

The "bottom line"

Business management is a complex and demanding field, and everyone has their strengths and weakness. The manager needs to be viewed as a total human being with strengths and weaknesses, challenges and opportunities. Locating, developing, and retaining the best talent requires that we accept each manager with all of their uniqueness. Whenever deficiencies and limitations impact performance, we must work with these individuals to help them improve.

DIS-INFORMATION OVERLOAD

With the digital age continuing to develop, we've been talking for years about "information overload," and problems this entails. Written knowledge doubles about every eighteen months, a phenomenal rate. However, with an increasing absence of data verification, a bigger concern is emerging - the problem of misinformation or disinformation. Essentially, the dearth of quality information on which to base decisions or opinions, or the intentional promulgation of "bad" information has unpleasant implications for business and society.

How Fast is Information Growing?

Peter Lyman and Hal Varian, professors at the University of California, Berkley, School of Information, determined that "world-wide information increased at 30% a year from 1999-2002"...and that "92% of new information is stored in magnetic media," further, ..."the U.S. produces 40% of the world's new...information." (*Los Angeles Times* article, July 7, 2007, as reported in *latimes.com/news*). The researchers' intent was to quantify people's feelings of being "overwhelmed by information."

More recent estimates are that total information is increasing at 66% per year (*The Speed of Information,* Kevin Kelly, Feb.20, 2006, Technium, Internet edition).

Quantity vs. Quality

Ok, so there's an overwhelming, almost inconceivable amount of new information being generated and stored, but what is the quality of the information? Not surprisingly, the fastest growing segments of information include "social networking" (e.g., *Facebook, MySpace, YouTube, Twitter, LinkedIn, Orkut, Bebo,* etc.). There are literally hundreds of these sites, some of which cater to a small niche, while others have broader appeal. The information offered is of little or no value except for curiosity or (practically) anonymous connection.

Sorting through fantastic amounts of data to retrieve a few pertinent, relevant and valid, pieces of knowledge requires powerful search "engines," and sophisticated research techniques. However, more and more people report: "I saw it on the Internet," as though that provides an element of credibility.

Business Implications

The demand for rapid decision-making when combined with a lack of quality and/or inaccurate information is a recipe for trouble. And, if we need to make fast decisions, often based on bad data, what kind of results can we reasonably expect? There's an old saying in Information Science/ Data Processing: GIGO, - "garbage in, garbage out." And, it seems we're drowning in piles of information garbage.

What Can You Do?

When trying to gather valid information:

--Be a critical consumer of data and information; use analytical and evaluative techniques

--Look for references, and/or expertise

--Seek out responsible publications, especially refereed Journals

--Know the background and experience of the author

--Review several articles or books to ascertain a sense of consistency

--"Opinion pieces" must be written by someone with credibility

The main point here is, there is plenty of informative and useful material on the Internet, just don't accept most of it as fact, or even educated opinion.

A SENSE OF URGENCY OR A PERCEPTION OF CRISIS

Everything seems to be moving very quickly in the world of business, In fact, it is so fast-paced that deliberation, good decision-making, smooth project implementations, and effective strategic planning may be getting lost in the process.

Hide Under Your Desk

I've recently encountered people who reportedly are so overwhelmed by the hectic pace that they feel like "hiding under their desk" to avoid the barrage of emails, voice-mails, assignments, messages, meetings, etc. Now, this, obviously, is not a practical solution. Besides that, hiding from the problem will not solve it - and you'd look pretty foolish down there anyway.

Out of Control

The perception of crisis is an uncomfortable one. It seems like things are out of control, and that management can't quite figure out how to plan and prioritize. It is stressful too!

Sometimes it seems like bosses want everything immediately. When everything is urgent - nothing is! It becomes a joke! There are no real priorities and with everything being equally important; no way to distinguish between something that needs to be done now, and something that might be nice to have now, but the world won't fall apart if it's not.

Sometimes it's an individual who can't keep up, other times it's an office, or department, or even a whole organization.

Although some believe that multi-tasking is the solution, recent research indicates that multi-taskers may be able to do more tasks, but they do each one poorly. "They're suckers for irrelevancy" says Professor Clifford Nass whose research was reported in the Aug. 24, 2009 edition of the "Proceedings of the *National Academy of Sciences*". "Everything distracts them." he says. Counter intuitively, the low multi-taskers outperformed them on every task.

So what is the solution? It may be to take a deep breath, put things in perspective, re-prioritize and re-organize, and tackle assignments one at a time. If you're a high-level manager, protect your subordinates, and yourself; keep things in perspective; resist the impulse to become frantic or overly demanding; and maintain your poise.

Here are some tips:

--Have the guts to say no! Enough is enough!

--Don't sacrifice your health or sanity.

--Realize that some people get their "kicks" from having everyone say "how high?" when they say "jump"

--Delegate as much as possible

--Resist the inclination to become an "adrenaline junkie" thriving on chaos

--Know when it's time to escape: your assignment, your office, or even your job

--Manage your own time and priorities as effectively as possible

--Ask for help when necessary

--It's important that you do things you like, so make time for them

--Don't be hard on yourself, realize that everyone's rot good at everything

--Use your common-sense and good judgment in deciding what's really important

--Perform your work methodically and at a reasonable pace

--Be available physically, and mentally, when the "real" crises emerge

THE SELFISH MANAGER

Selfish managers are much more common than you might suspect. The consequences of managerial selfishness can prove costly for the organization.

What is a Selfish Manager?

Let's try a little logic.

Many people are selfish. Managers are people. Therefore, some managers are likely to be selfish. People are selfish because they think primarily of their own needs and not others. One definition of selfish (adj.) is "holding one's self-interest as the standard for decision-making."

Some managerial style differences are acceptable, and should even be encouraged. The big problem is when the manager's style or goals are at odds with the mission and goals of the organization. Selfish managers believe that their approach is right, and may be unable or unwilling to change.

Conflicts with the Management Role

The definition of a manager is someone who "gets things done through other people."

It definitely complicates this role if the manager is unconcerned about these other people. How do you motivate people if you don't care about helping them meet their needs? The obvious answer is that it makes matters much more difficult. *Need Theory* postulates that people are motivated to meet **their** unmet needs (not necessarily the manager's). Of course you can order and direct people to do things but you have to be prepared for resistance or rebellion. At best, you will achieve marginal results, generally begrudgingly obtained.

The management tasks of Planning, Organizing, Leading, Informing, Controlling, and Enhancing all require the participation and commitment of others to be effectively accomplished. Furthermore, we all have individual strengths which can contribute greatly to the efficient and effective achievement of desired results.

Organizational Difficulties

An organization is a combination of people and other resources assembled to achieve a specified mission. Along the way there are various goals and objectives that focus energy and time on scope limited targets which support that overriding mission.

If the manager's goals are not in sync with the organization's mission, the enterprise will suffer. Subordinates will be dissatisfied, unmotivated or disengaged, or worse yet working on activities that are not in the firm's best interests. The end result will reflect in the "bottom line."

Interpersonal, Motivational and Inspirational Skills

Increasingly today's manager needs "people skills." The days when managers could treat people like machines are long gone. Theoretically, we all know this. But in practice many do not apply these concepts. Frequently there is the difference between knowing something on an intellectual level and implementing and practicing that same philosophy on a real level. The selfish manager is quite *Darwinian*. His survival comes first.

To be a successful manager there must be compromise. Everyone's needs will not always be met, including the boss'. The selfish manager will try to get most of his needs met without much regard to others.

The unselfish manager will inspire, support and motivate subordinates. This will be done with grace and ease. The mere fact of treating people with respect, consideration, and humanity will help. The unselfish manager's organization will obtain superior performance because the employees will experience satisfaction, recognition and accomplishment collectively and individually. They will realize that they are working for results and not just the manager's ego, insecurities or misguided goals.

Recommendations

Recruit and retain people with superior interpersonal skills. (Don't necessarily promote the employee with the most experience or the best technical skills.)

Conduct a managerial style and substance audit to ascertain what is currently going on.

Recognize the connection between people skills and organization performance.

Identify managers (this may be yourself) lacking in interpersonal abilities. Then, get those managers into training.

Inform managers, on a regular basis, of the company's philosophy, mission and goals. Make sure there is understanding and ACCEPTANCE.

Verify that managers are consistently and wholeheartedly embracing and supporting organization goals, and not just their own.

Make sure that managers give appropriate "credit" to subordinates. Praise and reward those managers for their team accomplishments.

Understand that unselfish managers ("I don't care who gets credit") generally achieve the best results.

Get ongoing feedback from subordinate managers and first-line employees.

Ideally, there would be complete concordance between the manager's goals and those of the organization. However, we don't live in an ideal world. The more selfish a manager is the less willing he will be to subordinate his own needs, goals and desires to those of the organization. To achieve your organization's profit, growth and strategic objectives there must be alignment. The first step is to recognize there may be a problem.

THE MARVELOUS MENTOR

Mentorship has been a powerful force in the business world. The transfer of knowledge, typically between more senior employees with greater experience and those who are more junior, contributes to workplace functioning. Sharing expertise in an informal and collegial manner benefits both participants in the exchange.

Background

The origin and evolution of the role and practice of mentoring is lengthy and significant. The term "mentor" is believed to have been derived from a Greek word describing the nature of the relationship between a friend of second-century (B.C.) Greek King Odysseus, and Odysseus' son Telemachus. (Webster's New World Dictionary) The friend was entrusted with the education of the boy and guided him throughout his developmental years. The practice of mentoring became rather widespread and gradually migrated to the business world as commerce and organizations developed.

Forms of Mentorship

Mentorship comes in various forms. A tutor, advisor, or coach can be a mentor. A teacher, business leader, counselor, or friend can be a mentor. The mentor role is voluntary, desired by both parties, and can be dissolved at the discretion of the participant(s).

What distinguishes the mentor is the nature of the relationship. Mentorship is most frequently an informal process, and one that is entered into willingly by both participants. The mentor role is voluntary, desired by both parties, and can be dissolved at the discretion of the participant(s). Unlike a teacher-student relationship, where there is a formal structure and set of obligations and expectations, the role of the mentor is generally informal without contracts, structures, compensation, or obligatory requirements. However, mentorship in certain professions or fields may be more structured, and some, particularly in the legal field, may even require written agreements.

Mentorship is not limited to the workplace and can take place outside that setting in professional or friendship networks. It has even gone into *Cyberspace* with forms of mentoring provided by bloggers, advisors, affiliates, distance colleagues and experts of all types over the Internet. Proximity and face-to-face contact are no longer essential. This evolution of the mentoring mode and process is, of course, a positive development.

The Importance of Mentoring

Mentoring doesn't seem to be as popular or widespread as it was a few years back. Perhaps this is because people change jobs and careers with greater frequency, and it takes time to develop relationships. However, mentorship may be particularly important at this time. With single parent families, and societal disconnects, isolation and individual alienation, the mentor can also fill a social void. It seems many young people are looking for a "father figure" or surrogate parent of either sex. And, with all of the time spent at work, the workplace offers a fertile environment for these types of interactions.

Mentoring can provide for inter-generational transfer of knowledge and history. It can provide continuity in an increasingly less stable environment. The recipient of mentoring can gain knowledge, techniques, approaches, etc. which will help them to avoid missteps, and develop the maturity and judgment of a more experienced manager.

Effective Mentoring

Mentoring can be quite rewarding. The rewards are available to each participant. The mentor enjoys sharing knowledge and experiences, while the "mentee" obtains valuable guidance and information from a trusted source. Mentors don't just share information; they place things in context, share life experiences, and provide guidance in surviving and thriving.

To be effective, each participant must freely share information, value the relationship and process, respect one another, support and trust each other and desire to grow. It cannot be a competitive or manipulative relationship. The mentor must desire to see the growth and success of the person they mentor without seeking or expecting credit or recognition for those accomplishments. Both parties will learn about themselves, gain insights, and strategies for increased personal and professional development. They will identify their strengths and weaknesses and determine which approaches work best. Mentees can expect to improve their professional performance and future career prospects.

Whether you are an experienced manager or a novice, this may be the time to consider entering into a mentorship relationship. And, while some of these relationships may be a natural occurrence, most require some initiative from one or both participants.

Considering the multiple benefits of mentoring, why not give it a try?

JUST A LITTLE BIT MORE

In business, some make it to the top, while most don't. Long ago I realized that small differences in effort and performance make huge differences in career possibilities.

The Mediocrity Mentality

The vast majority of employees settle for mediocrity. Sure, they want to advance, but they are unwilling to put forth the required effort to make them a stand-out performer. There is a socialization process that goes on in life, and youngsters learn at an early age that it is in many ways preferable to be "one of the guys," or girls. Acceptance and conformity seem important when you're defining yourself and developing a self-image.

However, making the transition to an "economic being," and trying to advance on the ladder of success require that we re-examine our notions of conformity and mediocrity.

Most are only partially successful in making this transition. Others just don't wish to expend the time and effort required to become a superior performer. Not that they're lazy, but a significant number of employees just "settle." They perform well enough to keep their job, and that may be sufficient.

Ambition

Ambition is not a rare quality; most of us have it to one degree or another. However, ambition is not enough. To attain one's ambitions requires effort and sacrifice. It's safe to say that everyone wants to improve their economic condition, but how many will do what is necessary to achieve this?

The desire to achieve must be matched with the willingness to excel. Desire and action are not the same, and neither are ambition and achievement. The myth is that it takes a genius or workaholic to attain the heights of one's profession or business. It doesn't. Generally what it requires is a little more - A little more effort, a modicum of dedication, and probably a reasonable amount of persistence. These are qualities we all have to one degree or another.

Achievement

If you embrace the "do a little more" mentality you will do yourself a great service. I have observed workplaces where the few employees who practice this concept "shine like a beacon." Obviously their chances for recognition and advancement are much better than their colleagues with the "just enough to get by" approach.

It's your life, and your career-- try to make the most of it.

THE ULTIMATE COMPETITOR – YOU!

Some consider themselves to be very competitive. Others seem to care less.

Of course, the biggest, most fierce and formidable competitor is not anyone other than ourselves.

The Internal Competitor

Competition is natural. Charles Darwin suggested that "*survival of the fittest*" is the natural order of things. Therefore, the best competitors should come out on top. But who are we competing against? In the business world we refer to the "competition," meaning those that are in a similar business, providing similar products and/or services, and who we try to gain market share or dominance over.

Our most difficult opponent is oftentimes not external, but instead internal, within us. Mastery of the competition is more of a "mind game" than a "one-upsmanship." Most obstacles in life or business have their origin in our own attitudes and behaviors. The "enemy within" can be characterized as self-defeating beliefs, negativity, lack of confidence, etc.

Beating the Competition

A critical step in besting the competition is to ascertain their strengths and vulnerabilities. When we're battling with ourselves, discipline and knowledge are essential. We need to know the competition in order to develop strategies to best them. When our ideas, desires, and goals compete with our achievement and success in life, instead of supporting these ends, we need to take action.

Strategies

Because our internal competitor is so clever and strong, we must be committed to winning. And, to beat the competition we must have a strategy.

-- Recognize that your toughest competition is yourself

-- Know yourself - understand when your attitudes and behaviors are out of sync with your life goals

-- Decide on your priorities

-- Determine which thinking patterns need changing - write them down

-- Have the courage and discipline to change your thinking - develop plans outlining required actions

-- Take action to correct the self-defeating attitudes and behaviors

-- Reward yourself for making changes which reduce the internal dissonance and help you further your real ambitions

-- Celebrate your victory over your toughest competitor (your established, non-productive thinking)

-- Remain vigilant, as your competitor may attempt to use devious strategies, or appeals to your emotions or fears to beat you down

IT'S YOUR JOB TO HAVE FUN AT WORK!

The workplace can be a very funny place. Sometimes it's even hilarious. Workplaces have their own special personalities, just like the people who work there. To a great extent, it's the personalities of the employees that, when combined, make up the workplace character. Like one big dysfunctional family!

To be a survivor in corporate America it helps immensely to have a sense of humor. This is not only an adaptive quality, but it keeps things in perspective. How can you possibly take some of your coworkers, managers, and customers seriously?

Business is Serious, but...

As a Business observer, consultant, and professor, I'm among the first to acknowledge that business is serious. The challenges of the marketplace, making your "numbers," achieving profitability, are not laughing matters. However, if you take things too seriously you'll end up a "basket case." After all, you're only human. And humans can only take so much stress. You have an obligation to yourself, and your loved ones, as well as your employer. And, you're of no value to anyone if you're sick or dead!

You are More Effective if You're Happy

Happiness is contagious. If you wear a smile others who you come in contact with are likely to react positively as well. If you show positivity to your customers they're likely to respond favorably and have an inclination to return. Likewise your coworkers will be disinclined to avoid you and more likely to cooperate. So there are collateral benefits to being happy at work, not just from a selfish perspective.

These are stressful times, and people have a right to be concerned. Many are struggling to make a living and keep their "head above water." A large number of employees dread going to work. They view their jobs in a single dimension. They work to make money. Of course, if you take away the paycheck, you won't find very many people in the workplace. But, income is only one reward. It's up to you to find the others. The feelings of accomplishment and satisfaction, the social interaction, the capacity to be of assistance to someone, the growth, stimulation, and challenge are all important aspects of our jobs and careers.

Stay Healthy

Norman Cousins (*Anatomy of An Illness*, Norton, 1979) claims to have even cured disease by being joyful and laughing. Even if his recovery cannot be entirely attributed to his laughter, why take a chance? There is some good scientific, as well as anecdotal evidence to support Norman Cousins' theory (*UCLA School of Medicine, Loma Linda University, New England Journal of Medicine, etc.*). Research has shown that in addition to releasing endorphins (a chemical in the brain which promotes a sense of euphoria), laughter also increases circulation, lowers blood pressure, and improves respiration. Yes "humor therapy" works. And, in the workplace you're not paying for the entertainment, in fact, they're paying you!

THE INCREDIBLE POWER OF SETTING LIFE GOALS

Lots of us have general goals like "travel," "make a million," or "buy a bigger home." A goal means an end point such as "achieving a goal," or "scoring a goal." Attaining a goal, whether in life, business, or sports, requires planning and effort.

Fail to Plan and You Plan to Fail

Many people seem to have no goals at all. Yes, they have plenty of "wants," "desires," or "needs." The problem comes in defining, establishing, and taking steps toward your goal. Yes, you can rely on "luck." but then you are trusting your future to fate or chance. Are you willing to do this? Isn't your future more important than that?

Setting Goals

The first step is figuring out what you want to achieve. Goal setting is frequently a challenge. There are so many things you'd like to have, or do, or accomplish. How can you possibly select one, or a few?

This will require some thought. It probably will require talking with others who are important to you, such as your spouse, family, or significant other(s).

Exploring the Options

You need to weigh and deliberate your options. For example, you may value leisure time, but also want to climb the corporate ladder. In fact, these goals may be contradictory, or have to be attained sequentially; first move up the ladder to become CEO, and with your wealth, find leisure in retirement. As you can see, some thought, prioritization, and considerable effort is necessary.

"Brainstorming" is an excellent approach to exploring and narrowing options. The rules of brainstorming are straightforward. First, everything is "fair game." Nothing is immediately ruled out. Try to generate as many ideas as possible. Second, a free thinking, non-critical, non-judgmental process is employed. Third, unusual ideas are actually encouraged so that ideas aren't discarded because they appear ridiculous, outlandish, or unattainable. Fourth, try to ascertain inter-relationships between the ideas.

SMART Goals

While brainstorming will generate lots of possibilities, some refinement is required.

In business courses we talk about **SMART** goals, a catchy acronym for a well-defined process. (You certainly wouldn't want to pursue "dumb" goals.) SMART GOALS are: 1) **S**pecific, 2) **M**easurable, 3) **A**ttainable, 4) **R**elevant, and 5) **T**imely. On a cautionary note, don't apply the SMART approach over-rigorously when it comes to your personal goals. For example, you might reject an option as unattainable, when, in fact, it could be. Finally, develop an Action Plan for goal attainment.

The Plan

Once the goal has been identified, and become "smart," you will need to develop a plan for implementation. My favorite approach is termed: "Action Planning." Action Planning involves determining a series of steps that will lead to the goal, putting them in appropriate sequence, then establishing "target dates" for completion. This way you will be able to monitor your progress toward your goal, gain some sense of accomplishment as you complete steps, and improve your odds of attaining your goal by the time you desire.

The Process

In summary: After engaging in the "brainstorming," technique and deciding on your BIG goal(s), apply the "SMART" approach, and then develop your Action Plan. This sequential process is intended to focus your thoughts, efforts and resources. It is also designed to break your big ideas into smaller, more digestible components. You will not typically attain your life's goal(s) in one giant leap.

Pursuing the Dream

A few comments on "dreams" is in order. The "DREAM" is a double-edge sword. Dreams can be overriding obsessions, or vaguely defined end-points. They can be extremely powerful motivators, and not infrequent cause for despair. Gamblers have dreams, schoolchildren have dreams, aspiring actresses have dreams, Broadway dancers have dreams, entrepreneurs have dreams, in fact, and perhaps most, or even all, of us have dreams. The intensity of the dream, the specificity of the dream, and the determination of the dreamer all play a role in whether or not the dream will ultimately be realized. So does opportunity, talent, and circumstance. Some say the universe will conspire to assist the dreamer, while others will consider the dreamer a fool.

I consider the dreamer fortunate. Life can be extremely challenging, very discouraging, or disappointing. A dream can help "keep hope alive," and sustain the dreamer through difficult times. And, your chance of being successful will undoubtedly be greater with a dream than without one.

Finally...

We've discussed goal-setting; however, the dream generally precedes the goal. The dream is the really big "picture." Just because you don't have an overarching dream, doesn't mean that you can't have perfectly ambitious, meaningful and challenging goals. Try the goal setting and action planning described and you may find that you can make your dreams a reality by achieving your life goals.

THE SECRET OF MOTIVATION

The secret of motivation is simple. It boils down to DESIRE. Psychologists might call it the drive to satisfy UNMET NEEDS. However, most of these "needs" are not really NEEDS at all. We deceive ourselves into believing that we need something, and that perception is what makes us pursue whatever it is we WANT. Our wants always exceed our needs. Many would say they're unlimited.

Desire Trumps Ability?

For those of you who like to watch or participate in sports, you see it all the time. It isn't the best team, or the most talented player that always wins, but the one that WANTS it most!. When Cassius Clay beat up Sonny Liston, or when Spud Johnson, at 5'7" height, beat all competition in the NBA "Slam Dunk" contest. When Milan H.S. won the Indiana State Basketball Championship (they made a movie about this) Or when NCAA team *Virginia Tech* prevailed over *Temple University*, or the Florida Marlins in 2003 beat the New York Yankees. These victories confirm the importance of desire,

Ability Matters

A caution is in order. You won't succeed on desire alone. The sports examples referred to above underscore the decisive impact of exceptional desire. However, although greater desire and motivation may be the determining factor in the outcome, a baseline of ability is imperative. You have to be capable, have the necessary experience, and know the "rules" in order to win.

And So It Is in Business

Your career success or lack thereof, is a reflection of your motivation more than anything else. Sure, luck, timing, skills, education, connections, etc., may play a huge part. Perhaps these factors were the basis for an employment opportunity, promotion or business start-up. But, your desire is what really makes the difference.

What is Important?

- Remember, we all want something (actually many things) for ourselves.
- Connect with, and cultivate, your desires.

- Visualize the outcome(s) of your efforts to attain your desires.
- Use your desire to motivate you to: win/achieve your goals/push you towards success.
- Welcome competition, and learn from your opponent(s).
- Learn from your successes (and failures); make changes as necessary.
- Keep desiring, fighting, pushing, competing, training, and eventually you will attain your goals.

NO! A SMALL WORD, WITH A BIG IMPACT

Have you noticed the number of people who will tell you NO? Of course you have, they're so numerous. People are always telling us: Don't do this! Don't do that! Don't take a chance! Be careful! Better safe, than sorry!

One of the first words we learn as a child is NO! And, the no's continue throughout our time on this planet.

Tough to Ignore

It's tough to ignore the naysayers; they're very pervasive and persistent, and you've heard them all of your life. And, there are often elements of truth, caution, good intentions, and genuine concern in their advice. Furthermore, we all have doubts and have experienced failures, so if we're not careful, we'll be receptive to their negativity.

It takes a strong individual to stay true to their convictions, ambitions and dreams despite this continuous onslaught of negativity, doubt, and rejection.

Dealing with the Naysayer

So how do you deal with the naysayer? Well, there's no quick and easy immunization against the self-doubt, anticipation of error or failure, fear, and lack of conviction we all experience from time to time. However, there are some things you can do to protect yourself.

--Confront your fear of failure

--Strengthen your resolve to succeed

--Recognize that we all have self-doubt and fear

--Emphasize the potential of new ideas, approaches and projects

--Realize that some people want to "kill your spirit"

--Value those who support and encourage you

--Don't allow yourself to be surrounded by "naysayers" or "yeasayers"-seek balance - the "no" people may discourage you, while the "yes" people will not provide objectivity

--Understand that most people are risk aversive and fear change

--Make a realistic appraisal of your strengths and prior successes

--Accept the advice and doubts expressed by others without losing your perspective; use this input to check your assumptions, potentially modify your approach, and/or solidify your resolve; be thankful for the opportunity to examine your assumptions and beliefs

DON'T JUST "GO TO WORK"

How many times have you heard employees say "I'm going to work"? It's a common refrain, and as an educator and as a businessman it always annoys me. Employees don't just "go to work" they have a career, a profession, or a business. "Going to work" sounds passive and unexciting.

A New Way of Speaking

How about "I'm going to teach young minds," for schoolteachers; I'm going to "show homes to new buyers," for Real Estate Salespersons; I'm going to "build automobiles," for autoworkers; I'm going to "greet customers," or "prepare taxes," or "make people happy," or... well, you get the idea.

The way we describe ourselves, and what we do, is important for our self concept and our motivation. How dreary it can be if we're only "going to work?" "Making a living" is an honorable necessity. We need work for a variety of reasons, not the least of which is to sustain ourselves and our families. However, employment provides us with many other rewards, particularly in the American society where so much time and energy are spent on our careers. We can gain in value and self-esteem when our careers are meaningful and satisfying. There's a certain dignity to work, that should not be diminished by just "going" there.

CHECK YOURSELF

Listen to yourself, and the way you describe spending a third or more of your life. Are you merely mouthing the fact that you must work, or are you expressing more of the quality and importance of this aspect of your life? Try an experiment to see how it feels. For example, in my case, "going to the College," sounds better than "going to work." In your case, invent some term or phrase to describe what you do, and/ or where you do it. Feels better, doesn't it?

PROTECT YOUR JOB – MAKE YOURSELF INVALUABLE

Invaluable employees are few and far between. The old management saying is: "Nobody's indispensible." And, I suppose it's true. However, some employees are more valuable than others. To enjoy a primo level of job security, become one of them!

Turnover

Many organizations have a high rate of employee turnover. High, can mean anywhere from twenty percent to close to 100% annually. Probably the average is more like 10%-25%. By historical levels that's very high. But with the typical employee changing jobs every two to five years, not too many (only about one in five) have been with their present employer for more than five years.

Of course, voluntary separation is still the most common reason for leaving a job. But with national unemployment hovering near 10% (officially), and around 22% (actually)[*New York Post*, Post Business, September 20, 2009] many employees have recently experienced "involuntary separation." In other words, they've been fired or "laid off." And, unfortunately, with the economy in the doldrums, lots of jobless people are experiencing difficulty re-entering the employment market and becoming, once again, gainfully employed.

What's the Solution?

To stay employed, get promoted, or leave by your own volition, you must have skills. An array of skills is preferable, unless you're so specialized that you're irreplaceable because no one can do your job, or because there aren't any, or many, with your talents or background.

Employers care about value. You must have value to the organization. Ideally your value should be multiples of your salary. This cost-benefit equation will generally not be explicitly calculated, but it will always be in your employer's mind. The key is-- are you bringing in more revenue, or contributing more to the organization, than you cost?

Take Action

--Realistically asses your value to the organization

--Recognize that you're vulnerable if the organization has declining revenue or a shrinking employee base, and double your efforts

--Build your skills. Take on new assignments, tasks and responsibilities

--Don't be bashful about your value to the organization. Let management know about your successes and contributions

--Determine what your boss wants- and deliver it

--Find new ways to generate revenue, or reduce costs

--Stay up-to-date with business processes, technologies, and competitive matters

--Cater to the customers; be the person they want to do business with

--Continue your education and learn new skills

BUILDING A TOP PERSONAL "BRAND"

Let's face it—in today's world, YOU are a BRAND!

Who are you? Increasingly it's not only you're a parent, manager, pianist, friend, churchgoer, adviser, "good person," skier, swimmer, hobbyist, lover, husband, wife, etc., etc. You're also a BRAND. Just like *Ford, Chevy, Kellogg's, Nabisco, Mercedes-Benz, Macy's, Wal-Mart, Coca-Cola, Geico, and Levi's.* Who ever thought so many of us would willingly, unwillingly, or inadvertently be in the marketing, advertising and image management "business"? And the "product" is ourselves.

The Wild West and Beyond

In the old West cattlemen branded their herd so that people would know what cattle belonged to which rancher. Cattle have this habit of wandering the range, and some sort of identification was necessary to sort things out. Likewise companies put their mark on products so that consumers will know who made them. Branding connotes ownership. A good product reinforces the company name and reputation, and ultimately sales and profitability.

Your Brand

Increasingly the "brand" terminology has made inroads into the business world, and the concept broadened to include individuals and their reputations. We refer to the *Obama* brand, the *Jack Welch* brand, Mary's brand the Carlsen brand and your brand. Your name is your brand, and the quality of your brand is based by your reputation, and the perceptions of others which, in turn, becomes your public persona.

Of course, you don't even need to be in the business world to have a brand. Like millions of others, you may have *Facebook* or *MySpace* account, a personal website, a Blog, or a *Twitter* account, or…so many other presences on the Internet, media, public records, or elsewhere. This represents your brand. It's your public face, and it probably is not limited to your business.

Do You Have a Good Brand?

If you think of yourself as a business or product, how would you be viewed? Dependable, reliable, high quality, valuable, competitive; maybe even "fantastic," or "best I've ever seen."

In the mass-communication, Internet, Social Media world, your name is out there. How do you want to be known? Perhaps you'd better consider image and reputation management and develop strategies to enhance your brand.

Considerations

Now it's not just movie stars and public figures that enjoy name-recognition, fame and access to publicity, it can be anyone! This can be a mixed blessing. Everyone can, as Andy Warhol so aptly coined the phrase, enjoy their - **15 minutes of fame.** Now it's more likely to amount to a few seconds or miliseconds, although it could be a reputation, perception or brand that will endure.

Here are some tips:

-- You can manipulate and promote your brand by using marketing and promotional strategies, even if you don't have a PR agent. Review your Internet content to portray the image you want others to see - look at your *Facebook*, *LinkedIn*, *YouTube*, *Twitter*, personal and business websites to make sure they convey the message you want. Remove content that may embarrass you or diminish your reputation.

--Seriously consider how much you want to be in the (Internet) "public eye." A private brand might be o.k. too. Some people value their privacy or anonymity. If you decide you want to be out there, gain visibility by regularly adding and revising content; review and improve your *Google* ranking (check: www.googlerankings.com); write articles and blogs, etc.

--Enhance your professional brand and work reputation by your professionalism, customer service, trustworthiness, willingness to do more than required, etc. Produce professional products with a professional attitude. Don't be bashful. Toot your own horn! (Just not too often or loudly.)

--Develop expertise, and specialized services and skill sets. You will want to be thought of as the best, most knowledgeable in your field. Try to promote other's perception of you as a "valuable asset." Get your name out there in a positive way. Continue sensing and monitoring feedback concerning your reputation, value, and abilities.

--Make adjustments/corrections as necessary. Re-brand, or begin a marketing campaign to enhance your brand. Do damage control, and crisis management when necessary, and promote and market your "Me Brand."

--Remember, the worth of your brand is determined by your reputation. It is how others perceive and value you. Guard it, protect it, enhance it, promote it, value it, and enjoy it!

WHAT JOB SKILLS ARE MOST IMPORTANT
FOR THE FUTURE?

Employers, employees and job seekers all want to know: "What are the important job skills for the future?" The problem is - nobody knows!

The Trouble with Job Forecasting

Every few weeks a business magazine, Internet site, or popular press publication produces an article forecasting the jobs and careers most in demand over the next year, few years, or even decade. The problem is that these predictions are based on current data and trends, and often rely on straight-line extrapolations of current employment data. Frequently demographic and technological information is incorporated into the equation. Additional projections and analysis may be performed but none of these techniques are particularly accurate for forecasting future conditions. This is because the "explosion" in technology means that many jobs that don't even exist today will represent major career opportunities in the future.

The Job and Career Situation

The U.S. Department of Labor estimates that today's graduates will have 10-14 jobs by the time they reach age 38! In the current workforce, only 25% of employees have been in their present job more than a year; while 50% have been there less than 5!

The top 10 "in-demand" jobs for 2009 did not even exist in 2004" (statistics from *"Did You Know?"* video created by Karl Fisch, Scott McLeod and Jeff Bronman, for *Corinthian Colleges*, Parthenon IV, 2009). *Corinthian Colleges* (which includes *Everest Universities, Colleges* and *Institutes* as well as *WyoTech*) says that they are "preparing students for jobs that don't yet exist...using technologies that haven't been invented"..."to solve problems we don't even know are problems yet." CCi (*Corinthian Colleges, Inc.*) has many initiatives to address these challenges, including technology, curriculum, modes of student contact and instructional interface. Most importantly, recognition of the challenge, a willingness to change, an investment in classroom technology, and a "can do" attitude pave the way to the future.

This is not to say that other firms and educational institutions do not share this vision of the future, or a willingness to change. But it is an example of a progressive and proactive approach.

How does One Prepare?

It's challenging to prepare for a future when there is so much uncertainty, and things are changing so rapidly. What is needed is not only a "skill set" but a "mindset." The technical skills you need to make a living in business, criminal justice, medical or legal fields are important, but given the rate of change, other abilities are at least of equal value.

You've probably guessed that one of the keys to success in the emerging environment is education. But education is not enough. You must have an attitude of openness, flexibility, and eagerness to learn, along with willingness, even desire, to embrace change. And, your education must be enriched with learning technologies, and approaches designed to engage the student and teach them to be a *"lifelong learner."* It must include technical skills, information technologies, interpersonal and communications skills. It must also incorporate planning, critical thinking and analytical skills. This is a good foundation for any career.

<u>AVOIDING UNEMPLOYMENT IN AN ERA OF JOB CUTS</u>

We're no way through this recession. Every week we look at the unemployment statistics and, with some minor exceptions, the trend is still UP. Employers continue to reduce their workforce, as a cost-cutting measure, in a difficult economy. With payroll costs the largest single expenditure for most businesses it's natural to look at possibilities for "doing more with less." And, in many organizations, that means "less" employees!   The unemployment rate as of publication is over 9%, and climbing. Most experts predict it will top 10%, and that may be optimistic.

We're Undergoing a "Sea Change"

"Sea Change" is a wonderful term, and seems to be particularly applicable to our current economy. A Sea Change is a massive, formidable occurrence. It sweeps everything in its path, and like a tsunami, may result in devastation and displacement. It's a transformational event. The U.S. economy is undergoing an economic sea change. We've been through this before, and it's a major challenge. Those of you familiar with economic history know that we've experienced, in the past century, a change from an agrarian society to an industrial one, an "information age," internationalization, and a global economy. Along the way we experienced several depressions, recessions and other economic turmoil. Many characterize this a post-industrial era of finance, commerce, and service, on a global scale.

With all this change, many workers have been displaced, replaced, or discarded. Employees, whether white-collar, blue-collar, managerial, or self-employed, are experiencing a sense of uneasiness, uncertainty, and economic vulnerability.

Protecting Your Economic Viability

In times like these, individuals need to be more adaptable, creative and strategic. It's important to have options and preparation to be able to "make a living," and, hopefully, to experience success and financial security. There are many ways to improve your odds. Here are a few:

-- **Get an Education**. We're in an era of "lifelong learning." You can't afford to suspend your education. If you don't have a high school diploma, get one. Continue on with your Associates Degree, and don't stop there. They say the Masters Degree of today is what the undergraduate degree once was - and not that long ago. In my lifetime I've seen the percentage of the adult population with a four-year degree increase from 10% to over 30%. Undergraduate degree educations are certainly commonplace now, and increasingly, so are post-graduate credentials.

-- **Resist Complacency.** Your greatest enemy may be an attitude of "it'll be OK." It probably won't. Changes occurring right now, and likely in the near future, will probably test your resourcefulness and initiative. Try to stay motivated and focused. After all, it's a money economy, and you need income.

-- **Be Competitive.** I'm not saying it's a "dog-eat-dog" world, although it may be. What's more realistic is to understand that the employer-employee contract has changed. It's more temporal, less permanent, and less committed, on both sides. With more people looking for jobs the differences in abilities and potential between candidates is more apparent and decisive. Whether you're seeking an entry-level job, or an executive position, there is competition, and you must be able to differentiate yourself from your competitors. Being competitive means being better prepared, sharper, and willing to do more to win than your "adversary."

-- **Become Strategic.** Analyze yourself and the employment market. What jobs and careers are most in favor for the immediate, short, and long term? Look at the newspaper want-ads. Check out *CareerBuilders.com,* and *Monster.com.* The *U.S. Department of Labor* has excellent career forecast information. Plan your career strategy so that you effectively position yourself. Growing areas include *healthcare, education, international business, professional and business services, environmental science," green" industries,* and some *public sector* careers, particularly at the Federal level.

-- **Learn New Skills.** Take seminars, courses, certificate programs, etc. Build your resume, and your arsenal of credentials. Sometimes that Certification in *Microsoft Office* will make the difference between unemployment and becoming gainfully employed. For the currently employed training and knowledge may give you an edge in a promotional opportunity.

-- **Use your Network**. Most positions are filled through contacts or referrals. Develop and maintain your network of friends, colleagues, business associates, etc, so that you can learn of new opportunities. Many positions are not advertised, and many companies prefer people known to their current staff. Some even pay referral bonuses for referred new hires.

-- **Practice a Customer Focus.** In these competitive times employers' value employees with a customer-first attitude. Retaining customers, and attracting new ones is a major challenge and employees who do not contribute to this process are not highly valued no matter what their level of technical proficiency.

-- **Invest the time**. Seeking a new job or promotion takes time and energy. There may be nothing more important than spending the time to identify, research, prepare for, and target new opportunities.

-- **Improve your Attitude.** Often overlooked, and sometimes underrated, is the importance of a positive, "can do," attitude. It's easy to slip into negativity when you are confronted with job loss, unemployment or limited career advancement. Don't fall victim or defeatism or self-pity. Use positive self-talk, motivational techniques, etc. Awareness is the biggest factor here. Listen to yourself. Ask trusted friends or family to give you feedback. Remember that to most employers ATTITUDE is the most important factor. You can always teach someone new skills, but it's difficult to change someone's attitude or outlook.

You're Unique

Remember, you are unique. In the entire world there's no one exactly like you. Recognize and capitalize on your strengths. Don't be afraid to showcase yourself. Modesty may be a charming trait, but in these times you have to be a salesperson for your special talents and abilities. To become employed or advance in your employment requires a lot more preparation, dedication and effort than it did just a few years ago. Make sure you're up to the JOB.

THE REALITIES AND UNEXPECTED
POSSIBILITIES OF UNEMPLOYMENT

Times are tough. Jobs are scarce and unemployment is up. According to *U.S. Department of Labor* reports, almost two million jobs have been eliminated in 2008, and almost four and one-half million are drawing unemployment insurance benefits (UIB). Perhaps you are a part of these statistics. Many people who never expected to be without a job are, in fact, jobless. However, employers are still hiring, workers are still retiring, and employees continue moving up or moving on.

Discouragement

Being without a job can be downright discouraging; maybe even depressing. It's not only a blow to the pocketbook; it's also a blow to one's ego. It is stressful, and you'll feel the pressure. All this is happening at a time when you don't want to deal with it, and can't quite handle it. Having to scramble to find employment can be a challenge in itself.

You will need to be gentle with yourself. You will need to discuss the situation with loved ones and close friends. However, you will also need to find the strength to take immediate and forceful action. You will need to swallow your pride and, if you're eligible, sign up for Unemployment Benefits as soon as possible.

Once you've started to deal with your loss, your pride, your sense of self worth, and all of the other issues you will be ready to move on. Of course this will be an ongoing process and you can't wait for resolution before you begin your quest for re-employment.

Having a Plan

Having a plan is essential, not only to your frame of mind, but also to provide the impetus, direction, goal, and persistence which will be required. Your plan does not have to be elaborate, but it should be written. Start by analyzing your strengths and weaknesses, your talents, skills and abilities. Write these down. Update your resume, and brush up on your interview techniques. Network, and contact your friends, colleagues and prior employers. See if you can get referrals or recommendations. Be sure to get Letters of Reference from your previous employers.

Make a list of potential employers. Don't necessarily limit your list to those that you are familiar with, or in your immediate locale, or in the industry in which you were most recently employed. Now may be the time to expand your employment horizons and consider employment in another field. More important than the industry, or type of business, is the match between your skills and the job requirements. Post your resume on line, although this works better in some industries than others. As an educator, I know that colleges are constantly looking for new instructors, especially part-timers. We place advertisements, and always check for resumes on line, although our primary resource is referrals.

Try to meet with potential employers in person whenever possible. They will want to "check you out," and most appreciate the level of interest shown in a personal appearance. Explore the on-line career-builder and employment sites (e.g., *Monster.com, CareerBuilder.com, HotJobs*, even *CraigsList*), check the newspapers, and follow the trends. Not all leads are in the "classifieds," sometimes the information on the business page or in the media can be even more useful. You may have to examine some of the "less glamorous" jobs, and even consider a "step backwards" in pay or responsibility in order to position yourself for future growth.

You may want to consider returning to school or learning another profession. Your education will also benefit you as you will make new contacts, develop new perspectives, and perhaps find new career interests. The medical fields are some potential options, as are certain high-tech positions, security and law enforcement jobs, and environmental careers. Consider going into business for yourself, or a work-at-home option. Maybe there's a hobby or business opportunity you always thought would provide an income. Entrepreneurs are frequently highly motivated, greatly satisfied and successful.

Once you are aware of the range of possibilities you will feel more confident and empowered.

Each Situation is Different

There is no "cookbook" approach to dealing with the loss, challenges, and opportunities associated with unemployment. Some people are more prepared to deal with it than others. Some people are more resilient, some have resources to "tide them over," others have extensive networks of colleagues and friends. For some there are decent severance packages and re-employment assistance. A few even welcome the freedom and possibilities that unemploymert brings.

Whatever your situation, don't withdraw or procrastinate, but get on with the business of exploring your options and re-inventing yourself.

SUCCESS IN LIFE AND BUSINESS

Success in life and success in business are not the same thing. Of course, business and finance are huge and important components of our overall lives. You'd be a fool not to pay considerable attention to these areas, without compromising the other aspects of your life.

The Challenge of Success

Being successful in business and finance is not a simple task; otherwise we'd all be rich. Unfortunately, this is not the case. There is no easy or direct path to financial achievement. People find an infinite variety of ways to amass wealth and attain success in business and commerce. Others never find a way to progress financially. People can't decide on a career or enterprise, or how to progress once they're there. Some squander their money. Still others have setbacks, physical or mental challenges, and so forth.

Advice from One who Made It

H. L. Hunt was, by any objective measures, a financially successful individual. His business acumen was well-known. He made his fortune in the oil business, and by investing.

When asked about his "success formula" Hunt offered some prescient advice. His approach is direct, but not as easy as it sounds. FIRST: "Decide what you want." SECOND: "Decide what you're willing to exchange for it." THIRD: "Establish your priorities, and go to work." *(quotesdaddy.com)*

Hunt's approach is definitely straight-forward. Let's think about it. If you complete the FIRST step, you'll probably be ahead of 90% of people, because few really know what they want. And the SECOND step represents another formidable hurdle, because, again, a majority will be unwilling to expend the effort and make the required sacrifices. The THIRD step is also tough. Getting started (and then maintaining your motivation, initiative, effort, enthusiasm, dedication, etc,) requires strength of character and uncommon persistence.

Putting it into Practice

I recommend writing things down. It seems to make it more real, and you can always refer to it. But before you write it down, you'll need to do a lot of work THINKING. Serious THINKING! Deciding "what I want to be, when I grow up," is as challenging at fifty as it is at twenty. No one can do this for you. Your parents, friends, spouse, or teachers may try to guide you, but ultimately the decisions and responsibilities are yours. Also, nobody can determine *your* priorities, or what you're willing to do - or give up - to get what you desire. And, after you decide if you're willing to "pay the price," can you continue for as long as it takes to achieve your objectives?

Follow *Hunt's* formula, do the "prep" work, and if you believe you are capable of making the sacrifices and doggedly pursuing "what you want," put that commitment in writing and to work. Best of luck!

IN YOUR WORKING LIFE - DO WHAT YOU GOTTA DO

Your life won't be easy. This I can guarantee. But it can be quite an adventure. Nowhere is this truer than in your work and career. They don't call it "making a living" for no reason. And the reason is "you have to make a living" to live.

A Lifetime of Work

In my working life, I've had more than thirty jobs. I'll bet that many of you have had, or will have, even more. Some of my jobs were held simultaneously. Most resulted from promotions; one only lasted one day. I was raised in a fishing family, so it was natural that "fisherman" was one of my first job titles. In that job I learned the importance of hard work, long hours, good planning, and a lot of luck. I also learned that I didn't want to do that for the rest of my life. So, after graduating from high school, I went on to college. I realized that college would give me more opportunities in life, but I also had to work part-time to pay for my education. More experience = more value.

After college I moved to Los Angeles (with $60), and I needed to work. Despite my freshly-minted Bachelor's degree, employers were reluctant to take a chance on this youthful newcomer. And, lacking the talent to enter the entertainment industry, I quickly became broke and desperate. I took a position at the first place that would hire me. That first available job in L.A. was a loading dock worker at a furniture store.

Since those first few jobs I've been: a "merchandise collector," correspondent, O.E.M. (Original Equipment Manufacturer) rep., a social worker, and an "appeals worker." I've also been a supervisor, space manager, productivity manager, marketing manager, business consultant, office manager, program director and an administrative aide. --Now I'm starting to sound like Frank Sinatra in "That's Life."-- But, I'll continue with more job titles: division chief, house parent, painter, salesman, "day trader," small business owner, systems analyst, fiscal analyst, department head, real estate agent, mortgage consultant, office manager, CEO, entrepreneur, teacher, professor, and college president.

I can't begin to count the task forces, committees, public service organizations, professional associations, charitable and volunteer groups, mentoring, etc., I've been involved with. I'm neither bragging, nor complaining. I'm sure that some of you have had even more jobs, out of curiosity or necessity. But a point can be made, that you need to be flexible, adaptable, prepared, and opportunistic, in making a livelihood.

Don't "Pigeonhole" Yourself

Your life experience, education, work history, skills, talents, and abilities prepare you for many options. Take some chances. You're not an automobile worker, a teacher, or bus driver. You're much more complex than that.

Opportunities will occur, or be created. Get out of your comfort zone, and don't hang on to a job that no longer provides you with satisfaction or opportunities. Seek variety and challenge. In difficult economic times people become more conservative and risk-aversive. They want to keep that job, income, and security. This is practical and necessary. However, try to open your mind to new possibilities with your present employer, or perhaps a new career. Promotions, transfers, new assignments, new jobs and new careers are all attainable.

Your adventurous working life will be a testimony to your courage, knowledge, flexibility, experience, abilities, ambition, and persistence. So keep growing, changing, experimenting.... There are many ways to earn money; be sure to try a bunch of them.

LIFE IS ABOUT BUILDING OPTIONS

What a curious title. It does not refer to physical buildings or financial options. Instead, the title, and this discussion, is about the building, development or creation of options for yourself, and your life. Options mean "choices" and we all want to have them. And in business and life, options are important.

The Satisfying Life

Everyone wants satisfaction in their life. Even if your satisfaction is in the misery you are experiencing, it is still a form of satisfaction. Since we all strive for satisfaction it is important that we understand the means to attain it, because it can be quite elusive. It is so elusive that almost no one seems to have it completely.

The constant striving to identify what will satisfy us, and the efforts to obtain those things, feelings, relationships or perspectives are primary human motivators. In fact, *"Need Theory"* is a psychological framework which suggests that only unsatisfied needs are motivators, and that once satisfied, needs cease to be motivators. Here we have key elements of our paradigm. We all have needs, wants and desires. These unsatisfied needs provide motivation. Satisfaction is a universal goal, although complete satisfaction is undoubtedly unattainable.

The Dilemma

Like the *Rolling Stones* hit song from the 60's *"I Can't Get No Satisfaction"* (1965) we become frustrated in our pursuit. The song goes on to say: *"I try, and I try, and I try..."* And, this is what we humans do-- we keep trying!

Here's the dilemma. We can either "settle," stop trying, and be satisfied with our circumstances, or we can keep trying with the certainty that we will never attain complete satisfaction. The problem with the "settling" option is that we stifle our growth and limit our opportunities. People who are "pigeon holed" are limited in their possibilities and thus less able to adapt to changes in their environment.

In order to improve your probability for success and satisfaction, you must have options. And, the more options the better. Think about it. If your career is limited to "Caboose Tender" and trains no longer have cabooses, what do you do? In the case of a railroad employee, they have a strong union and the displaced caboose tenders and engine firemen were offered a transfer to another position, or a graceful retirement. But what about you? If your profession, skill, or employer was gone, how would you cope?

Building Options

The best way to build options is by being an active participant in your own life. Some people "go with the flow" while others challenge themselves and others. For example, are you continuing your education? Learning new skills? Advancing in your career? Trying new things? Participating in clubs and professional Organizations? Pursuing your hooby(ies)? Reading a lot? Etc.

Don't get stuck in a dead-end job, relationship, career, or mindset. Challenge yourself to try new things, take a few prudent risks, go back to school, or learn something new. Each time you limit yourself by not venturing out, you limit the possibilities you have and your options for future satisfaction.

The current pace of change continues to accelerate. Don't be left behind because you haven't learned what you need to know to adapt to these changes. Remember the *Serenity Prayer.*

> *God grant me the serenity*
> *to accept the things I cannot change;*
> *courage to change the things I can;*
> *and wisdom to know the difference.*

One implication of this prayer is: The fewer things you cannot change, and the more things you can, will only work to your advantage. Empower yourself by increasing the areas in which you can change, and create more options for yourself.

NOBODY RETIRES ANYMORE

Blame the economy. Blame the stock market. Blame the housing crash. Blame the demise of fixed benefit retirement plans. Blame Social Security. Blame longevity! There are lots of reasons why people don't retire anymore.

The Retirement Mentality

Retirement is a relatively new concept. It emerged in the late twentieth century following the enactment of the *Social Security Act* of 1933, the expansion of unionized labor, the temporary proliferation of retirement plans, a boom in wages and benefits, and a leisure mentality. People began to believe that there was an end to work, and a life of leisure, travel, and contentment awaited them. And for many people, for a window of time, it was real. Then things changed.

A Wake-Up Call

We're creatures of habit, and after a lifetime of work, it's difficult to change. Think about it. Most people begin working full-time between ages eighteen to twenty-five, and continue to work until they're 55-65 years old. This means they typically spend between 25 years (beginning work at 25 and retiring at 50), to 47 years (starting at age 18 and working to age 65). Some work a shorter period, while many continue to work even longer. During our working years the only activity we spend more time doing, is sleeping. Habits are difficult to change, and work is one of our most enduring.

During our employed years we spend around one-third of our total day (eight hours) working. This may be considerably longer depending on our job, our commute and other circumstances. Sure, we enjoy weekends, vacations, and holidays away from the office or factory, but a huge proportion of our life is spent working, thinking about work, preparing for work, getting to and from work, etc. And, recently even more of our time is "sucked up" by electronic tethers (cell phones, *BlackBerry*'s, laptops, and the like) to the office.

Prepare to Continue Working

The fact is, you should prepare to continue working, indefinitely. Not only does work provide income and benefits, it also provides social connections, mental stimulation, challenge, opportunity, meaningful activity, fulfillment, etc. For some people retirement is wonderful, for others it's a feeling of uselessness.

Studs Terkel summed it up: "Work is about a search for daily meaning as well as daily bread, for recognition as well as cash, for aston shment rather than torpor; in short, for a sort of life rather than a Monday through Friday sort of dying." (*Working*, [1974] New Press)

Today's reality is- most people will have to continue working. If they didn't, chances are they would "outlive their money." However, there are many options. Part-time employment, self-employment, at home work, Internet businesses, etc., are all possibilities. So, don't be discouraged by the possibility of lifetime work. Instead, see the opportunities for creativity; lifelong learning and value.

5

CREATING YOUR OWN BUSINESS

NURTURING THE ENTRPRENURIAL MINDSET

Entrepreneurs are special people. They often look at things differently than most. They see opportunities where others do not, and are willing to take risks, despite pitfalls and downside potential. Somehow they are able to persevere and maintain their enthusiasm.

The Entrepreneur

An entrepreneur is not a job title, position or even description, as much as it is a mindset --a way of thinking. Like any other thought patterns these perspectives can be nurtured and developed. Entrepreneurs are creative and creators. They create new products and ideas, new businesses and new ways of doing business. How do they arrive at this mentality, where they see possibilities and opportunities when others do not?

Entrepreneurial mindsets don't only exist for those who create businesses or inventions; this way of looking at things through the lens of possibilities also exists among employees and managers in many companies, even in government offices. In organizations they're called "*intrapreneurs*" because they are performing their "magic" within an existing organization. Wellsprings of ingenuity, they advance their concepts, ideas and novel approaches to existing problems and enterprises.

The key element in becoming an entrepreneur is willingness to accept risk. Most people are cautious and risk-aversive, whereas the entrepreneur enjoys, or at least tolerates, the uncertainty which accompanies business ventures. There is no "safety net" for many of these entrepreneurs. They will plow their life savings, borrowed money, time, effort and security into a new scheme, approach or possibility. Others may not understand or appreciate this risk-taking mindset, and there are plenty of people to say "I told you so" when things don't work out. But the entrepreneur presses ahead in the hopes of success and the enjoyment of following a dream. Without romanticizing this notion, these dreamers are a major engine of change, progress, and economic development. Thousands of new businesses, making billions of dollars, and employing millions of workers are constantly created by these folk.

Becoming an Entrepreneur

The entrepreneur mindset is difficult to capture or develop. Its elusiveness is rooted in a counter-intuitive approach where the need for security is over-ridden by the willingness, even desire, to accept, or embrace, risk. Many will say this mindset is an elemental part of the person. Either you have it, or you don't, and most do not. However, what if the mindset could be nurtured and developed? How would you go about this?

--First, understand the risk-reward equation. Greater risk CAN result in greater reward.

--Second, begin looking at the world with "fresh eyes." Challenge your established ways of thinking. Discard your old notions of impossibility and unlikelihood, and replace those ideas with possibility thinking. See the opportunities and potential in new ideas, and new ways of doing things. Keep a notepad with you to jot down new ideas. Some refer to this as their *"idea book,"* and soon it will be filled with interesting, and perhaps potentially profitable, business or product ideas.

--Third, start thinking like a business owner, even if you are working for someone else. This perspective will advance your knowledge, attitude, and mentality, and prepare you for the day when you are the owner of your own enterprise.

--Fourth, try taking a few chances, small ones at first until you test your assumptions of risk.

--Fifth, make sure you understand that entrepreneurship is competitive. You will have to be prepared to get in the muck and wrestle with the competition.

--Sixth, associate with those who have an entrepreneurial bent, perhaps small business owners, and/or creative types. Schools or your Chamber of Commerce provide opportunities for this. And, your personal network of friends and associates may encompass many like-minded entrepreneurial types.

--Seventh, actually develop one of your ideas into a business concept or plan. Test the plan on others. Try to pick successful people, and entrepreneurs. Stay away from the negative people and naysayers.

--Eighth, like every habit, your entrepreneurial way of thinking will need to be practiced until it becomes ingrained, and "second nature."

--Ninth, develop your knowledge about all aspects of business (e.g., management, marketing, entrepreneurship, legal requirements, etc.) by enrolling in college and/or participating in seminars or training sessions. The *SBA* (Small Business Administration) also offers several valuable courses either on-line or in person.

--Tenth, never give up. Persistence is a major factor in success. Most entrepreneurs have endured many setbacks and failures before becoming successful.

Try these approaches and see if they make a difference. Perhaps you will become a successful entrepreneur one day.

LET'S GET RICH

My undergraduate economics professor insightfully said: "There are three ways to get rich in America: 1) Be born Rich, 2) Be awfully lucky or very smart, 3) Marry rich." He went on to say: "For most of us, by far the easiest way is to marry rich, and that's what I did!" Most of my Business students want to know how to get rich. After all, that's why some of them study business. In this country "bigger is better" and that includes bank accounts. People want more of everything - especially money. Many authors have made tidy sums writing books about getting wealthy. It's a very popular subject.

The book *"Rich Dad, Poor Dad,"* (Robert Kiyosaki & Sharon Lechter, 2001) emphasizes knowledge, experience, and attitude. This information is useful and sound. The Rich Dad mindset touts investments before consumption. But we are a nation of consumers, and 70% of our GNP is based on consumer spending, so spending money (often unnecessarily) is almost a national pastime.

Suzie Orman, internationally acclaimed financial advisor, has a TV show (CNBC) where she consistently emphasizes "financial responsibility." She believes that Americans (especially women) have a "totally dysfunctional" relationship with money (Time, CNN, April 5, 2007).

What is the secret to becoming rich? Well, if I knew I'd be there. And, the authors of "Money" magazine(s), books, newsletters, etc., can't tell you either. You see, wealth is as much a state of mind as anything. Like anything else, it's all a matter of perspective. And, there is not a handy roadmap with clear directions to your wealth destination.

Is there a Science for Getting Rich?

In his book *"The Science of Getting Rich"* (2001 ed., orig. pub. 1910) William Wattles tries to make a case for a "scientific" approach to becoming wealthy. His theory is built upon "financial success through creative thought," and the interconnectedness of all elements in the universe, including thoughts. The use of mental imagery and vision are cornerstones of the approach. The premise is that if the vision is strong enough the universe will conspire to develop a realization of the subject of the thought, i.e, $$$$. Wattle's book is claimed to be a precursor to the wildly popular *"The Secret"* (movie [2006], and book [2007]).

The Secret refers to the "Law of Attraction" which insists that you will attract what you think about most. Interestingly, a "down on his luck" lottery player earning about "$300 a week" practiced this method concentrating on money, and in 2007 won a Florida Lottery prize of $33 million (*Miami Herald*, Aug. 8, 2007). Draw your own conclusions.

Luck, Hard Work, Intelligence

Many people think rich folk are smarter or work harder than the rest of us. And, oftentimes that's true. However, many of the hardest workers are not rich, and most of the smartest people aren't either. So, what is the explanation? Obviously, the secret to becoming rich does not depend so much on these attributes as it does on some other factor(s).

How about "luck"? Yes indeed, luck does seem to play a role: Choosing the "right" business or career, living in the "right" area at a fortuitous period. Taking advantage of a "once in a lifetime" opportunity, or "falling" into a favorable situation. How many people prospered from buying a home or other real estate during a good period? Were they omniscient, or particularly analytical? Usually not. Although some of them recognized a trend and jumped on the bandwagon. However, probably an equal number didn't realize what was going on, or failed to get out before the situation reversed. Much of our wealth can often be attributed to "dumb luck" rather than astuteness.

Obviously, luck seems to play a role in good fortune, misfortune, or amassing a fortune.

Discipline

One of the more data-based studies of wealth involved surveying wealthy individuals. *"The Millionaire Next Door"* (Thomas Stanley & William Danko, 1996) captured attitudes and experiences of wealthy people and found that most had accumulated their riches by being disciplined over the years. The old-fashioned attitudes of thrift, even frugality, spending less than you earn, and long-term goals were in clear evidence in the study.

Preparation

Of course, there is something to be said for preparation. Taking courses, studying, reading books, accumulating information, are all helpful. The old axiom "a fool and his money are soon parted" rings true. Unknowledgeable individuals will make uninformed decisions which have a higher probability of being poor ones. Study and try to become expert in those areas which will enhance your probability of financial success.

Make Getting Rich a Priority

Napoleon Hill wrote what is perhaps the most famous of all wealth books. His *"Think and Grow Rich"* (pub. 1937) described "Laws of Success" including such characteristics as: desire, faith, conquering your fears, and persistence. He recommends "self talk" to reinforce your motivation, attitudes, and commitments.

Just deciding that accumulating wealth is a top priority will help. Accumulating wealth is not necessarily dependent on making more money. Frequently, our investment and spending priorities are the deciding factors. Evaluating your life's priorities to decide what is personally most important is a requisite step. Establishing a top priority necessarily means that other priorities will have to take a subordinate place. And your top priorities will consume most of your attention, time and energy. This may not be exactly what you want, after all. There are tradeoffs and family, personal life, and your desire to lead the so-called "balanced life" may suffer.

Goals, Focus, Effort

Perhaps a more direct, commonplace and business-like approach is called for. People with goals are more likely to succeed. "Goal Theory" indicates that having specific, well-defined goals make us focus on outcomes, direct our energies, and increase our likelihood of attainment. Of course merely wanting to be rich will not result in our becoming wealthy. The goal(s) needs to be "specific," "measurable," "attainable," "realistic," and "timely." These *SMART* goals, as they are referred to, will significantly improve your odds.

Most people do not have very specific financial goals. As a result, they are easily distracted from their general objective of "getting rich." Also many individuals do not have measurable goals. They have not decided on what wealth actually means to them, and how they will measure it. A simple "net worth" statement, calculating the difference between assets and liabilities should suffice. In order to attain a goal it needs to be reasonably within your reach. There are many millionaires-- around 1% of the population (*New York Post*, June 25, 2008) so attaining that goal seems fairly realistic.

Finally, timeliness includes developing "benchmarks," interim steps and periodically assessing your results. Attaching dates to these interim goals will help you achieve your ultimate goal. And you need sufficient time. If you're eighty years old with $5,000 in total assets and your goal is to accumulate $1 million by the time you're eighty-five, although it may be specific and measurable, your goal is not realistic, attainable and TIMELY. On the other hand, if you're twenty-five and have the million dollars net worth goal you have plenty of time, and opportunities to realistically attain it providing you apply the SMART principles.

Getting Rich the SMART way

Maybe getting rich is not so mysterious and elusive after all. It doesn't require having the "right" relatives, super-intelligence, extraordinary luck, or "marrying rich!" It may not even require esoteric, mystical or sacrificial approaches or techniques. Perhaps it's just like any other goal or ambition. What we must do is apply ourselves, and focus on developing a SMART goal. Then comes the essential part, finding the discipline, energy and focus to attain the SMART goal.

WHO YOU NEED ON YOUR SMALL BUSINESS TEAM

The days when an entrepreneur could open and manage a small business all on his own are long gone. Today, it takes a team. It probably always took a team, especially for the most successful enterprises. You will need support from a variety of sources from the beginn ng. Let's look at some of the resources you'll need, or at least wish to consider.

We'll begin with the Big Four. The first thing you'll notice is that they all have something to do with MONEY. And, money is the lifeblood of business. It's the business's air, food and water. It's a necessity. Sure, we all know stories of someone who started a multi-million dollar enterprise with a couple of hundred bucks. But, just like the lottery winner, these examples are exceptions.

The BIG FOUR

Here are the "critical few" you will need:

--Banker

You'll need money, perhaps for start-up, and later on for expansion. You'll also need a business account, perhaps credit card processing, etc. You should establish a line of credit.

Small local banks are frequently more friendly to small business than are their larger counterparts.

--Attorney(ies)

An attorney is an important resource, hopefully one that won't be required too frequently. Your attorney can protect and defend your interests, help you legally structure your business, (e.g., partnership, corporation, etc.), and provide advice to keep you out of legal "hot water."

--Accountant(s)

Your accountant will set up your accounting records, (payroll, financial statements, cash flow, accounts payable and receivable, etc.), Small Businesses frequently use *Quicken,* or some other commercially available software package, but an accountant can do so much more. You'll inevitably need advice on taxes, major expenditures, financing, etc. Choose carefully.

--Insurance Agent(s)

Small businesses frequently skimp on insurance. However, a lawsuit, illness, fire, natural disaster, etc. may put you out of business permanently.

Here are Some Additional Resources You May Need:

--Marketing Consultant - increase visibility and sales, improve image, etc.

--Web Designer - almost all businesses have some Internet presence.

--*SBA* - the Small Business Administration offers courses and seminars, advice and support.

--*SCORE* - this was originally the Service Corps of Retired Executives; it's a great non-profit organization to help you.

--*Chamber of Commerce* - your local "chamber" is comprised of small business owners like you, and it's a good place to learn and network, as well as promote your business.

--*Better Business Bureau:* at some point you may want to join the BBB.

--Personal Contacts (your friends, family, and acquaintances may be customers, advisers, supporters, encouragers, critics, or be of value in unexpected ways)

DON'T NEGLECT PLANNING IN YOUR SMALL BUSINESS

Small business owners frequently don't know or fail to practice, what management in large companies knows is essential--PLANNING. Planning can make the difference between failure and success; between survival and going out of business. A small business with a plan will outperform a similar or bigger one, without a plan.

Planning Requires Discipline

In order to plan effectively you must be disciplined. It requires thoughtful analysis to plan, and regularly revisiting your assumptions, goals and strategies. The discipline of developing and implementing plans must also be combined with the discipline of monitoring, evaluating, modifying and maintaining your plan. Plans must be re-examined periodically to re-test their viability and validity. A regular schedule of planning updates must be developed and adhered to.

Planning Requires Participation

Planning is best when it is done as a TEAM. The old adage, "everyone knows more than anyone" applies here. Of course, in addition to gaining other perspectives in the planning process, the benefit of support is also important. People are much more committed to a plan that they helped develop, than to a plan developed without their participation, and "crammed down their throats."

Planning Requires Goals

What is the purpose of your plan? What are you trying to achieve? The plan is there to help you arrive at your destination-- like a roadmap. Ambitious goals require comprehensive plans. In the business world we speak of SMART goals: Specific, Measurable, Attainable, Realistic, and Timely (King, et.al.). A goal which is not specific will be difficult to communicate, monitor, and attain. Without measurements you will have no way to track progress. Unattainable goals are a waste of time and a set-up for failure. Realistic goals are not grounded in fantasy or illusion; rather, in fact and concreteness, with of a probability of attainment. Finally, timely goals are those which are synchronous with the window of opportunity, meet a need which is apparent, and include achievable milestones and deadlines.

Planning Requires Analysis

You're probably tired of hearing about the *SWOT* (Flagenbaum, et.al.) analysis, but it remains at the core of the strategic planning process. Each small business has some unique attributes. It is important to identify and build upon these Strengths, but also to recognize and minimize any Weaknesses. Likewise, Opportunities must be recognized to capitalize on them and Threats discovered so that strategies can be developed to mitigate or avoid them. The *SWOT* analysis is an excellent process to discover and record the realities of the internal and external environments. Armed with this information, plans can be created to address each area.

Planning Requires Data

Your planning assumptions should be grounded in data. Mere speculation will not suffice. Gather data and determine the most important data elements, for incorporation into the monitoring process. Estimates are fine if they have a historical, or benchmark, basis. Whether you're preparing a comprehensive business plan, a marketing plan, a sales plan, a relocation plan, an expansion plan, a retrenchment plan, a contingency plan, a competitive strategy, etc., you will need data and realistic forecasts. Some of this data may already be available to you in industry reports, government data (especially demographics), *Chamber of Commerce* or Business Association analyses, or even reports produced by the competition.

Planning Requires Creativity

Playing it safe when developing a plan is not enough. Plans need to be made with "stretch" goals that will significantly, perhaps dramatically, advance the enterprise. The most effective plans reframe reality. They look at problems from fresh perspectives and new angles. "Brainstorming" is a useful technique so that as many ideas as possible can be created and considered. (There are excellent references and Internet sites which will provide the ground rules.)

Plans Focus Energy, Resources, Attention, and Effort

Plans are useful to direct available resources and talent toward the solution of a problem, or attainment of a goal. With this focused attention and support, successful implementation of change becomes far more probable.

There is no Best Formula for Planning

Writing a plan is far superior to one carried around in your head. The act of writing seems to make it more real and concrete. Written plans tend to reflect more analysis and thought, and are easier to share with others. There are excellent planning software packages, great books on the subject, even workbooks. However, your business is unique, and as such you will need to only use any references as basic guidelines. Adapt your planning process to meet the exigencies of your situation and don't rely on "cookie cutter" solutions.

You may think you don't have the time, resources or energy to devote to developing a comprehensive strategic, business, marketing, financial or other important plan(s) for your business. However, even a plan scribbled on the back of a napkin, at a lunch, is better than no plan at all.

DON'T LET YOUR BEST IDEAS VANISH!

Carrying a small memo pad with you at all times will provide protection that your best ideas won't slip away. Most of us don't remember many of our most creative thoughts, because we neglect this simple step - write it down.

Insights, creativity, and "flashes of brilliance" can be fleeting thoughts, which, unprotected, will escape us. All of us have thousands of thoughts, daily. Most of these thoughts are of minimal consequence, or even "noise," -- unimportant "chatter." However, every so often we come up with a particularly good idea which can even be "life-changing." Typically, we neglect to record these important thoughts, and rely on our faulty faculties of recollection.

Some people realize how important their ideas can be and jot them down on scraps of paper, business cards, the palm of their hand, etc. This is obviously better than failing to write them down, but paper scraps get misplaced, end up in the washing machine, or cannot be found. All the more reason to keep a memo pad/ notebook.

The Idea Book in Practice

I teach a course called "Small Business Management," and the content concentrates on entrepreneurship. Of course, in order to have a small business to manage you first have to create one. And, every business begins with an idea. So, I purchase a spiral-bound memo pad for each student. I'm sure you're familiar with the type. It's a 3x5 inch notebook that can easily be carried in a shirt pocket or purse. The students are encouraged to write down ideas that occur to them relating to improvements in existing businesses, or thoughts concerning new products, services, and business opportunities. Unfortunately many students do not take the practice seriously, and fail to regularly record their business ideas. They view it as yet another school assignment and task, not appreciating the power of the technique.

In class we share our ideas and sometimes recognize a new perspective or insightful thought. However, many students "pass," saying that they did not have any noteworthy ideas during the past week. This paucity of ideas does not generally indicate a lack of ideas or creativity, but rather a failure to observe, or negligence in developing or recording insights. The discipline required to have a readily available notepad, although minimal, seems to be beyond the motivation of many even though simple, spontaneous ideas have resulted in the creation of great business empires.

Creative "Types"

Creativity needs nurturing. Not that it is, necessarily, a learned habit, but it is synergistic. You know the concept; ideas create more ideas, additional linkages and inter-relationships. There are some outstanding examples of this. People like Thomas Edison, Leonardo daVinci, Issac Newton, Albert Einstein, Benjamin Franklin, etc. Most of these inventors and innovators kept extensive journals, recording their concepts in detail. Modern innovators like Ron Popeil, Steve Jobs, and Tyler Perry, may make less extensive written, or computer notes, but recording ideas is important.

Get Started

Hopefully you're convinced, or at least recognize the potential value in carrying a small notebook to record your ideas. Some people may prefer to record their thoughts on a pocket recorder, *"Palm Pilot,"* or *Blackberry*. Whatever approach you may use is preferable to trying to remember these ideas. Most notes may prove to be of little consequence, although there may occasionally be that flash of brilliance which may start a business or create a product. Why trust your admittedly untrustworthy memory with your precious ideas?

MAKING PARTNERSHIPS WORK

There's an old saying: "Two heads are better than one!" And, so it is in business. In a partnership, each partner brings something unique to the "table." Whether it's perspective, talents, resources, judgment, finance, initiative, motivation, creativity, discipline, etc, a combination of attributes of two (or more) people is superior to an individual. That's what makes partnerships so powerful.

Synergy

Just like a good marriage, the best partnerships have a synergistic quality. That is, the result of the combination is not only better, but greater than the sum of the individual parts. There's a multiplier effect; it's more than just adding the skills of the individual participants. Something "magic" may happen that will exceed the expectations of those involved, and would be far more successful than either party could ever be, alone. Some familiar examples might include: *Laurel & Hardy, Dean Martin & Jerry Lewis, Thomas Edison & JP Morgan*, The *Google* Boys (*Larry Page & Sergney Brin*), *Microsoft's Bill Gates & Paul Allen, Hewlett-Packard,* McDonnell-Douglas, *Bush/Cheney* (or *Bush/Karl Rove* [fondly referred to as "Bush's Brain"]), "*Pep Boys*," *Wilbur & Orville Wright, Coco Chanel & Pierre Wertheimer, Steve Jobs & Steve Wozniak* (*Apple*), or ice cream moguls *Ben & Jerry.*

Know Thy Partner

To paraphrase *Socrates*, I would say in a partnership above all know thy partner. Yes, it's true a great partner can make a company. Alas, the reverse holds true as well and the wrong partner can erode and hinder success. The question you need to ask yourself is does this person strengths complement my deficiencies? Or, moreover, will his weakness impede my progress? Remember being joint owners of the business makes you joint owners of the problem. And that's true whether you, or your partner, are at fault. These are just some of the considerations for being a part of a business partnership. Therefore it's incumbent upon you to due diligence and make sure the person you are entering a partnership agreement with is well vetted. Communication is the key element here. Knowledge is power, and that knowledge is obtained through effective and frequent communication.

Losing to Win

Next to communication, the single most important element to a winning partnership is each party's ability to compromise. If you expect to always have your way, then you are probably not the sort of person who will excel in a business partnership. Having fixed opinions about how a particular task should be done misses the bigger picture - i.e., "what's best for the business?"

Structure

Let's say you want to enter a partnership. You believe that it's preferable to a "sole proprietorship." What should you do about formalizing your agreement? Many would advise that you define roles, responsibilities and obligations from the beginning, to avoid misunderstandings and conflict. Although there is a strong rationale for this approach, legal expenses may best be avoided in a "start-up." There will be time for the legal formalization. However, agreement should be reached informally, and then placed in writing, as soon as practicable. This is business-like and responsible. After all, money will undoubtedly become an issue at some point. The relationship needs to be legally defined, and registered accordingly. This will prevent misunderstandings, frivolous lawsuits, unnecessary operational threats, and ensure the continuity of the business.

Power Struggles

It isn't always easy to work together. There will be disagreements. Someone will need to take the lead, and there could be resentments. We've all witnessed family, and unrelated business partners feud, and the results are frequently catastrophic.

The best relationships have as a foundation, mutual respect. This lays the groundwork for cooperation and progress. When petty jealousies and "one-ups-manship" enter the picture, cooperation suffers.

The sharing of responsibilities, efforts and rewards should be fair. Responsibilities should be assigned based on expertise, judgment, and ability. Smart partners realize it's sometimes best to "give away" power. A person's power is often increased by this sharing tactic. But however it's done it needs to be done for a good purpose. The primary objective is the success of the endeavor. The next most important consideration is to strengthen the partnership (essentially, the leadership of the organization).

Making it Work

If, despite all the challenges, obstacles, and pitfalls, you still want to create a partnership, picking the "right" partner is the first step. Generally, there is a natural alignment due to common interests, friendship or familial considerations, or a strategic combination of resources. Just remember to preserve the partnership and foster its preservation by developing a mindset that this is bigger than either (or any) of us. And, keep in mind that there is a rich and lengthy history of successful, enduring, even famous, partnerships. Perhaps yours will be one, too.

OPPORTUNITIES NEVER END

Many people are discouraged with the lack of opportunities in the current economic climate. They see their net worth evaporating, worry about their job and career; their house may be in jeopardy, their future is uncertain. However bleak the outlook may seem, there are always opportunities. Opportunities abound. Our problem is to: 1) Recognize them, and 2) Exploit them.

Recognizing Opportunities

It's important to look at the world with "fresh eyes." Many times we don't see the opportunities that surround us. There's a book called "*Acres of Diamonds*" (Conwell, Richard, pub. Arc Manor, 2008), and the point of the story is that the individual is seeking fortune far and wide, while riches are in abundance in his own backyard!

A child sees with "fresh eyes." Everything is new and wondrous. The child explores, seeks, enjoys, and finds excitement and stimulation in everything around him.

A newcomer, for example, a recent immigrant to this country, sees opportunities that many of us who have lived here all of our lives cannot. They too are seeing with fresh eyes.

It's human behavior to ignore extraneous stimuli. Something can be "right in front of our nose" and not be recognized. Look around you; is there anything that could be done differently or better? Are there any products or services that aren't available, but would make your life better? Are there investment opportunities that present themselves? How about educational opportunities?

Horse trainers often use "blinders" to help train the animals and keep them focused. No one will put blinders on you, except yourself. Self imposed blinders, or "tunnel vision" will not only restrict your vision, in terms of the view, but your life in terms of inability to see the opportunities that are out there.

Think like a child or a newcomer and you will see things you never noticed before.

Exploiting Opportunities

Once you have recognized an opportunity, you must immediately record it (i.e., write it down) then focus on it, develop it and create a plan to exploit it. Missed opportunities are legendary. We have all committed this mistake.

In a land of opportunity, there are always more that can possibly be recognized, and/or taken advantage of. Some of these opportunities will be life-changing. It's your task to find them and do something about them.

ENTREPRENUIAL SHIFT

The Great Recession of the early twenty-first century has awakened a new spirit of entrepreneurship. America has always been a country of entrepreneurs. We have a frontier spirit, and this is a land of opportunity. There is no reason to think this will change.

A Sea Change in the Economy

We are undergoing a monumental shift which is causing workers to rethink their plans for earning a living and attaining financial security. We are all too familiar with the scenario of declining asset values (particularly homes -most people's largest one), employment insecurity, layoffs, dismantling of traditional pensions, foreign competition, wage stagnation, etc. We see the national debt rising exponentially; hear of government programs -including Social Security- going broke, banks and financial institutions closing, and corporations struggling to stay profitable. We see millions out of work, "upside-down" in their homes, scrambling to keep or find a job, and a public which are generally pessimistic or stressed.

There are Still Opportunities

Because of all the negativity swirling around American workers, many are looking for other income opportunities. Poverty, insecurity, and dissatisfaction can be powerful motivators. The allure of "working for yourself" and being a business owner, has always had great appeal. With the present circumstances many who would have not considered being an entrepreneur, are reconsidering their options.

Not an Easy Choice

Small business owners typically spend a lot more time and effort to make a living than regular employees. It is frequently said that you won't find a tougher boss than yourself. It is not only the hours, but the responsibility involved. As an employee you don't have to worry about Payroll; only that you get paid. As a business-owner you must "make" payroll. As an employee you probably have a reasonably well-defined job; as an entrepreneur, you're responsible for everything.

Then there's the failure rate. Most small businesses don't make it. In fact, that's an understatement, because about 90% don't last three years.

Plus, instead of making money from the outset of your enterprise, you will be spending money. Start-up costs they call it, and the biggest problem with neophyte businesses is under-capitalization. The owner(s) underestimate, or simply don't have, the capital required. Well, can't you just go to the bank? After all, you have a great idea, and you're a hard worker. The Small Business Administration doesn't loan money, but they will help you get prepared to apply for financing. *SCORE* will help, too. But it's tough to get money to start a new business, so most start-ups are financed with cash from the entrepreneur, her friends and family, credit cards, or savings.

If You Still Want to Try It

Being business for yourself may be more rewarding than any other type of economic activity. You have an opportunity to build something from "scratch." You might even build a legacy. You have that self-determination that no employer can offer. Yes, it's all yours, for good or bad!

So, if in spite of all the challenges, downside risk, and expectation of a laborious future, you still want to proceed, please consider the following:

--tap into your creative mind to come up with innovative and unique approaches which will distinguish your business from the millions of others out there

--resist the temptation to risk everything, particularly if you have a family dependent on you

--be realistic in your assessment of reward vs. risk

--develop a business plan - put it in writing, even if it is brief and not entirely complete

--seek sources of funding; use resources like the *Small Business Administration,* and *SCORE*

--use the aforementioned resources to become more savvy, informed and knowledgeable about the opportunities, hurdles, and requirements for successful business development

-do your research, check out similar ideas, do your undercover visits to the "competition"

--share your plans openly with your family and close friends; gain their support and buy-in

--avoid the naysayers, but not entirely. Consider valid concerns and objections; don't be blinded by your optimism; take the "rose colored glasses" off sometimes

--maintain your optimism and enthusiasm, you'll need it when the inevitable problems and discouragement set in

--seek help and advice when necessary -you don't know all the answers

All this being said; if you're independent, determined, maybe stubborn, a hard-worker, not overly risk-aversive, upbeat, forward thinking, and have a good business concept, then go for it! If you don't, you will regret the missed opportunities and satisfactions. And, as a motivating thought, remember: you may just escape from the "rat race," have more freedom, and avoid dancing to someone else's tune.

THE ABBREVIATED BUSINESS PLAN

Business Plans do not have to be lengthy, formidable, detailed documents. Often 2-3 pages will suffice. The primary objective is to get your ideas, strategies and resource requirements out of your head, and onto paper. This documentation is important for a number of reasons. First, plans have a tendency to become more "real" once they're written down. Second, for planning purposes it's important to be organized and objective. It's easier to accomplish this in writing. Third, a written plan is important to share with others and gain their reaction. Fourth, investors and financers will want to see the numbers.

An abbreviated Business Plan forces the writer to be concise, and include only essential information. The Plan will be more focused, and understandable. Also, the plan should receive more favorable attention, and a thorough reading.

Plan Components

Although there are different opinions, some variation of essential elements for your business plan may include:

Introduction/Executive Summary (or Background)

Mission & Vision

Key Products/Services

Management/Operating Plan

SWOT Analysis

Finance & Funding

Marketing

Basic Information for Each Section

Introduction and background may not seem too important, but how did you come up with the idea? Is the concept original? The Introduction/Executive Summary/or Background Statement is to gain the reader's attention, and prepare them for what follows.

In the Mission Statement/Vision area, try to describe exactly what the purpose of your organization is, and where you see it going in the future. Key Products or Services is where you describe what you will be producing and selling.

Management is the section where the principals (founders) are identified along with an indication of staffing requirements.

The SWOT analysis identifies your proposed company's strengths, and perhaps more importantly, its weakness as well as the opportunities available in the marketplace, and the threats (primarily from competitors).

Finance and funding specifies the money required to begin and sustain your operations, and the source of "start up" funds.

Marketing identifies your customer (targeted segment) and how you propose creating/satisfying their need/desire for your products/ services. Pricing, packaging, sales and distribution may also be included.

How Much Detail?

In preliminary Business Plans, often "less is more." Your purpose is to convey essential information, not to answer every quest on, or to provide every detail. At some point in the future, you will need to flesh out the specifics, although there is plenty of time to do this. I'm not suggesting that you be superficial, just concise and "tight." Aim for two or three substantive paragraphs in each section. Remember: get that plan out of your head and onto paper!

A MILLION DOLLAR MARKETING PRESENCE – FOR FREE!

Small businesses often have trouble competing with the big guys because of limited marketing resources. Big companies purchase television commercials, radio ads, newspaper and magazine advertising, and telephone outreach, while small businesses have typically relied on: word-of-mouth, neighborhood flyers, placards, storefront promotions, etc. Both small and large businesses typically sell their goods and services on the internet, at least to some degree. At a minimum, almost all businesses now have a website.

Well, there is a recent game-changer that small businesses are just discovering -- the *Social Media*.

What is Social Media?

Internet based social media has exploded on the scene over the past few years. Ask your children, I'm certain they know more about it than you do. *Facebook* recently announced that they surpassed 500 million members. (Wauters, *Robin, Zuckerberg Makes It Official*: "Facebook Hits 500 Million Members," *TechCrunch.com,* July 21, 2010) Yes, a half billion people. Now, that's a big audience. *Twitter* is also huge. Twitter consists of tiny, sentence or two "blogs" that are instantly posted on the Internet and reach millions of viewers. And, speaking of blogs, there are thousands of "*bloggers*" with millions of readers on the web, too! Bloggers usually concentrate on an area of interest and post brief "articles," or statements about their area of interest and specialization.

So what?

You may be thinking "so what?" It's great that all of these people, who have nothing better to do, are blogging, and tweeting, and "facebooking." How does this apply to my business? Think again. With a huge audience of participants who are also consumers available to contact for **free**, could the *Social Media* give your business a boost? The obvious answer is: Almost certainly!

Get started!

What are you waiting for? Free advertising is a golden opportunity, and it may not last forever. Governments and businesses are currently thinking of ways to charge for internet services, and tax them as well.

But while it's here and free, you'd be foolish not to take advantage of this once-in-a-lifetime opportunity. You can begin by opening *Facebook* and *Twitter* accounts. This should take you a total of about five minutes. Then, begin looking at what is out there. Become an active participant. At some point in the near future I'm sure you'll recognize the opportunities, and begin to think of the possibilities for your business to become a part of the *Social Media* craze.

6

MANAGING
ETHICALLY

THE TEMPTATION TO CHEAT IN BUSINESS

When forces of compensation and limitations on performance collide the pressure to "fudge" a little is immense. There is little doubt that, in an effort to look good on the statistics most valued and incentivized by management, employees may be tempted to "doctor" the numbers. The best advice: Don't do it!

Those Pesky Performance Targets

Performance "stats," "goals," "targets," "standards," "indicators," or whatever they're called in your business, may directly or indirectly affect your compensation and promotional opportunities. So, if the performance isn't so "good," why not make yourself "look good" on paper.

For some, the temptation to cheat may be too strong to resist. For those with an unethical bent, this inclination may lead to even more manipulation of numbers as a way of doing business. It may be "creative accounting," misstatements, liberal interpretation, or downright fraud. With *ENRON* or *Bernie Madoff* it reached unimaginable proportions, involving billions of phantom dollars.

A Culture of Cheating

Cheating may begin at the top of the enterprise with intentional misstatements of quarterly profits or estimates, or at the bottom, with a salesman inflating his expense claim or sales numbers. Wherever it begins it corrupts the integrity of the organization and has a tendency to proliferate. It's kind of a "she got by with it, so can I," mentality which ultimately progresses to contaminate and corrupt the entire organization. And, it's not harmless, no matter how inconsequential it may seem. At some point it may be discovered in an internal audit, or, worse, unearthed in an outside audit. It may be reported by employees, or found by regulatory agencies. If it is sufficiently egregious, it could result in the destruction of the business and/or the incarceration of its leaders.

A "Wink"

Many companies have beautifully crafted and comprehensive ethics policies However, in too many cases they are ignored either intentionally or inadvertently. If the company just has the policy as a requirement or a publicity document, or to include in a motto e.g., "we have the highest integrity in the business," and it is not backed up by a rigorous code, practice, and performance of these values, it's worse than no policy at all. Not only is it hypocritical, it's unethical, and maybe illegal. If management "winks" at violations it promotes a culture of miscreants and demonstrates a tacit approval of morally unacceptable behavior.

What to Do

Here are a few tips:

--Lead by example

--Protect your organization's reputation

--Recognize the capacity for performance goals and incentives to promote "cheating"

--Communicate the consequences of cheating to your employees

--Make an example of wrong doers

--Promote a culture of authentic integrity

--Review your compensation system so that pay isn't too heavily influenced by one or two performance criteria

--Rigorously review and "test" reports and data

--If it is "too good to be true," it probably is; so investigate

--Establish, realistic, attainable, and meaningful measures of performance

--Examine your firm's Ethics Policy for clarity, appropriateness, directness and practicality

--Continuously review and update your Ethics Policies

Finally, whatever the temptation, don't give in. The personal sacrifice of integrity and the risk of detection are not worth any potential temporary gain from unethical behavior.

R-E-S-P-E-C-T

In the late 1960's *Aretha Franklin* had a top hit. This popular song was titled *R-E-S-P-E-C-T*. Perhaps you remember the words, as this song has endured as a Rock-and-Roll classic. This discussion is not about music, or Aretha Franklin, however it is about R-E-S-P-E-C-T.

The Importance of Respect

Why is RESPECT so important? If you watch the prison episodes on TV you will see the inmates constantly referring to respect or "dissing" (i.e., disrespecting someone). Disrespect can, and often does, result in a fight for one's honor. It seems when you have lost everything all you have left is RESPECT, and you will defend it at all costs.

RESPECT and Relationships

While in a doctoral program at the *University of San Francisco*, I had a professor by the name of Robert Lamp. Dr. Lamp taught me something that I'll always remember. He had a "*Relationship Model.*" that he was fond of sharing with his students. The theory is that relationships develop in stages, one step at a time. In this staircase model the first step is RESPECT. The second step on the staircase is SUPPORT, and the top step is TRUST. So imagine yourself walking up this three-step staircase, beginning on step number one – RESPECT; then proceeding on to SUPPORT and so on. This sounds reasonable and simple. But simple it is not.

You see, the *RST* model requires mutuality. In order to achieve relationships, you must first expend effort in developing them, one step at a time. However, your efforts alone are not enough. The other person must reciprocate. For example if I respect you, and you don't respect me, do we have a basis to move forward in our relationship? The answer is NO. Conversely if you respect me, and I don't respect you, we cannot move forward either.

Mutual respect provides the foundation from which to proceed ascending. This is a clue to why relationships are so difficult. You can only control your actions and not anyone else's.

Application of the Concept

If relationships are important in our personal and professional lives why do we spend so little time and effort in cultivating them? First, it is difficult. Second, you are not completely in control. But there are other factors as well; something as elementary as ignorance of how relationships work. People generally know when they like someone, and similarly when someone likes them. Frequently, however, they do not know why. They also know that they would like to be able to trust people who are important to them, and be considered trustworthy.

Our adventure down the journey of relationships is filled with challenges and obstacles. When we have just mastered one step there is often a setback, due to our actions or those of the other party. Missteps in relationships are commonplace. One slip-up can undo considerable progress and cause us and/or the other party to go backwards and descend to a lower level.

For example, deception can lead to mistrust. So, we either go back to support, or even respect, or worse yet we go back to the point where we had not even climbed the first step.

As fragile as our relationships are, they require constant monitoring, attention, reevaluation and corrective action. These maintenance activities will ensure an enduring, strong relationship.

How About Business?

I have spent considerable time discussing the concepts and almost no time on business. This is undoubtedly because the concepts are much larger than the business world. However, we all know the importance of business relationships, partnerships, employee relations, customer service, etc. And, intuitively we know that these relationships are important, necessary, productive or counterproductive, and must be maintained and improved. Also, in the current business environment these issues have become increasingly important. With international and multi-national business connections it is essential that managers have an understanding of, and appreciation for, not only relationships within the American culture, but other cultures as well.

So how about it? Are you ready to apply the RST approach in your personal and professional life?

--Begin by finding something to like about the other party. Not everything, just something.

--Respect the other individual for this/these quality/qualities.

--Treat the other person with respect and see if they reciprocate.

--Now, you're off to a fine start. Show support for the other person and see if they demonstrate support for you. Mutual support means: I help you, and you help me.

--Once you are at this point, you will start to trust the other person, and if all goes well, they will trust you too.

The above described process is a "cookbook" approach. Most relationships develop naturally, and through consistency of actions and attitudes over time. But, an awareness of the process will be valuable in determining where you're at, and how to remedy relationship problems.

Best wishes for happy, enduring, successful relationships.

IN BUSINESS, TRUST IS ESSENTIAL

Does dishonesty in business pay? The answer to this question is: Yes, No, Maybe, and Sometimes. Dishonesty may pay, but usually only over the short run, and the consequences may be severe. Honesty may not always pay, although it's still the "best policy."

Examples

Bernie Madoff, the famous Wall Street Investment Advisor is a prime, and recent (December, 2008) example of business dishonesty on a large scale, and for a long period of time. While, at this writing, details of his scheme are still emerging, it appears as though an elaborate *Ponzi* scheme was perpetrated over at least a twenty year period. The total amount involved could be as much as $50 billion, as the $17 million that Mr. Madoff had under management was highly leveraged. In the meantime, Mr. Madoff was released on $10 million bail. The primary concern about this story is that Madoff was a highly regarded Advisor, practically above reproach, with heretofore unquestioned integrity. The man was an icon, as one of the founders of the *NASDQ* exchange. The damage to investor confidence may be considerable.

There are numerous other examples of fraud, deception, and thievery on an even larger scale. Some scandals reach into the hundreds of millions, perhaps billions. The *Forbes* Magazine "*Corporate Scandal Sheet*" (Patsurius, 2002) listed over twenty big ones, while acknowledging "chronicling every corporate transgression would be impractical." Names like *Enron, Global Crossing, Adelphia, Time-Warner, Bristol-Meyers, Haliburton, K-Mart, Tyco, WorldCom*, and *Xerox* are on the list. But there have been many more. In fact, cheating, falsification, and "crooked" accounting seems rampant. Everyone from big brokerages, accounting firms, manufacturers and retailers had their turn.

So who can you trust?

Enforcing Corporate Honesty

The *Sabanes-Oxley Act* (2002) was enacted following the *Enron* scandal. The law strengthens reporting requirements and directs corporate oversight and internal controls. But can external requirements work when the rewards for a little corruption can be so astonishing?

Obviously not. Corporate scandals continue unabated. There is a "risk-reward" equation in operation that seems to favor taking chances. Ethics and honesty often lose out when confronted with the possibility of huge financial rewards, the profitability demands of shareholders, and the relatively small chance of legal recourse.

The Consequences of Dishonesty

The consequences can be severe. Not the jail terms, personal disgrace and business failure, but the taint of the entire business community and the distrust of even reputable businesses. Commerce can grind to a halt, liquidity shrivels, and financing may be practically unattainable. Consumers may curtail their spending, investments and purchases. Promises, guarantees, and contracts will be under suspicion, or of limited meaning. These are the consequences of dishonesty. If we can't trust each other how do we transact business?

THE CONVENIENT, DISPOSABLE EMPLOYEE

It is often said that we live in a "throwaway" society. It is frequently easier, maybe even cheaper to dispose of things, rather than repair them. When was the last time you had your TV repaired, or your toaster, or your cell phone? When it breaks or is obsolete, or a new model appears on the scene, junk the current version.

Disposability

We live in a world of convenience. When something, or someone, is no longer convenient our first reaction is to dispose of the offender. Even people have become disposable. Tired of your wife? Get a new one. Tired of your parents? Ship them off to an "old folks" home. This "out with the old, in with the new" mentality has become pervasive, and it is not without implications and consequences.

In the workplace the emphasis is on productivity. New employees typically bring more up-to-date knowledge and skills. It is easier to acquire these new "models" than it is to "repair" the old, by investing the time and cost of training. And there is frequently not an acknowledgment of the value of organizational memory and experience.

A Cost-Benefit Analysis

Business decisions are dollar-driven. The costs and benefits of each course of action is calculated and weighed. Emphasis is on cost-effectiveness, as the business must generate profits to survive. Although we may not always do a careful analysis when making personal decisions, hopefully in business we will be more objective, as the overriding concern is profitability.

William Bliss, President of *Bliss & Associates*, has a formula for calculating the cost of employee turnover. In *The Advisor* (www.isquare.com) he outlines a detailed list of considerations totaling over thirty-five separate cost items. The primary categories include: Costs Due to a Person Leaving, Recruitment Costs, Training Costs, Lost Productivity Costs, New Hire Costs, and Lost Sales Costs. The calculations reach an impressive 150% to 250% of annual salary, depending on the position. So, before you terminate that $50,000 employee think of the $75,000 to $150,000 you will spend in replacing them.

Of course the turnover costs may not apply to every situation. If you don't plan on replacing the employee you are not confronted with this problem (although you may have others). With a straight layoff you will not experience many of the turnover costs but you may have severance pay and benefits, decreased productivity, and other direct and indirect costs.

Decisions

Human Resources decisions are seldom easy. Whenever these decisions involve employee separation, either by the employee's volition or a business decision it can be a painful and costly process. Company policies and practices which contribute to a reduction in employee turnover usually pay off. Employee retention has its benefits and these benefits can be dollarized. Other intangibles like morale may also be considerations.

The decision to terminate an employee should not be taken lightly as it impacts both the employee and the employer. Carefully consider the decision before taking action. It might be cheaper to retain and retrain the employee, transfer them to another assignment, or just keep them on the payroll. You don't really know what the replacement employee will be like, how they will perform, or how long they'll stay.

We may live in a "throwaway society" but this norm is based on convenience and low cost. When it comes to people it may be neither.

VALUE YOUR EMPLOYEES DIFFERENCES

We're all different. Some of us are downright peculiar! But these differences, aside from making us unique, also make us valuable. Managers who try to make employees think or act alike may be doing their employees, themselves, and their organization a disservice.

Uniqueness

An organization is a combination of individuals, resources, and management, working together for a common purpose. The manager's job is not to fit the employee into a pigeonhole. An employee will not be best utilized by forcing him into a specific Job Description, but rather to identify the strengths of that worker and assign tasks and duties in accord with those abilities. Now this flies in the face of common organizational principles, however, it is effective. Of course I'm not recommending that designated tasks, assigned responsibilities, and Position Descriptions be thrown out the window. Instead, I'm suggesting that to the extent feasible, we try to be flexible and accommodate the unique personalities and skill sets of our subordinates; just like we want our superiors to accommodate our eccentricities.

You Hire a Person, Not a Job Description

It's tempting to hand a new employee a "Position Description" and send them off to perform. However, there are lots of failures with this technique. Position Descriptions are often out-of-date, inaccurate, incomplete, or completely worthless. These documents generally don't reflect the realities of the position, or the best way to do the work. In fact, the quickest way to kill a business might be if everyone performed only their assigned duties and responsibilities.

It's a Social Entity, Not an Organization Chart

The workplace is a community, whereas an organization chart is an idealized depiction of relationships which totally ignores the social aspects of the entity. This can present problems or open new opportunities. The network of interpersonal connections can lubricate the business processes, facilitating communications, gaining cooperation, and promoting teamwork.

A Manager Needs to be Creative

Managers need to be thinking individuals. As people, all managers have seen the dysfunctionalities and eccentricities of our own families and friends. However, we somehow expect that our co-workers and subordinates will behave in a rational manner while at work. Yet, we all know this isn't the case. Bridging the gap between our unrealistic expectations of employees, and the reality of human individuality is a challenge. Managers must figure out ways to utilize the differences, unique characteristics, and, yes, eccentricities of employees to their advantage, and the organization's success.

SOME SUGGESTIONS

--Welcome and appreciate individuality

--At least tolerate, if you can't embrace, the eccentricities of your employees

--Realize that an organization of "clones" will not be a top performer

--Recognize that when you deal with one employee, your actions will have a "ripple effect" throughout the organization

--Productivity and customer service must be your top priorities, and if someone is not contributing, they must be removed, reassigned, or re-educated

--Different perspectives help groups arrive at better decisions

--It's true that outliers, peculiar people, or individualists are often the biggest contributors to the organization

THE HAPPIEST PEOPLE IN BUSINESS

The happiest people I know LOVE what they do. Not that their work is their life - although it's a significant, meaningful, and rewarding component. Moreover, and perhaps even more importantly, they are PROUD of what they do. They may not have an easy work schedule, or even make a lot of money, but they're fundamentally satisfied. Their profession, occupation, business, etc, is fulfilling and contributes to society.

Perhaps you've never been involved in a job that has an element of deception, or unfair treatment of stakeholders or is, on some level, dishonest. Congratulations. However, many jobs, perhaps even a significantly increasing number, have some unsavory, unethical, or downright dishonest, component. Many employees and businesspeople rationalize their behavior. They say: "that's business," or "gotta make a living..." or "everybody's doing it."

I've heard people comment: "Yes, I know the company's unethical, but I just try to do the best job I can, in my area of responsibility." My response is: "Even if you're the best messenger for the Mafia, you're still a part of organized crime!"

Consequences

Working for an unethical, deceptive, unfair, or dishonest employer, or in a capacity that requires you to make unethical or compromised decisions may take it's toll on your physical, mental, and/or emotional health. As we know, there are consequences for our actions. In business you may not do something against the law, and you will probably not go to jail. However, escaping consequences on a technical or legal basis does not mean you're "home free." So if you feel uneasy, "dirty," or less than "proud," about your workplace activities, your employer's expectations, values, ethics, or behavior, you are in danger of personal health problems. Few people can act contrary to their values, or be a part of an organization that expects, encourages, or facilitates such actions, with impunity. They will suffer consequences, and perhaps not "connect the dots," to fully understand the origin of their unhappiness or illness.

GUARD YOUR PROFESSIONAL REPUTATION

A person's reputation is important and valuable, and must be protected. In July, 2010 a *U.S. Department of Agriculture* employee, Shirley Sherrod, was all over the nightly news, with allegations of racism. Even the *NAACP* denounced and repudiated her. Shortly after the controversy surfaced, Ms. Sherrod was summarily fired by *USDA*. In fact, she was driving to a meeting when she received a series of calls, one of which indicated the "White House" wanted her out of there. Under extreme pressure Ms. Sherrod submitted her resignation. All of this took place in a little over one day. It turns out it was all one giant, public, misunderstanding, with statements taken out of context, facts in complete contradiction to the reports, and a much bigger story.

How Could it Go this Far (this Fast)?

Ms. Sherrod is a respected manager, a positive "face" for the government, and represents her employer well. One day she was competent, highly regarded, and secure. The next day her name was in all the national media, she left her job in disgrace, and was unemployed; almost a national pariah.

Ms. Sherrod is a black (African-American) woman. She was alleged to have discriminated against a white farmer- *some twenty years ago.* Unfortunately, Ms. *Sherrod* recently recounted her experience, which occurred some decades earlier, at a public meeting. Like almost everything these days, her speech was videotaped. When an edited version of her comments were leaked to conservative blogger *Andrew Breitbart* it set the stage for a rapid sequence of events.

What REALLY Happened?

Ms. Sherrod did have professional contact and interaction with the white farmer. The farmer was in financial difficulty and was about to lose his farm through foreclosure. Ms. Sherrod was called to help. She initially felt the man was acting "superior" because of his Caucasian race. Because of her perception, she even considered not helping him as much as she was able to. In the end, her ethical and moral nature triumphed over those baser instincts, and she offered full assistance and support. The farmer's farm was saved, everyone was happy, the farmer and the government employee even became friends. (The man even came to her defense in televised interviews.) The real story was not one of racism, discrimination, and unfair treatment; instead it is an inspiring tale of moral and ethical redemption and victory.

Instead of silently walking away with her head held down, Shirley Sherrod confronted her accusers. She spoke on national television. She told her side of the story. She questioned her accusers' motives. She fought for her reputation. She prevailed. She received public apologies from White House spokesperson (Robert Gibbs) and was offered another position (probably at a higher level) at USDA.

Was There a Happy Ending?

The damage has been done. Some people will only recall the allegations. The government looks bad from mid-level, all the way to the President. Civil Rights protectors (like the NAACP) may jump on the "bandwagon" and fail to protect the interests of those they're in place to represent. The media reputation, as low as it is, suffered even more. There was plenty of disgraceful and unwarranted conduct to go around. Only through the courage of the victim (Ms. Sherrod) were corrective actions taken.

Lessons to be Learned

There are many lessons to be learned from this incident, here are some:

--You may be falsely accused

--Your words can be taken out of context

--People will jump to unfair conclusions

--Your integrity may be impugned

--Despite your authentic views, you may be viewed, or characterized, as racist, sexist, ageist, homophobic, or having some other prejudice

--Your actions or words could be misinterpreted, taken out of context, or falsely reported

--Your employer may act without all the facts

--The innocent are frequently accused, maligned, or convicted of perceived misdeeds

--You could end up on the nightly news (for something you did, or DID NOT do)

--**You need to protect, and fight for, your reputation**

When employers, professional colleagues, or the public think of you, will they think of an *Edsel* or a *Mercedes*?

IN THE WORKPLACE – CHOOSE YOUR
CONFIDANTS CAREFULLY

By nature, some of us are open and trusting. We share information too freely, and expect that others will guard our personal information. This isn't always the case, and perhaps more often than not, confidential information is shared either inadvertently or intentionally.

"Loose Lips Sink Ships"

During World War II the military became concerned that our enemies would gather useful strategic information from the casual conversations, and letters sent home, by soldiers overseas. A government policy was established that prohibited the discussion of certain subjects either verbally, or in writing ("Loose Lips Sink Ships," EyeWitness to History, *eyewitnesstohistory.com* [1997]). The government's concerns were warranted and the stakes were high. The risk to life and military assets could not be tolerated.

While the stakes might not be as high in the workplace, certainly YOUR SHIP could be figuratively SUNK! By this, I mean that you could suffer loss or damage through loose conversation. Your "secrets" could be revealed and your reputation and prestige could suffer.

Similar to the wartime effort, companies are often engaged in a form of "economic warfare." They have "trade secrets," strategic directions, products or programs about to be unveiled, etc. You could also sink your company's "ship," inflict some damage, or cause opportunity or economic loss.

Keep Your Opinions To Yourself

One of the more common violations is to voice your opinions, particularly negative ones, about your organization, your boss, the leadership, the established programs or policies, the competence or character of other employees, etc. This is tempting and normal, after all "free speech" is one of the Constitutional foundations of our democracy. However, if you engage in this type of conversation, do so with the realization that it could "come back to bite you." Your co-workers or superiors could overhear your remarks or be told of them. They may be irritated or offended by your comments, or consider them a breach of "confidentiality."

Be Selective About Your Confidants

People have bonds, friendships, associations, etc. The informal organization is often as powerful and influential as the formal one. We're social beings, and this implies a need to connect. We confide in our friends, and most of us have friends at work. Often the subjective information is equally as valid in forming judgments and assessments. That being said, be cautious in whom you choose to confide. Don't be indiscriminate - be selective! We've all had experiences with people sharing information we specifically asked them not to.

Capsulized Advice

- If you talk about subjective work matters, be careful
- Avoid gossip
- Go through your boss: keep him, or her, informed
- Pick your confidants carefully
- Respect confidences, and do not repeat them
- Recognize your reasons for sharing information with others (is it friendship, power, being in the know, frustration, discontent, a desire to help, etc.?)
- Advice should be private
- Be ethical
- Practice loyalty; don't betray
- Exercise discretion
- Protect yourself, and others
- Remember some confidential information is protected by law (e.g., employment, health insurance, credit, etc.)

<u>LOVE, SEX, AND MONEY – THE WORKPLACE HAS IT ALL!</u>

Are the steamiest relationships on the Big Screen? Hollywood certainly has no monopoly on torrid romance, hot sex, or obsessive infatuation. In fact, the most intense intrigue is probably where you spend much, if not most, of your time - at your workplace.

The Setting

The office is a giant cauldron with all of the ingredients for sordid, or innocent entanglements. The combination of money, status differentials, different sexes (and orientations), and power hungry individuals thrown together for prolonged periods of time on a regular basis; is bound to result in interesting outcomes. What better place to meet, learn about others, work together, socialize, flirt, develop friendships or relationships, and stimulate the senses? Experiences can include everything from "mild interest," to friendship "hugs," to stalking, "making out" in the parking lot, "quickies" in the elevator, "hands under the conference table," or "having your baby."

It Even Happens in the "White House"

Remember the *Clinton* affair? President *Clinton* quickly said "I didn't have sexual relations with that woman..." when confronted with a scandal about an affair with a White House intern; the young, voluptuous *Monica Lewinsky*. Mr. Clinton's vocabulary was tried as he revealed his definition of "sex." The exceedingly amiable, erudite and adroit President's understanding of sex apparently did not include the oral variety. Fortunately for him, there was no prosecution, impeachment, or removal from office, only embarrassment, and humiliation.

There are Boundaries – Both Legal and of Propriety

Some people draw personal boundaries, not unlike the military code of conduct, and will not "fraternize." Others have no such prohibition. Many want to avoid personal and romantic entanglements, and follow the old school advice: "Don't shit where you eat!"

The legal system also has something to say about this. Sexual harassment is a form of sex discrimination that violates Title VII of the *Civil Rights Act of 1964*. (In Fiscal Year 2008, the government received almost 14,000 charges of sexual harassment.) *Title VII* applies to employers with 15 or more employees as well as state and local governments. The United States EEOC (*Equal Employment Opportunity Commission*) recognizes that some unscrupulous bosses will take advantage of the "power differential" and attempt to coerce underlings into unethical compromise. The technical term is "quid pro quo;" essentially "this for that!" As an example, the boss may explicitly say, or imply, something like: "You sleep with me, and I'll give you a promotion." "Quid Pro Quo" is one type of discrimination and "sexual harassment" which is prohibited under the law.

The other form of sexual harassment is a "*hostile work environment*" which can involve workplace behavior that is "sexually charged." Everything from sexual innuendo like "I'll bet she can really please a man," to off color jokes or comments, sexy pictures on the wall, and the like.

For more comprehensive information concerning legal requirements visit www.eeoc.com.

Most of the questionable or even illegal behavior never comes to light. Sometimes the boss will even marry the secretary, and raise eyebrows about what may have been going on. And, frequently office romances do not have any legal or ethical consequences - they just happen.

Watch Yourself!

--Be fully aware of your employer's policies in this area.

--Prevention is the best approach.

--Let your co-workers and managers know when you find their behavior offensive.

--Tell people to STOP objectionable or unwelcome behavior.

--Remember that retaliation for reporting unwelcome behavior is prohibited.

--Don't participate in questionable practices (including touching, joking, "locker room talk," etc.)

--Be aware there can be seducers in the copy room or the Boardroom or the bathroom, even the cubicle or office next to you.

--Be cautious, considerate, and respectful when it comes to workplace behaviors, or activities.

--Be on your best behavior when it comes to interaction with co-workers, customers, managers, suppliers, even the UPS deliveryman.

--Just exercise good judgment in this area, to protect yourself, your job, and your reputation.

7

A NOTE TO STUDENTS
WHY STUDY BUSINESS?

DECISIONS...DECISIONS...DECISIONS...

Students frequently have difficulty in selecting a career path. Should they major in Law, Criminal Justice, Nursing, the Sciences or the Social Sciences? Selecting a Major course of study is not an easy task for anyone, let alone a teen-ager or twenty-something year old.

Of course experts say the first step is to do an examination of yourself. What are your interests and abilities? What do you like to do and what are you good at? What are your strengths and weaknesses, and what would excite you? What career would appeal to you?

The SWOT Analysis

One of the common business tools is the SWOT analysis. The SWOT model is designed to help you organize and categorize. This technique is useful in making decisions, formulating strategies, and adaptable to the process of deciding upon a field of study.

The "**S**" stands for STRENGTHS, the "**W**" for WEAKNESSES, the "**O**" for OPPORTUNITIES, and the "**T**" for THREATS. Strengths and weaknesses are internal (within you, in this case) and opportunities and threats are external (in the environment).

Start by identifying and listing your strengths, and don't underestimate yourself. Then, list your weaknesses, and be brutally honest. After that, decide on what the opportunities are in a particular field, such as: management positions, potential for advancement, plenty of potential jobs, good levels of compensation, a wide range of career paths, etc. Finally, determine the threats which may include business down-turns, technological obsolescence, management cutbacks, out-sourcing or off-shoring, etc.

The strengths required for business generally include: strong communications skills, good analytical ability, decision-making capabilities and some facility with facts and numbers. If you're strong in these areas you may want to consider a business major and career.

The Business Curriculum and Professional Credentials

Business degree programs typically include courses in management, finance, accounting, and computer applications. Courses in Strategic Planning, Entrepreneurship/Small Business Management, Project

Management, Customer Service and International Business are also important. Since communication and planning are so crucial, pay particular attention to programs that offer courses in written communications, business communications, or have English Composition components.

Students interested in specialized areas of study should aim for Certification and/or licensure at some point. Designations such as CPA (*Certified Public Accountant*), CFP (*Certified Financial Planner*), RFC (*Registered Financial Consultant*), CMA (*Certified Management Accountant*), CSP (*Certified Systems Professional*), or CPM (*Certified Project Manager*) are all professional credentials which assure a standard of knowledge and competence. Each of these designations has separate requirements for education and experience.

The Case for Business

Business is one of the broadest fields and traditionally one of the most highly compensated. For four-year college graduates it typically ranks in the "top ten" most profitable majors. (*National Association of Colleges and Employers*) The *U.S. Department of Labor* statistics also report favorable earnings results for business graduates. As a broad field (as opposed to specialized career or job training) there are a wide range of employment opportunities in the private sector, public sector and non-profits. And, since the business world is highly competitive, those equipped with some business knowledge and credentials are at an advantage.

Business can also be exciting. The competitive environment, the challenge of marketing and selling goods or services, the successful conclusion of a deal or project, negotiations, and making profits can produce an adrenaline "rush."

If you want to be an entrepreneur and start your own business, or if you wish to be a corporate manager, the investment in studying business administration is good preparation. Whether you begin with an Associate's Degree, attain a Bachelor's in Business, or complete your MBA, your business education should pay you personally and professionally. Everyone makes buy or rent decisions, struggles with investments or taxes, and faces motivational or organizational challenges where a business background /education would be valuable.

Candidates with a business background and education are frequently sought after by employers, regardless of the field. One of the "hottest" combos is to have a professional license along with a business degree. For example: R.N./MBA's are in high demand.

Employers recognize that having employees who speak the "language" of business and understand business concepts and techniques will facilitate training, increase productivity, help in providing focus on organization priorities and contribute to the "bottom line." Sharp employees with business acumen, in fact, give employers that "competitive edge."

Where Do You Go From Here?

Once you have made a decision about your major, examine some programs and schools pick a program that meets your needs, challenges you, and feels comfortable. You will need to spend lots of time, effort and energy to succeed, so make sure you're up to the commitment. Next, select a school in a business-like manner.

Some tips for prospective college students include:

--Check out the school, look for complaints on the web; the reputation of your college is important

--Speak with your family, friends, school counselor, current or former teachers, or others during your decision-making process, even if you are an adult

--Ask about accreditation. While national accreditation is OK; regional accreditation is superior

--Ask about transferability of credits, this is particularly important if you plan to continue your education at another college or university

--Inquire about graduation rates, placement rates, school programs, student services, etc.

--Make sure the faculty is well-qualified, with advanced degrees from highly regarded schools

--Take time to make your decision, check out other colleges, and make comparisons

--Don't sign any contracts, financing, or loan agreements until you fully understand what you are getting into

--You may want to have a trusted adviser (friend, banker, or accountant) review your proposed school financing terms and conditions

--Make sure you're making a "good deal" and getting value for your

money

--Avoid high interest private loans or other costly financing arrangements

--Ask to speak with faculty and students before making your decision

--Don't be bullied, coerced, or fooled by glowing, unwritten, comments and promises

--Don't be overly impressed by appearances or rhetoric

--Take time to decide on your program or major, make sure it's right for you

8

 CONCLUSION

CONCLUSION

This brings us to the end of our business journey. As stated in the Introduction, my purpose in this book was to provide managers, both aspiring, and practicing, with "Bites of Business" in a practical, relevant, concise format. The intent was to create a "guide," focusing on the most important aspects of business and management. As you discovered, this is not a theoretical book. Rather, it is "down-to-earth" advice from one manager to another. In it I have drawn on years of experience as a manager, executive, CEO, Board member, educator, writer and consultant. I also drew from the questions, concerns, ambitions, and input of thousands of college students over more than two decades.

This was intended to be a positive, motivational, and inspirational book, without shying away from obvious problems and challenges. The content is informal, non-technical, and written in a rather informal style. While dealing with serious business, management, ethical and career issues, I tried to be engaging and entertaining.

In our society "everything is business." By that, I mean that as a post-industrial society, practically everything we do involves a business of one sort or another. Think of the businesses you have dealings with in a single day. You go to work, and may visit a bank, drive to a gas station, buy fast food, go to a grocery store, eat dinner at a restaurant, or take in a movie. If you read the newspaper, or watch TV you will encounter scores of ads from various businesses in short order. When you pick up your mail, or your phone you may have solicitations, bills or other contacts from other enterprises. Business is everywhere and everything.

Management is also pervasive. These ubiquitous businesses have managers and supervisors to run things. Increasingly, especially in a service economy, the management of relationships is a priority. The importance of the human side of business cannot be over estimated. It is the essence of success, customer satisfaction, growth and profitability.

Management is an honorable and meaningful profession, and business is essential to our society. Everything from the sole-proprietorship to the largest corporation requires leadership and management. Please exercise the care and afford the reverence which it deserves. In the final analysis, business may be about the money, but that's not all it's about!

ADDENDUM
REINVIGORATING AMERICAN BUSINESS

The United States of America succeeded in the last century largely as a result of business acumen. We had the best leadership, the best "know-how," and the most productive workers. We enjoyed a motivated workforce, a rising standard of living, a tremendous amount of ingenuity, a wealth of natural resources, and millions of foreign consumers hungry for our exports. We built a manufacturing base, a political niche, a stable society, and enjoyed entrepreneurial energy without parallel.

We also benefited from world events, and had a competitive edge following World War II, when major countries in Europe and Asia had their factories and productive capacity decimated. We, on the other hand, had an intact infrastructure, a highly developed workforce, an economic engine developed rapidly during wartime, and an educated consumer-oriented population. There was practically no competition, and our goods were highly prized and sought after. Under those conditions it would be hard to fail.

As a result of these circumstances, the USA prospered.

TIME to WAKE UP!

We're no longer the only major industrialized country with productive capacity intact. We no longer have a monopoly on the best leadership, and most productive populous. We no longer have the strongest (although it's still the biggest) economy. We no longer have a huge international trade surplus; instead, it's a substantial, problematic, and growing deficit. We no longer monopolize innovation.

We still have the best higher education system in the world, despite our seemingly intractable problems with the K-12 programs. We educate foreign leaders and business people in our Business Schools, and export management theories and practices to our competitors. This is healthy and appropriate. However, it diminishes our competitive edge.

A world economy benefits all of us. In the U.S. Consumers are treated to a wide range of low cost products. Business people and investors find infinitely more choices and opportunity. In foreign lands there are increasing incomes and standards of living.

WHAT SHOULD WE DO?

We can't roll the clock back. It's too late for protectionism; too late for many choices. Obviously, we need to accept the realities, and develop new models and strategies to preserve our economy and standard of living. And, while independent businessmen can make a difference, a more comprehensive approach may be required to achieve these broad objectives.

Here are some initiatives that come to mind...

--Business Incubators

Small businesses fail at an alarming rate. We need to protect and nurture fledgling enterprises.

--National strategic initiatives and support

Business is at the core of the success of this nation. We need to decide which businesses, products and services are essential for future positioning and effective international competition, and help them achieve success. Labor needs to be included in this process, as well as academia, so that prepared workers can be ready for new demands.

--Government grants and awards for innovation

We celebrate the Academy Awards (the film industry is very successful internationally), we celebrate much in entertainment, and other industries. We need to provide support and recognition for business excellence, in recognition of its indispensable role in our society.

--Financial Support mechanisms

Many new and existing strategic businesses are extremely capital intensive. Instead of our current "too big to fail" philosophy, we should consider a "too important to our future to fail" mentality. Ensuring that capital is available to industries essential to our future competitive and strategic future should be a national business priority. Also, the current tax structure provides more disincentives than incentives to entrepreneurs, established companies, and those seeking expansion. With foreign competition, and cheaper labor overseas, we need to revise our tax structure to encourage business at home.

--National Business Leadership Academy

The best business brains and talent should be tapped and asked to share, as a public service, their knowledge and skills in a government-business-academic partnership. The Academy could be jointly sponsored by government and business, and orchestrated by a consortium of universities.

--National Business Advisory Board

An advisory board to the Executive and Legislative branches of government should be considered. This entity would have a broad mandate, encompassing: international competitiveness, strategic industries essential to U.S. future interests, strategies to support business enterprise, foster innovation, develop alliances, and cut "red tape." To be effective, this body must include top business leaders; people with clout and reputation.

--Rotation of leaders among business and government

Part of the current business problem seems to arise from a lack of understanding of respective roles, responsibilities, challenges, priorities, etc. Many government officials have been insulated from the harsh realities of the business world for much of their career. Likewise, business leaders may not have a sound appreciation for the compromises, public policy considerations, and legal ramifications of governmental process. The role and importance of human capital in the equation would be strengthened through labor leadership being involved in the rotation or experiential processes.

--Revisit QUALITY and SERVICE

Despite our progress in improving quality of products and services, we still have a need to do more. America should develop a reputation as the highest quality provider in the world. Business, Labor, and Government will have to cooperate in this effort.

--Emphasize ethics

Ethical, honest, and fair business practices are at the core of business relationships. Successful business dealings are based on trust and an expectation of fairness. Until this expectation is a universal reality our business progress will be thwarted. Business and government are equal culprits. Unfair, and/or preferential treatment is well-known. Illegal and unethical business (or Government) dealings should be harshly punished. Minimal consequences, or knowing "winks," encourage unethical behaviors which are corrosive to our economy and society.

FINALLY...

There are many other factors that need to be considered, and certainly the recommended initiatives are not the only areas that need attention. However, we seem to have been in a prolonged period of denial and neglect. We will certainly be on our way to a lesser nation, society, and economy, unless we soon address fundamental business concerns. All of the initiatives suggested should be led and operated by volunteers, not extensions of the cumbersome and costly government bureaucracy. Support services could, in some areas, be provided by contract employees with minimal government financial support.

We need to reaffirm our capitalistic roots. We are a nation of risk-takers, a society of independent thinkers and frontier spirit, a hard-working people of accomplishment, results, and well-deserved success. We recognize the changes and trends in international business and its crucial connection to our national well-being and future prospects. We know that new approaches are necessary. We're definitely up to the challenge. Let's get started.

ABOUT THE AUTHOR

BEN CARLSEN has a uniquely broad perspective of business and management. He has extensive experience in the public and private sectors, consulting, and academia. He has written over one-hundred published articles. He served as President, Board member, or Director of numerous professional organizations, and non-profit agencies. He was Chairman of the Los Angeles County Productivity Managers Network, chaired the Marketing Managers Association, and was President of the Association of Systems Management (SoCal Chapter) as well as serving on the association's International Publicity Committee.

He has held management and leadership positions almost his entire adult life with titles such as President, Board Member, Provost, Director, Program Manager, Section Head and Supervisor. He worked for City Products Corp., Union Carbide and other large corporations. He was Chief of the Management Systems Division at the Los Angeles County Department of Health Services, and President/Provost of the L.A. County College of Nursing & Allied Health. He also created, owned and managed several small business enterprises.

Dr. Carlsen earned his Bachelors Degree at the University of Washington, an MBA at Pepperdine University, and a Doctorate, majoring in Organization and Leadership, at the University of San Francisco. His teaching and research experience was gained at the *University of San Francisco, University of California (Davis), Pepperdine University, California State University (Dominguez Hills), Western International University, Axia College (University of Phoenix), and Corinthian Colleges.* He has taught extensively at both the under graduate and graduate levels.

Dr. Carlsen was selected "Teacher of the Year" at the University of San Francisco, and "Instructor of the Year" for Corinthian Colleges.

Throughout his career, Carlsen won numerous Leadership and Service Awards including the Distinguished Service Award by the *Association for Systems Management*, and a Commendation scroll from the *Los Angeles County Board of Supervisors*.

He firmly believes in developing an ambitious organizational vision, exploiting opportunities, providing consistent and exceptional leadership, supporting, mentoring and developing subordinate staff, and being fair and ethical in business dealings.

REFERENCES AND RESOURCES

Allen, David, *Getting Things Done,* New York: Penguin Classics, 2002.

Barnard, Chester, *The Functions of the Executive,* Cambridge, Mass: Harvard University Press,1971.

Bennis, Warren, *On Becoming a Leader*, New York: Basic Books (4th ed), 2009.

Bennis, Warren, *and* Nanus, Burt, *Leaders: The Strategies for Taking Charge*, New York: HarperBusiness, 1997.

Bing, Stanley, *Crazy Bosses,* New York: Collins, 2007.

Baumeister, R., (2001) "Violent Pride," *Scientific American*, 284, No.4, (pp.96-101).

Blake, R, and Mouton, J, *The Managerial Grid: The Key to Managerial Excellence*, Houston: Gulf Pub., 1964.

Blanchard & Johnson, *The One Minute Manager,* New York: William Morrow, 1982.

Bliss, William, *The Advisor*, (www.isquare.com).

Bucholz, Todd G., *New Ideas from Dead CEO's: Lasting Lessons from the Corner Office*, New York: Collins, 2007.

Business: The Ultimate Resource, various contributors, New York: Bloomsbury Pub., Perseus Pub., 2002.

Bryne, Rhonda, *The Secret*, New York: Atria Books, 2006.

Carnegie, Dale, *How To Win Friends And Influence People,* New York: Simon & Schuster, 2009 ed.

Caulfield, J., & Wang, P., Science Weekly, vol. 149. Issue 10, (January, 2003), pp.1-12.

Collins, Jim, *Good to Great: Why Some Companies Make theLeap, And Others Don't*, New York: HarperBusiness, 2001.

Comaford-Lynch, Christine, *Rules for Renegades: How to Make Money, Rock Your Career, and Revel in Your Individuality*, New York: McGraw-Hill, 2007.

Cornwell, Russell, *Acres of Diamonds*, Robert H., Harrington Park, NJ: Sommer Publisher, 1987 ed., (orig., 1915).

Cousins, Norman, *Anatomy of an Illness as Perceived by the Patient: Reflections on Healing and Regeneration,* New York: W.W. Norton & Co., 2001.

Covey, Stephen R*., The Seven Habits of Highly Effective People,* Forest City, N.C., Fireside, 2003.

Drucker, Peter F., *Management: Tasks, Responsibilities, Practices*, Harper & Row, 1974.

Drucker, Peter F, *The Practice of Management,* New York: Harper-Collins,1954.

Elish, J., (2004, 03/01) "FSU Study Finds Self-Esteem Programs Don't Work," *FSU.com.*

Evatt & Field, *The Givers and the Takers*, Paramanibo, SA: Papaya Press, 2008.

Fisch, Karl, McLeod, Scott, Braunman, Jeff, (2009) *"Did You Know?"* (video), Parthenon XIV, Corinthian Colleges.

Flagenbaum, Hart & Schendel, (1996) *"Strategic Reference Point Theory," Strategic Management Journal, vol. 17,* pp.219-235

Gladwell, Malcom, *Blink: The Power of Thinking Without Thinking,* New York: Little, Brown & Co., 2005.

Gladwell, Malcom, *The Tipping Point: How Little Things Can Make a Big Difference*, New York: Little, Brown, & Co., 2000.

Hallowell & Ratey, Driven to Distraction: *Coping with Attention Deficit Disorder from Childhood through Adulthood,* Baltimore: Johns Hopkins University Press,1995.

Hammer and Champy, *Reengineering the Corporation*, New York: Harper-Collins,1993.

Herzberg, F.I.(1987) 'One more time: How do you motivate employees?', *Harvard Business Review*, Sep/Oct., Vol. 65 Issue 5, pp109-120.

Herzberg, F. I., Mausner, B., & Bloch-Snyderman, B., The Motivation to Work, Piscataway, N.J., Transaction Publishers, 1993.

Kelly, Kevin, (Feb. 20, 2006) *"The Speed of Information,"* Technium, (Internet edition).

King, Oliver, Sloop & Vaverek, *"Planning and Goal Setting for Improved Performance,"* Participant's Guide, Washington, D.C: Thomson Executive Press, (1955)

Kiyosaki & Lechter, *Rich Dad Poor Dad*, Philadelphia: Running Press, 2001.

Kubler-Ross, Elizabeth, and Kessler, David, *On Grief and Greiving: Finding the Meaning of Grief Through the Five Stages of Loss*, New York: Scribner, 2007.

Levitt, Steven D*., Freakonomics,* New York: William Morrow, 2006.

Malloy, John, *Dress for Success*, New York: Grand Central Publishing,1988.

Maslow, Abraham (1943) A Theory of Human Motivation, *Psychological Review*, Vol. 50 #4, pp. 370-396.

MacNeilage, Peter F, (January 24, 2003) "Left Brain/Right Brain," *Science Weekly*, pp. *1-12*

McGregor, Douglas. *The Human Side of Enterprise*, New York: McGraw-Hill, 1960.

Murphy, Mark, *What Great Managers Do Differently*, Singapore: Select Books, 2007.

Naisbitt, John, *Megatrends: Ten New Directions Transforming Our Lives*, New York: Grand Central Publishing, 1988.

Nasbitt, John & Doris, *China's Megatrends*, New York: Harper-Collins, 2010.

Nass. Clifford, et.al, (August 25, 2009) "Multitasking Muddles Brains," *Proceedings of the National Academy of Sciences, vol. 106, no. 33.*

Patsurius, (2002), "Corporate Scandal Sheet," *Forbes.com.*

Peale, Norman V., *How to Win Friends, and Influence People*, New York: Simon & Schuster, 1934.

Peters and Waterman*, In Search of Excellence,* New York: Harper-Collins,1982.

Peters, Tom, *The Brand You 50: Or, Fifty Ways to Transform Yourself from an Employee into a Brand*, New York: Knopf, 1st ed., 1999.

Pfau and Kay*, The Human Capital Edge,* New York: McGraw-Hill, 2001.

Poras, Jerry, *Built to Last: Successful Habits of Visionary Companies,* New York: HarperBusiness, 2004.

Roman & Raphaelson*, Writing That Works: How to Communicate Effectively in Business,* New York: Collins Reference, 2000.

Ross, George, *Trump Style Negotiation*, New York: Wiley & Sons, 2006.

Sarkis, Stephanie, *10 Simple Solutions to Adult ADD*, Oakland, CA: New Harbinger Pub., 2006.

Senge, Peter M., *The Fifth Discipline: The Art & Practice of the Learning Organization, rev.,* New York: Broadway Business,1990.

Skinner, B.F, *Science and Human Behavior*, New York: Macmillan & Co., 1953.

Stanley, Thomas, *The Millionaire Next Door: The Surprising Secrets of America's Wealthy*, Atlanta: Longstreet Press, 1996.

Stein, Edgar H., *Organizational Culture and Leadership*, New York: Jossey-Bass, 2004.

Stevens, Mark, *Your Management Sucks: Why You Have to Declare War on Yourself...and Your Business,* New York: Crown Business, 2006.

Taylor, Frederick Winslow, *The Principles of Scientific Management, (rev,)*, New York: Harper and Bros.,1911.

Terkel, Studs, *Working: People Talk About What They Do All Day Long and How They Feel About What They Do,* New York: Pantheon Books Random House, 1974.

Wattles, Wallace, *The Science of Getting Rich*, CreateSpace Pub., 2009 ed., (orig. pub.1910).

Wauters, Robin, (July 21, 2010) "Zuckerberg Makes It Official: Facebook Hits 500 Million Members," *TechCrunch.com.*

Weber, Max, *The Theory of Social and Economic Organization*, OUP, orig. pub., 1947.

Weiss, Margaret, *ADHD in Adulthood: A Guide to Current Theory, Diagnosis and Treatment*, New York: Simon & Schuster, 2001.

Yahoo Answers: "TV Preachers," (Nov. 18, 2003) *St. Louis Post-Dispatch*, Retrieved from: *Yahoo.com, Questions Index: 0080331053715AA21tXY* on May 20, 2010.

Additionally...

www.money.cnn.com (CNN Money – Business news)

www.drudge.com (Drudge Report – links to current news and events)

www.eeoc.com (Equal Employment Opportunity Commission)

www.bbb.com (Better Business Bureau)

www.scorecommunity.org (Small Business Community- free consulting forentrepreneurs and small business owners)

www.sba.com (Small Business Administration)

www.hbr.org (Harvard Business Review)

www.toastmasters.org (Toastmasters – public speaking help)

www.finance.yahoo.com (Yahoo Finance)

www.hoovers.com (Business Solutions and Company Information)

www.inc.com (Inc. business news and resources)

www.allbusiness.com (Ideas, resources, info. Geared to small biz)

www.business.gov (Official link to U.S. government – services, international trade, business laws & regulations, labor laws, etc.)

www.youngentrepreneur.com (Entrepreneur help & info – be sure to check: Warren Buffet's 10 Rules for Amassing Wealth)

www.monster.com (Job search)

www.careerbuilder.com (Job search)

www.hotjobs.com (Job search)

INDEX

A

accountants/accounting,47, 53, 54, 109, 141, 255, 276, 261, 296,

accreditation, 300

acquisitions, 22

"*Acres of Diamonds*", 265

ADD, 199, 200

Adelphia, 261

AIG, 43

Ajilon, 127

ambition, 162, 212, 216, 223, 241, 254, 304

American Airlines, 131

American Banknote Company, 55

analysis, 10, 32, 33, 34, 50, 60, 61, 71, 74, 88, 93, 107, 128, 139, 149 ,169, 193, 196 ,229, 230 ,257, 258, 259, 270, 271, 283, 296, 305

Anatomy of An Illness, 217

Andy Warhol, 229

Apple, 27, 262

" *Art of the Deal!*", 35

AT&T, 85

attitude surveys 49, 109

authoritarian, 114

B

Bad debts, 23

"bailout", 43, 82

Bakker, Jim & Tammy, 117

Bank of America, 85

Baumeister, R, 150

Bear Stearns, 43

Bebo, 202

Bennis, Warren, 152

*Benton,*Brook, 195

BlackBerry, 126, 244, 261

C

Industrial Revolution, 73

influence, 3, 40, 44, 55, 56, 130, 160, 161, 162, 181, 186, 186, 189, 190, 196, 200, 314

informal network, 143

Information Systems, 64

Informing, 18, 111, 141, 191, 206

intrapreneurs, 248

invention, 26, 80

inventory, 22, 26, 63, 107, 108

investor, 32, 261

J

Jakes, T.D., 177

James, LeBron, 130, 131

Jay-Z, 130

Job Description, 284, 285

Jobs, Steve, 261, 262

Johnson & Johnson, 67

Johnson, Lyndon, 45

Johnson, Spud, 221

JP Morgan, 262

K

KB Toys, 30

"Keep the Faith, Baby", 195, 196

Kellogg's, 228

Kelly, Kevin, 202

"kiss ass", 187, 188

Kubler-Ross, 183

Kiyosaki, Robert, 251

L

""Law of Attraction", 252

leadership, 9, 10, 11, 27, 41, 45, 46, 68, 71, 111, 112, 116, 125, 126, 134, 141, 152, 153, 154, 160, 171, 292, 304, 308, 309, 310, 312, 313

"Leaders: The Strategies for Taking Charge", 152

Leading, 12, 14, 18, 68, 92, 111, 141, 164, 169, 170, 171, 191, 206

Left Brain/*Right Brain,* 126

productive, 9, 154, 155, 156, 165, 200, 213, 227, 255, 332, 361

productivity, 9, 23, 29, 32, 38, 10, 56, 61, 75, 76, 94, 98, 107, 113, 114

profit/ profitability, 5, 9, 11, 14, 17, 20, 21, 22, 29, 30, 32, 37, 48, 58, 60, 62, 64, 81, 82, 85, 86, 87, 88, 100, 113, 114, 134, 146, 159, 163, 181, 208, 216

Progressive Discipline, 104

public speaking, 159, 176, 177, 178, 318

publicity, 30, 131, 277, 312

punctuality, 51, 52

Q

quality, 20, 21, 29, 32, 33, 34, 53, 61, 63, 79, 84, 85, 86, 88, 93, 1405, 123, 148, 155, 175, 180, 202, 203, 212, 216, 225, 262, 279, 310

quality control, 21

Quicken, 255

Quid Pro Quo, 295

R

recruitment, 94, 95, 107, 130, 283

Registered Financial Consultant, 299

Reinforcement Theory, 118, 123, 137

"Rich Dad, Poor Dad,", 251, 316

reinvention, 17, 80, 82, 83

relationship(s), 11, 25, 29, 30, 33, 36, 39, 56, 75, 95, 98, 108, 141, 149, 196, 209, 210, 211, 218, 242, 243, 251, 261, 263, 278, 279, 280, 285, 294

Relationship Model, 278

reputation, 17, 21, 29, 52, 61, 68, 69, 85, 86, 144, 146, 147, 180, 181, 187, 188, 189, 190, 194, 275, 277, 289, 290, 292, 296, 300, 310

reserve, 22, 23, 24, 25, 55

responsibility, 27, 47, 59, 71, 77, 86, 102, 11, 113, 114, 136, 141, 153, 155, 163, 164, 165, 169, 171, 174, 183, 236, 251, 267, 287

Robbins, Tony, 177

robotic, 45, 91, 133

Rockettes, 130

Rolling Stones, 242

Ross, George, 25, 316

RST model, 278

rumors, 91, 143, 144

S

S.M.A.R.T., 61

Sabanes-Oxley Act, 281

sales, 21, 23, 29, 30, 35, 47, 53, 55, 56, 58, 60, 63, 81, 84, 86, 1409, 136, 137, 143, 164, 167, 176, 225, 234

"sandwich" approach, 147

"scale of one to ten", 49, 50

Schadenfreude, 181, 182

Science of Getting Rich", 254, 317

Scientific Management, 73, 152, 317

scientific method, 32

SCORE, 30, 301, 319, 320

"Secret""The, 252, 314

self-actualization, 137

self-esteem, 137,149, 450, 181, 182, 187, 225, 314

selfish manager, 159, 206, 207, 208

Serenity Prayer, 243

severance package, 104, 237

sexual harassment, 190, 294, 290

shareholders, 11, 22, 43, 114, 148

Sherrod, Shirley, 289, 290

Simon, Paul, 118, 119

Skinner,B.F. 118

Small Business Administration, 250, 256, 268, 318

SMART, 218, 219, 253, 254, 257

Social Media, 228, 272, 273

Social Security, 244, 267

Sprint-Nextel, 85

stakeholder(s), 19, 68, 70, 130, 167

standards, 21, 23, 49, 60, 61, 98, 103, 133, 166, 171

strategic planning, 53, 204, 258, 298

strategy, 23, 39, 41, 67, 84, 109

Sullivan, Anthony, 117

"success formula", 238

Swaggert, Jimmy, 117

SWOT, 193, 258, 270, 271, 298

T

Taco Bell, 81

www.ingramcontent.com/pod-product-compliance
Lightning Source LLC
Chambersburg PA
CBHW021429180326
41458CB00001B/186